Praise for *Azure Data Fundamentals*

An outstanding guide for anyone beginning their Azure data journey—clear, structured, and full of real-world context. This book demystifies core concepts and builds a solid foundation for both certification and modern cloud data work.

> —*Fisnik Doko, senior cloud & AI architect, vector8;*
> *Microsoft Certified Trainer*

The Azure Data Fundamentals exam (DP-900) can be challenging because it covers such a breadth of topics. Michael has done a great job of covering so many topics in an up-to-date way that will help you to pass this exam. I particularly liked the chapter summaries that let you focus on the key points of each chapter and how they relate to the exam. And a special bonus was the hints that Michael has sprinkled throughout the book, which help you to know what to look for in exam questions.

> —*Dr. Greg Low, founder and principal mentor for SQL Down*
> *Under; long-term data platform MVP and member of the*
> *Microsoft Regional Director program*

Navigating the new world of data and AI demands a foundational understanding of data's core elements. *Azure Data Fundamentals* masterfully distills these complex concepts—from core relational concepts to Azure cloud workloads—into an easily understandable starting point, giving everyone the fundamental know-how to build their data future.

> —*Rodney Joyce, managing director, Data-Driven*

This is a great book, not just for preparing for the DP-900 exam, but for learning about Azure Data in general. In particular, I love the "Beyond the Exam" sections at the end of each chapter, which give practical advice to anyone getting into this space.

> —*Rob Farley, owner and principal consultant,*
> *LobsterPot Solutions*

Michael's extensive experience in Data, AI, and Azure is seen through in this book. He makes it easy to understand how to get started with these technologies, whether you're a beginner starting your career in tech, or a seasoned professional looking to refine, refresh, or re-learn your skills. His practical insights and clear explanations make this an invaluable resource for anyone passionate in tech, especially data.

—*Philip Domingo, account technology strategist, Microsoft*

It is rare to find someone with Michael's deep expertise in data and AI who writes for beginners. He distills decades of real-world experience into crystal-clear fundamentals. This book is a must-read for anyone seeking to master modern data practices and ace the exam.

—*David Ding, lead data consultant, SDInnovation Pty Ltd;*
author; Microsoft MVP

Working with Michael over the years has really shown me how uniquely he can take deep data and AI concepts and make them feel simple and approachable. He has a knack for explaining things in a way that just makes sense, always backed by real experience rather than theory. This guide reflects exactly that, giving readers a solid and practical starting point for understanding Azure's data ecosystem.

—*Bryan Anthony Garcia, senior consultant, Versent*

Michael provides the key to passing the DP-900, with bonus best practices and patterns that go beyond the exam, all in a single book. A must study for those that are looking to jumpstart their career in data or looking to refresh on Azure data fundamentals.

—*Miles Cole, principal program manager, Microsoft*

A rare guide that balances exam preparation with real-world utility. This book offers practical tips and foundational knowledge that every data engineer needs, making it useful long after you've passed the DP-900.

—*Rafferty Uy, cloud infrastructure manager*
in the financial sector

Azure Data Fundamentals

A Guide to DP-900 Certification and Beyond

Michael John Peña

O'REILLY®

Azure Data Fundamentals

by Michael John Peña

Copyright © 2026 The Trustee for Repollo Peña Investment Trust. All rights reserved.

Published by O'Reilly Media, Inc., 141 Stony Circle, Suite 195, Santa Rosa, CA 95401.

O'Reilly books may be purchased for educational, business, or sales promotional use. Online editions are also available for most titles (*http://oreilly.com*). For more information, contact our corporate/institutional sales department: 800-998-9938 or *corporate@oreilly.com*.

Acquisitions Editor: Megan Laddusaw
Development Editor: Rita Fernando
Production Editor: Christopher Faucher
Copyeditor: Audrey Doyle
Proofreader: Dwight Ramsey

Indexer: Krsta Technology Solutions
Cover Designer: Susan Thompson
Cover Illustrator: Karen Montgomery
Interior Designer: David Futato
Interior Illustrator: Kate Dullea

December 2025:   First Edition

Revision History for the First Edition
2025-12-08:   First Release

See *http://oreilly.com/catalog/errata.csp?isbn=9781098164737* for release details.

978-1-098-16473-7

[LSI]

Table of Contents

Part IV.   Analytics on Azure

Part V.   Beyond DP-900

Preface

In a time when AI dominates headlines, it's easy to forget that intelligent systems rely fundamentally on the quality of their underlying data models, storage decisions, workload designs, and governance practices. This book is about mastering those foundations so that you can build, reason about, and evolve Azure data solutions with confidence.

Rather than overloading you with disconnected facts, I'll use stories, analogies, and real-world mental models—coffee shops, loyalty systems, streaming dashboards, global social apps, role collaboration, and future-facing governance challenges—to help you grasp these concepts. These are not embellishments. They serve as learning anchors to aid recall under exam pressure and in real project conversations.

Who Should Read This Book

Whether you're an IT professional, a data analyst, or a data scientist, I wrote this book for you. If you're studying for the DP-900 certification exam, this could be your new best friend. And hey, even if you're new to cloud computing and data concepts, don't worry. We'll start with the basics before we delve into the more complex stuff.

Why I Wrote This Book

Azure's data platform has grown from a few services into an expansive, integrated ecosystem. That breadth creates a paradox: more capability—but also more decision friction. When do you choose a fully managed relational platform versus a distributed NoSQL option? How do workload characteristics influence architecture? How do roles collaborate across ingestion, modeling, analytics, governance, and visualization? I wrote this book to connect those dots through enduring principles rather than short-lived marketing slogans.

My goals are twofold:

1. Help you pass the DP-900 exam by truly understanding—not memorizing—the conceptual domains.

2. Prepare you to make informed architectural and career decisions in real-world Azure environments.

Navigating This Book

The book is divided into five parts:

Part I, "Core Data Concepts" (Chapters 1–4)
We establish the vocabulary: how data is represented; fundamental storage considerations; distinctions between transactional and analytical workloads; and how evolving data roles collaborate in Azure. You'll develop a solid intuition before navigating the array of service menus.

Part II, "Relational Data on Azure" (Chapters 5 and 6)
We dive deep into relational concepts such as normalization, constraints, indexing logic, and integrity, then map them to Azure SQL offerings and managed open source options—highlighting the trade-offs between control, scalability, and operational responsibility.

Part III, "Nonrelational Data on Azure" (Chapters 7 and 8)
We distinguish between Azure Storage modalities—object, table, queue, file, and core patterns—and then explore Azure Cosmos DB's globally distributed model, including its consistency, partitioning, replication, and latency and the architectural shift it represents.

Part IV, "Analytics on Azure" (Chapters 9–11)
We progress from large-scale batch and lake-centric analytics to real-time streaming patterns, then move into visualization, modeling, and self-service insight delivery with Power BI—bridging raw telemetry data to executive dashboards and data storytelling.

Part V, "Beyond DP-900" (Chapter 12)
We look beyond the exam to holistic governance, the role of Microsoft Purview, security posture evolution, performance patterns, AI integration, and emerging large language model (LLM)–assisted data interaction. This is your "future readiness" accelerator.

Each chapter follows a consistent structure:

1. A scenario or analogy to establish context
2. Progressive layering of concepts with comparative framing
3. Figures or mental models to aid understanding and retention
4. Decision-making heuristics or selection frameworks

How you use this book will depend on your goals:

First-time learner
Read the book sequentially. Avoid skipping the foundational chapters, as they reduce cognitive load later on.

Exam preparation under time pressure
Skim the objectives, then attempt quizzes without prior review, and finally revisit the concepts you missed.

Experienced practitioner
Start with Parts II–IV, then return to Part I for conceptual alignment.

Governance/AI curious
Read Part I thoroughly, skim Parts II–IV for vocabulary continuity, then focus on Chapter 12.

Staying Current

Azure evolves. Core patterns—workload classification, consistency trade-offs, governance principles, performance thinking—are far more durable than naming changes or UI shifts. Treat this book as your conceptual compass; verify SKU minutiae and pricing in the portal or official docs when implementing.

Conventions Used in This Book

The following typographical conventions are used in this book:

Italic
Indicates new terms, URLs, email addresses, filenames, and file extensions.

`Constant width`
Used for program listings, as well as within paragraphs to refer to program elements such as variable or function names, databases, data types, environment variables, statements, and keywords.

This element signifies a tip or suggestion.

This element signifies a general note.

This element indicates a warning or caution.

Using Code Examples

If you have a technical question or a problem using the code examples, please send email to *support@oreilly.com*.

This book is here to help you get your job done. In general, if example code is offered with this book, you may use it in your programs and documentation. You do not need to contact us for permission unless you're reproducing a significant portion of the code. For example, writing a program that uses several chunks of code from this book does not require permission. Selling or distributing examples from O'Reilly books does require permission. Answering a question by citing this book and quoting example code does not require permission. Incorporating a significant amount of example code from this book into your product's documentation does require permission.

We appreciate, but generally do not require, attribution. An attribution usually includes the title, author, publisher, and ISBN. For example: "*Azure Data Fundamentals* by Michael John Peña (O'Reilly). Copyright 2026 The Trustee for Repollo Peña Investment Trust, 978-1-098-16473-7."

If you feel your use of code examples falls outside fair use or the permission given above, feel free to contact us at *permissions@oreilly.com*.

O'Reilly Online Learning

O'REILLY® For more than 40 years, *O'Reilly Media* has provided technology and business training, knowledge, and insight to help companies succeed.

Our unique network of experts and innovators share their knowledge and expertise through books, articles, and our online learning platform. O'Reilly's online learning platform gives you on-demand access to live training courses, in-depth learning paths, interactive coding environments, and a vast collection of text and video from O'Reilly and 200+ other publishers. For more information, visit *https://oreilly.com*.

How to Contact Us

Please address comments and questions concerning this book to the publisher:

O'Reilly Media, Inc.
141 Stony Circle, Suite 195
Santa Rosa, CA 95401
800-889-8969 (in the United States or Canada)
707-827-7019 (international or local)
707-829-0104 (fax)
support@oreilly.com
https://oreilly.com/about/contact.html

We have a web page for this book, where we list errata and any additional information. You can access this page at *https://oreil.ly/azure-data-fundamentals*.

For news and information about our books and courses, visit *https://oreilly.com*.

Find us on LinkedIn: *https://linkedin.com/company/oreilly-media*.

Watch us on YouTube: *https://youtube.com/oreillymedia*.

Acknowledgments

To my wife, Maria—your patience and partnership grounded this entire journey. To my children—thank you for the perspective and energy you bring to every day. To my family and friends—your encouragement turned deadlines into momentum.

To Rita, Megan, and Virginia from O'Reilly—thank you for being very patient with me throughout the development and production of this book. To the publishing team—thank you for supporting a concept-first approach.

To these awesome book reviewers, who made this book possible by providing excellent and sound feedback:

- Pio Balistoy
- John Paul Ada
- Caleb Lent
- Håkan Silfvernagel

To the Microsoft MVP community—your collaborative spirit continually sharpens my thinking. To the Azure product teams—your relentless innovation powers mission-critical systems globally.

And to you, the reader: thanks for investing your time here. I hope these pages accelerate your growth and amplify your impact.

Let's dive in.

PART I
Core Data Concepts

Core foundations establish the fundamental mental models you need before you make any Azure service decisions. This part of the book grounds you in how data is represented, how storage choices shape performance and cost, how workloads differ in intent and design, and how modern data roles collaborate in cloud environments. Getting these concepts right early prevents architectural drift, avoids overengineering, and speeds up later decision making.

The chapters in this part supply the conceptual vocabulary you will reuse in the rest of the book:

- Chapter 1, "Introduction to Data Representation", explains the spectrum from structured to unstructured data, why format and schema flexibility matter, and how evolving digital complexity influences storage and processing strategies.

- Chapter 2, "Data Storage Fundamentals", explores storage characteristics—performance, durability, cost, access patterns—and shows how trade-offs shape architectural direction before you ever name a service.

- Chapter 3, "Understanding Data Workloads", differentiates transactional (OLTP) and analytical (OLAP) workloads, showing how latency, concurrency, and query shape drive design decisions.

- Chapter 4, "Data Roles and Responsibilities in Azure", maps modern Azure-aligned data roles and how their collaboration reduces friction and governance gaps across the data lifecycle.

By the end of Part I, you should be able to distinguish data categories with concrete examples; classify a workload as transactional or analytical based on observable traits; articulate why premature service selection causes later rework; and describe how role clarity supports governance, quality, and delivery speed.

Common pitfalls addressed here include assuming that all data belongs in the same storage tier, skipping workload classification, and allowing blurred role boundaries to create duplicated effort. The heuristics you develop (e.g., "high-frequency, row-level writes with strict consistency → transactional pattern") become guardrails for Parts II–IV.

Exam Alignment: This part maps strongly to DP-900 core domains on data concepts, workloads, and roles. Mastery here reduces memorization pressure later because you'll recognize patterns instead of forcing recall.

CHAPTER 1

Introduction to Data Representation

Data is everywhere around us—from the customer information in a retail store's database to the photos on your smartphone, from financial transactions at banks to sensor readings from manufacturing equipment. However, not all data is created equal, and understanding how different data is structured and stored is fundamental to making informed decisions about data management in the cloud. This understanding becomes important when working with Azure's data platform, where choosing the right approach to data representation can significantly affect performance, cost, and functionality.

Coverage of Curriculum Objectives

This chapter addresses the following DP-900 exam objectives:

- Understand different types of data representation.
- Understand characteristics of structured, semi-structured, and unstructured data.
- Identify appropriate Azure storage solutions for different data types.
- Understand data format considerations in Azure environments.

Think about your own daily digital interactions. When you check your bank balance, you're accessing structured data stored in neat rows and columns. When you post a photo on social media with a caption, you're creating unstructured data that combines visual content with descriptive text. When you share a product review with ratings and comments, you're working with semi-structured data that has some organization but flexible content. When you upload that vacation video, you're adding unstructured data to the digital universe. Each of these data types requires different storage approaches, processing techniques, and management strategies.

The evolution from simple, predictable business data to today's complex digital ecosystem reflects a fundamental shift in how organizations operate. A traditional retail store once tracked inventory with simple spreadsheets—product codes, descriptions, quantities, and prices in neat columns. Today's ecommerce platforms must handle customer profiles (structured), product catalogs with varying attributes (semi-structured), customer reviews and images (unstructured), and real-time behavioral data from millions of users simultaneously.

Understanding the Data Spectrum

Data representation exists on a spectrum rather than in rigid categories. Imagine a sliding scale where one end represents data that fits perfectly into spreadsheet-like rows and columns while the other end represents completely freeform content like videos or social media posts. Between these extremes lies data that has some organization but doesn't conform to strict rules.

Figure 1-1 illustrates how data exists along a continuum of organization and flexibility. Structured data sits at the left with rigid organization and predictable formats. Semi-structured data occupies the middle ground with flexible schemas and self-describing formats. Unstructured data spans the right side with maximum flexibility but minimal inherent organization. Understanding where your data falls on this spectrum is the first step toward choosing appropriate storage and processing approaches in Azure.

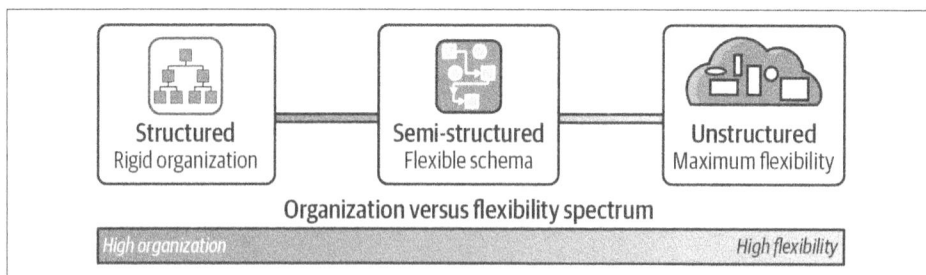

Structured
Rigid organization

Semi-structured
Flexible schema

Unstructured
Maximum flexibility

Organization versus flexibility spectrum

High organization   High flexibility

Figure 1-1. The data representation spectrum—from highly organized structured data, through flexible semi-structured formats, to completely freeform unstructured content

This spectrum concept is crucial because real-world business scenarios rarely involve pure implementations of any single data type. A customer relationship management (CRM) system might store contact information as structured data, communication preferences as semi-structured data, and email attachments as unstructured data—all within the same business process.

The DP-900 exam emphasizes understanding the characteristics and appropriate use cases of each data type rather than memorizing specific Azure service details. Focus on when and why you would choose each approach, as these concepts will be foundational for the specific Azure services we'll explore in Chapters 5–8.

Let's explore each type of data representation in detail, starting with the most traditional and well-understood: structured data.

Structured Data

Structured data represents the digital equivalent of a well-organized filing cabinet where every document has exactly the same format and fits into predefined folders. It's data that follows a rigid schema or format, with information organized into clearly defined fields, columns, and relationships. Think of structured data as information that fits neatly into a spreadsheet in which each column has a specific data type and every row represents a complete record following the exact same format. In Azure, structured data typically resides in services like Azure SQL Database, Azure Database for PostgreSQL, or Azure Synapse Analytics.

Imagine you're managing a library's book catalog. Each book record contains exactly the same information: ISBN, title, author, publication date, genre, and number of pages. Every book follows this structure—you can't easily have a book with an extra field for *translator* unless you add that field to every book record in the system (though it can be null for books without translators). This predictability and consistency exemplifies structured data.

Figure 1-2 demonstrates this concept with a library book catalog database, showing how every record follows an identical structure with predefined columns for ISBN, title, author, publication date, genre, and pages.

Library book catalog database						
ISBN	**Title**	**Author**	**Publication date**	**Genre**	**Pages**	**Available**
978-0134685991	Effective Java	Joshua Bloch	2018-01-06	Technology	416	Yes
978-0135766307	Clean Code	Robert Martin	2008-08-01	Technology	464	No
978-0596511748	JavaScript: The Good Parts	Douglas Crockford	2008-05-08	Technology	176	Yes
978-0321125215	Domain-Driven Design	Eric Evans	2003-08-22	Technology	560	Yes
978-0201633610	Design Patterns	Gang of Four	1994-10-21	Technology	395	No

Figure 1-2. Structured data example: library catalog system

Characteristics of Structured Data

Structured data exhibits several key characteristics that make it particularly suitable for certain types of applications and analysis.

Schema enforcement represents its most defining characteristic. Every record must conform to a predefined structure that's established before any data is stored. You cannot simply add a new field to one customer record without modifying the entire database schema and potentially affecting every application that uses that data.

Strong consistency makes structured data ideal for applications where data integrity is paramount. Relational database systems that store structured data typically provide ACID (Atomicity, Consistency, Isolation, Durability) properties that ensure reliable transaction processing. When you transfer money between bank accounts, the system must guarantee that money is never lost or duplicated, even if thousands of other transactions are happening simultaneously or if a power failure occurs mid-transaction.

Powerful querying capabilities through languages like Structured Query Language (SQL) enable complex analysis and reporting. The schema-driven structure allows for sophisticated operations like joining data from multiple tables, calculating complex aggregations, and performing statistical analysis that would be difficult or impossible with unstructured data.

Storage efficiency results from not storing schema information with each record. The structure is defined once and applied to all records, minimizing storage overhead compared to formats that embed schema information within each data element.

Common Examples of Structured Data

The most familiar example of structured data is the traditional *relational database.* Consider a retail company's customer management system where the Customer table includes columns for customer ID, first name, last name, email address, phone number, and registration date. Every customer record follows this exact structure, and relationships between customers and their orders are clearly defined through foreign key relationships that connect tables together.

Spreadsheets represent another ubiquitous form of structured data. When you create an Excel file with columns for employee information—name, department, hire date, salary—you're working with structured data. Each row represents one employee, each column contains a specific type of information, and the structure remains consistent throughout the spreadsheet.

Financial data provides excellent examples of structured data in action. Bank transactions have predictable fields: account number, transaction date, amount, transaction type, and description. Credit card processing systems rely on this structured approach to ensure that every transaction includes all the information necessary for processing, fraud detection, and regulatory compliance.

Enterprise resource planning (ERP) systems demonstrate structured data at massive scale. These systems manage everything from human resources to supply chain operations using highly structured data models that ensure consistency across complex business processes involving multiple departments and thousands of users.

Use Cases in Azure Environments

In Azure, structured data finds its home in several service categories that we'll explore in detail in Chapters 5 and 6. *Traditional relational database services*, such as Azure SQL Database and Azure Database for MySQL, provide fully managed environments for structured data, handling everything from backup and recovery to security and compliance while maintaining the familiar SQL interface that developers and analysts expect.

Modern data warehousing solutions in Azure, such as Azure Synapse Analytics, are specifically designed for structured data analytics at scale. These services can handle massive volumes of structured data while providing the performance needed for complex business intelligence and reporting scenarios that examine millions of records across multiple dimensions.

Hybrid and migration scenarios represent another important use case, where Azure provides solutions, such as Azure SQL Managed Instance and Azure Database Migration Service, which allow gradual transition from on-premises structured data systems to cloud-based platforms while maintaining all the benefits of structured data representation during the migration process.

> **Note**
>
> While this chapter focuses on data representation concepts, we'll explore specific Azure services for structured data in detail in Chapters 5 and 6, where we'll cover relational data concepts and Azure's database offerings. Understanding these fundamental concepts now will make those technical implementations much clearer.

Benefits and Limitations of Structured Data

Structured data offers significant advantages for many business scenarios, but it's important to understand its strengths and its limitations to make informed decisions about when to use this approach.

The benefits are substantial. Structured data's predictable format makes it ideal for applications requiring strong consistency, complex relationships, and sophisticated querying capabilities. The mature tooling ecosystem means that many business users are comfortable working with structured data through familiar interfaces like Excel, SQL reporting tools, and business intelligence platforms. Performance is often excellent for the types of queries structured data was designed to handle—looking up individual records, joining related tables, and calculating aggregations across well-defined dimensions.

However, structured data also has limitations that become apparent in modern digital environments. The rigid schema requirements can make it difficult to adapt to changing business needs. Adding new fields or changing data types often requires significant planning, testing, and system downtime. Additionally, structured data formats don't naturally accommodate the varied, unpredictable data generated by modern applications, Internet of Things (IoT) devices, social media interactions, and other digital touchpoints. Modern Azure services, such as Azure SQL Database Hyperscale, help mitigate some limitations through horizontal scaling capabilities, but the fundamental trade-offs remain.

The key to success with structured data lies in understanding when its benefits outweigh its limitations. For core business processes requiring strong consistency and complex relationships—like financial transactions, inventory management, and customer records—structured data remains the best choice. For scenarios requiring flexibility and rapid adaptation to changing requirements, other data representation approaches may be more appropriate.

As we move along the data representation spectrum, we encounter semi-structured data, which attempts to bridge the gap between the rigidity of structured data and the flexibility needed for modern applications.

Semi-Structured Data

Semi-structured data occupies the sweet spot in our data representation spectrum, offering significantly more flexibility than structured data while maintaining enough organization to be useful for applications and analysis. Unlike structured data, which requires a predefined schema that applies to all records (schema-on-write), semi-structured data includes the schema information within the data itself, enabling schema-on-read approaches. This self-describing characteristic makes it both more flexible and slightly more storage intensive than structured data, but the trade-off often proves worthwhile for modern applications. Azure services, such as Azure Cosmos DB and Azure Blob Storage with JSON support, are optimized for semi-structured data.

Think of semi-structured data like a collection of business cards. While all business cards serve the same basic purpose, each one might have a slightly different layout, different information fields, and different amounts of detail. One card might include a person's Twitter handle and LinkedIn profile, while another might have a fax number and physical address. Each card is self-describing—you can understand its structure just by looking at it—but there's no rigid template that every card must follow. This flexibility extends to the data's hierarchical and nested nature, allowing complex relationships to be represented naturally within a single record.

Characteristics of Semi-Structured Data

Semi-structured data exhibits several distinctive characteristics that set it apart from both structured and unstructured approaches. *Flexible schema* represents its most important characteristic: different records can have different structures within the same dataset. One customer record might have five fields while another has eight, and this variation is not only acceptable but expected and supported by the storage system.

Hierarchical or nested structures enable semi-structured data to represent complex relationships naturally. Instead of requiring separate tables with foreign key relationships like structured data, semi-structured formats can embed related information directly within a record. For example, a customer record might include an embedded array of order information rather than requiring a separate Orders table, making the data more intuitive and reducing the complexity of queries.

Semi-structured data has a *self-describing nature*, which means each record contains both the actual data and information about how that data is organized. This eliminates the need for external schema definitions but increases storage requirements since field names are stored with each record rather than being defined once for the entire dataset.

Human-readable formats characterize most semi-structured data types. These formats are both machine parseable and relatively easy for developers to understand and debug, which has contributed significantly to their adoption in web development, API design, and modern application architectures. However, binary semi-structured formats such as Apache Avro and MessagePack also exist, providing schema flexibility with better performance characteristics for specific use cases.

Common Examples of Semi-Structured Data

JSON (JavaScript Object Notation) represents the most prevalent form of semi-structured data in modern applications. Originally developed for web applications, JSON has become the universal standard for APIs, configuration files, and document databases. Its popularity in web development stems from its native support in JavaScript and ubiquity in modern web APIs. A JSON document can contain text, numbers, arrays, and nested objects, all within a single record.

Consider the following example of a customer record in JSON format:

```json
{
  "customerId": "CUST-12345",
  "personalInfo": {
    "name": "Sarah Johnson",
    "email": "sarah.johnson@email.com",
    "memberSince": "2019-03-15"
  },
  "addresses": [
    {
      "type": "billing",
      "street": "123 Main Street",
      "city": "Seattle",
      "state": "WA",
      "postalCode": "98101"
    },
    {
      "type": "shipping",
      "street": "456 Oak Avenue",
      "city": "Portland",
      "state": "OR",
      "postalCode": "97201"
    }
  ],
  "preferences": {
    "newsletter": true,
    "notifications": "email",
    "language": "en-US"
  },
  "loyaltyProgram": {
    "tier": "gold",
    "points": 2847,
    "nextTierRequirement": 5000
  }
}
```

This single JSON document contains structured elements (`customerId`, `email`), array data (`addresses`), and nested objects (`preferences`, `loyaltyProgram`). In a traditional structured database, this information would require multiple related tables with complex join operations to retrieve complete customer information.

XML (eXtensible Markup Language) predates JSON but remains important in enterprise systems, document processing, and scenarios requiring more sophisticated features like namespaces and schema validation. While more verbose than JSON, XML provides powerful capabilities for document-oriented applications and systems requiring strict validation rules.

YAML (YAML Ain't Markup Language) has gained popularity for configuration files, deployment scripts, and infrastructure-as-code scenarios. Its human-readable format and meaningful whitespace make it particularly popular for DevOps tools and cloud deployment templates.

Logfiles with consistent patterns represent another form of semi-structured data. Application logs, system event logs, and web server logs typically follow predictable patterns with timestamps, severity levels, and message fields, making them semi-structured rather than unstructured. Similarly, IoT sensor data often arrives in semi-structured formats like JSON, with different sensor types providing different fields while maintaining enough structure for processing and analysis.

Use Cases in Azure Environments

Semi-structured data has found numerous applications in Azure's ecosystem, particularly in scenarios requiring flexibility and rapid development cycles. *Document-oriented databases* in Azure, particularly Azure Cosmos DB, are specifically designed to handle JSON and similar formats, providing the flexibility needed for modern application development while maintaining enterprise-grade features like security, backup, and global distribution.

Cloud storage solutions in Azure, such as Azure Blob Storage and Azure Data Lake Storage Gen2, can efficiently store and retrieve semi-structured data files, providing cost-effective options for large volumes of JSON, XML, or other semi-structured formats. These solutions often include built-in capabilities for indexing and querying semi-structured content without requiring data transformation.

Modern analytics platforms in Azure, including Azure Stream Analytics and Azure Databricks, can process semi-structured data directly, extracting insights without requiring conversion to structured formats first. This capability is particularly valuable for analyzing web logs, IoT sensor data, social media feeds, and API response data that naturally arrive in semi-structured formats.

API integration scenarios heavily rely on semi-structured data formats for communication between different systems and services. Azure's integration services, such as Azure Logic Apps and Azure Functions, are designed to work seamlessly with JSON and XML data, enabling sophisticated data integration workflows without complex data transformation requirements.

Exam Tip

The DP-900 exam often presents scenarios requiring you to choose between structured and semi-structured approaches. Focus on understanding the trade-offs: structured data offers consistency and performance for well-defined requirements, while semi-structured data provides flexibility and development speed for evolving or varied requirements.

Benefits and Limitations of Semi-Structured Data

Semi-structured data offers compelling advantages for modern applications, but like all approaches, it involves trade-offs that must be carefully considered.

The benefits are significant. Flexibility allows rapid application development and easy adaptation to changing requirements. Developers can add new fields to records without database schema changes, enabling agile development practices that can respond quickly to user feedback and business requirements. The self-describing nature makes semi-structured data ideal for data exchange between different systems, even when those systems have different internal data structures.

Semi-structured formats also handle complex, nested relationships more naturally than structured data. This makes them ideal for representing real-world entities that don't fit neatly into tabular structures—like product catalogs with varying attributes, user profiles with different information fields, or configuration data with hierarchical relationships.

However, the trade-offs must be understood. The embedded schema information increases storage requirements compared to structured data, sometimes significantly. Query performance may be slower than structured databases for complex analytical operations, particularly those involving large datasets or complex joins. Additionally, the flexibility that makes semi-structured data appealing can lead to inconsistent data quality if not properly managed through application logic and governance processes.

The choice between structured and semi-structured data often depends on specific requirements and organizational context. Applications requiring maximum flexibility and rapid development cycles often benefit from semi-structured approaches, while those needing optimal query performance and strong consistency may be better served by structured alternatives.

As we continue along the data representation spectrum, we encounter unstructured data, which abandons predefined schemas entirely in favor of maximum flexibility and the ability to handle any type of content.

Unstructured Data

Unstructured data represents the most flexible and, in many ways, most challenging end of our data representation spectrum. This category encompasses any information that doesn't follow a predefined schema or organizational structure—everything from text documents and emails to images, videos, audio files, and social media posts. The defining characteristic of unstructured data is its lack of inherent organization; any structure that exists must be derived through analysis rather than being predefined at storage time.

Consider the explosion of unstructured data in our daily lives. Every photo you take creates unstructured visual data. Every email you send contains unstructured text. Every video call generates unstructured audio and visual content. Every social media post, blog article, or document you create adds to the vast universe of unstructured information. This data often contains incredibly rich information about customer sentiment, market trends, and business opportunities, but extracting that value requires different approaches than traditional database queries.

The rise of unstructured data reflects the digital transformation of business and society. While traditional business systems generated primarily structured data in predictable formats, the modern digital ecosystem creates vast amounts of unstructured information through customer interactions, IoT devices, social media platforms, mobile applications, and digital content creation. Organizations that learn to harness this unstructured data often gain significant competitive advantages. These files are often stored as Binary Large Objects (BLOBs), and traditional Online Transaction Processing (OLTP) systems are not optimized to handle and store such data efficiently.

Figure 1-3 reveals the true nature of unstructured data through authentic examples that show why traditional database approaches fall short. Notice how each example—from the informal customer email with emojis and personal asides, to the rich visual content of product images, to the real-time audio waveforms of customer service calls—defies any attempt at standardization. The customer email contains spelling variations, emotional context, and unpredictable length, while the social media posts blend text, hashtags, engagement metrics, and sentiment in ways that would require dozens of database fields to capture partially. Most telling is how the audio and video examples contain layers of meaning—tone of voice, visual context, background information—that simply cannot be reduced to structured fields without losing critical business intelligence. Because this data is so varied and complex, it needs specific AI and machine learning to be useful, but it also provides the most helpful information for today's companies.

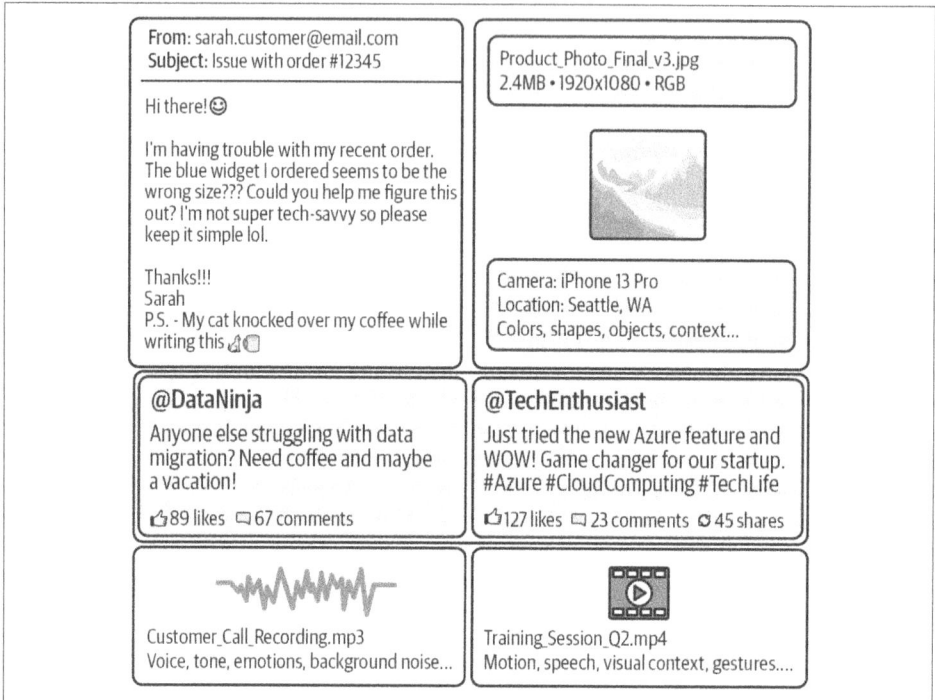

Figure 1-3. Examples of unstructured data in the wild

Characteristics of Unstructured Data

Unstructured data exhibits several key characteristics that distinguish it from structured and semi-structured formats. *Lack of predefined schema* represents its most fundamental characteristic. A collection of customer service emails, for example, might include messages of varying lengths, different languages, various attachment types, and no consistent structure for information like contact details or issue descriptions.

Unstructured data has special processing requirements, which means unstructured data can't be queried directly with SQL. Instead, extracting meaningful information typically requires techniques like natural language processing for text analysis or image recognition for visual content.

Rich contextual information often exists within unstructured data that isn't easily captured in structured formats. A recording of a customer service call contains not just the words spoken but also the tone, emotion, timing, and other nuanced information that could be valuable for understanding customer satisfaction, agent performance, and process improvement opportunities.

Variable size and format characterize unstructured data, which can range from small text files to massive video files, with no consistent pattern in how much storage space each piece of data will require. This variability creates challenges for storage planning and cost management.

> **Warning**
>
> Don't assume unstructured data is less valuable than structured data. While it requires different processing approaches, unstructured data often contains insights and opportunities that aren't available in structured formats. The key is understanding when and how to extract value from each type.

Common Examples of Unstructured Data

Text documents represent one of the most common forms of unstructured data in business environments. This category includes Microsoft Word documents, PDF files, email messages, social media posts, customer reviews, and support tickets. While these documents might have some internal formatting or structure, they don't conform to a consistent schema that would make them suitable for traditional database storage.

Multimedia content forms another major category of unstructured data. Digital images from marketing campaigns, product photography, security cameras, and user-generated content create massive volumes of visual data. Video content from training materials, marketing campaigns, surveillance systems, and customer interactions represents an even larger volume of unstructured information. Audio recordings from customer service calls, meetings, podcasts, and voice messages add another dimension to unstructured data collections. Even when images contain metadata (EXIF data with camera settings, location, etc.), the core image content itself remains unstructured—the metadata may be structured, but the actual visual information is unstructured.

Web content creates enormous volumes of unstructured data through social media posts, blog articles, forum discussions, and user reviews. This content provides rich sources of customer opinions, market insights, and competitive intelligence, but its varied formats and informal language make it challenging to process with traditional analytical tools.

Scientific and research data frequently exists in unstructured formats, including experimental observations, survey responses with free-text fields, interview transcripts, and field notes.

Use Cases in Azure Environments

Unstructured data has found numerous applications in Azure's cloud ecosystem as organizations recognize the value hidden within their unstructured data assets. *Content management and collaboration* scenarios leverage the capabilities of Azure's Blob Storage to handle large volumes of documents, images, and multimedia content while providing secure access, version control, and team collaboration features. In Azure, unstructured data is typically stored in services such as Azure Blob Storage and Azure Data Lake Storage Gen2.

Advanced analytics and AI applications increasingly rely on unstructured data to gain deeper insights into customer behavior, market trends, and operational patterns. Azure's AI and analytics services, such as Azure Cognitive Services and Azure Machine Learning, can process text, images, audio, and video content to extract business intelligence that wouldn't be available from structured data alone.

Machine learning and AI model training scenarios often depend heavily on unstructured data. Image recognition systems need large collections of photos for training, natural language processing models require extensive text corpora, and recommendation systems benefit from unstructured user behavior data and content analysis.

Compliance and archival scenarios frequently involve unstructured data, as organizations need to preserve documents, communications, and multimedia content for regulatory, legal, or historical purposes. Azure's storage solutions provide cost-effective, secure options for long-term retention of unstructured data with access controls and compliance features through services such as Azure Archive Storage.

Digital asset management for marketing, media, and creative organizations involves storing, organizing, and providing access to extensive collections of images, videos, audio files, and documents. Azure's services can handle these requirements while providing search, categorization, and workflow capabilities through integration with Azure Cognitive Search.

Real-World Insight

Many organizations initially focus on structured data and later realize that their unstructured data contains some of their most valuable insights. Starting with a strategy that acknowledges both types of data often leads to better long-term outcomes.

Benefits and Limitations of Unstructured Data

Unstructured data offers unique advantages for capturing the full richness of real-world information, but it also presents challenges that must be carefully managed.

The benefits are multifaceted. Unstructured data can preserve context, nuance, and complexity that might be lost when forcing information into structured formats. Customer reviews contain emotional context and specific details that numerical ratings can't capture. Images contain visual information that text descriptions can't adequately represent. Audio recordings preserve tone and emphasis that text transcripts lose.

Flexibility represents another major advantage: organizations can collect and store unstructured data immediately, then develop processing approaches as understanding of the data's value emerges. This capability is valuable in rapidly changing environments where the structure of critical information isn't predictable in advance.

With unstructured data, *new types of analysis* become possible that simply aren't workable with structured data alone. Sentiment analysis of customer feedback, image recognition for quality control, natural language processing of support tickets, and video analysis for security monitoring all rely on unstructured data sources.

However, the challenges are significant. Storage requirements can be substantial, particularly for multimedia content, and costs can escalate quickly without proper management strategies. Processing unstructured data typically requires specialized tools, skills, and techniques, making it more complex and potentially more expensive than working with structured data.

Query and analysis capabilities for unstructured data are more limited and slower than for structured data. While you can search for keywords in text documents or analyze image content, these operations are typically more resource intensive and less precise than SQL queries against structured databases.

Data quality and consistency can be challenging with unstructured data since there's no schema enforcement to ensure completeness or accuracy. Managing data quality requires different approaches, often involving automated content analysis and manual review processes.

The key to success with unstructured data lies in understanding when its unique capabilities justify the additional complexity and cost. For applications requiring rich context, maximum flexibility, or processing of naturally unstructured content, the benefits often outweigh the challenges.

Bringing It All Together: Data Representation in Practice

Real-world data scenarios rarely involve pure implementations of structured, semi-structured, or unstructured data. Instead, successful modern organizations typically implement hybrid environments that strategically combine multiple data representation approaches to meet diverse business needs. Understanding how these different types work together—and when to use each approach—is crucial for designing effective data solutions in Azure.

Let me illustrate with a comprehensive example. Consider a modern healthcare organization that operates both traditional clinical services and telemedicine platforms. Its patient management system stores core medical records as *structured data* in Azure SQL Database. Patient demographics, insurance information, appointment schedules, lab results, and billing codes all fit neatly into predictable database tables with strong consistency requirements for regulatory compliance and clinical safety.

The same organization captures patient-generated health data through mobile apps and wearable devices as *semi-structured data* stored in Azure Cosmos DB. Blood pressure readings, activity levels, medication adherence, and symptom reports arrive in JSON format with varying fields depending on the device type and patient condition. This data needs to be flexible enough to accommodate new device types and changing health metrics while remaining queryable for clinical analysis.

Meanwhile, the organization also manages vast amounts of *unstructured data* in Azure Blob Storage, including medical imaging files, physician notes, patient communications, research documents, and telemedicine video sessions. This content contains critical clinical information, but it doesn't fit into structured database schemas, and it requires specialized processing for analysis and clinical decision support.

> ### Real-World Insight
>
> The most successful Azure implementations I've worked with use multiple data representation approaches strategically, choosing the right format for each specific use case rather than forcing all data into a single model. This approach maximizes both flexibility and performance while controlling costs. Real-world applications often don't fit neatly into clear textbook example implementations.

Figure 1-4 depicts how this healthcare organization strategically employs all three data representation approaches within a single patient care ecosystem. The structured layer ensures regulatory compliance and clinical safety for core medical records, while the semi-structured layer adapts to the constantly evolving landscape of patient-generated health data from diverse devices and applications. The unstructured layer preserves the rich clinical context and diagnostic expertise that would be lost in rigid data formats. Most importantly, the figure shows how a patient's complete care journey touches all three data types—from initial registration in structured systems, through continuous monitoring via flexible device data, to clinical consultations involving images and physician expertise, ultimately enabling AI-powered insights that combine all data sources for optimal patient outcomes.

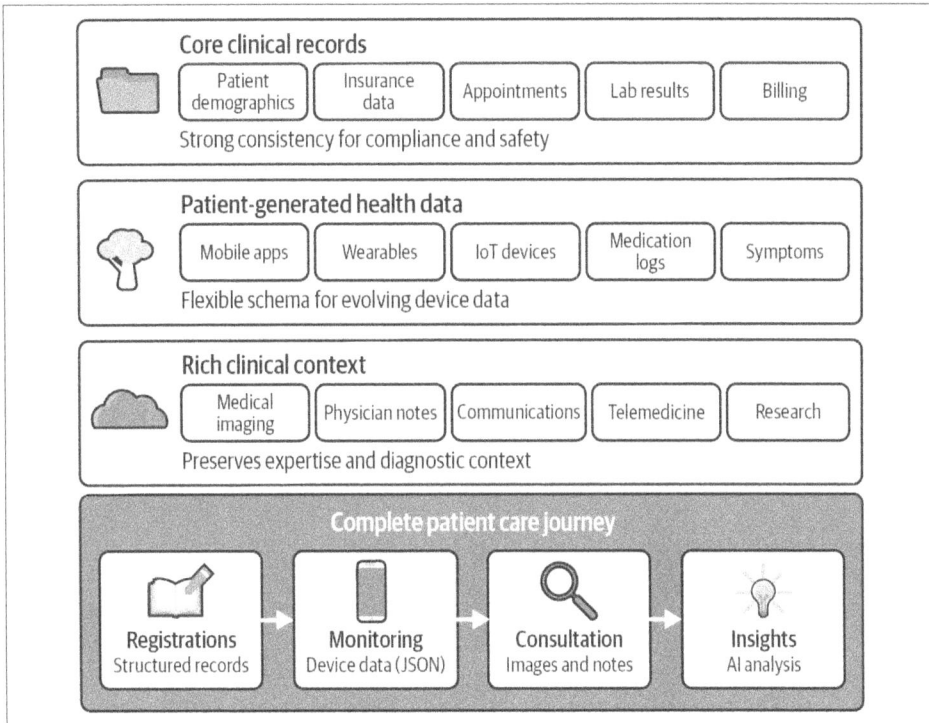

Figure 1-4. Healthcare organization example

Making an Informed Decision About Data Representation

Choosing the appropriate data representation requires careful consideration of multiple factors that extend beyond pure technical requirements. *Performance requirements* often drive decisions between structured and other formats. Applications requiring subsecond response times for complex queries typically benefit from structured data approaches, while applications that can tolerate higher latency for greater flexibility might use semi-structured or processing-intensive unstructured approaches.

Consistency requirements significantly influence format selection. Financial applications requiring strong transactional consistency typically use structured data with ACID properties, while content management applications might accept eventual consistency in exchange for greater flexibility and scalability.

Development velocity considerations often favor semi-structured and unstructured approaches for rapid prototyping and agile development environments, while structured approaches might be preferred for mature applications with well-understood, stable requirements.

Cost considerations involve both storage and processing expenses, which vary significantly by format and usage pattern. Structured data typically offers efficient query performance but might require expensive database licenses or specialized infrastructure. Unstructured data can be stored very cost-effectively but might require expensive processing for analysis and insight extraction.

Integration requirements often influence format choices based on how data needs to be shared with external systems, partners, or future applications. Systems requiring extensive data exchange might favor standard semi-structured formats like JSON, while internal systems might optimize for performance with structured formats.

Skill availability within your organization affects the practical feasibility of different approaches. Teams comfortable with SQL and traditional database tools might achieve better results with structured data, while teams experienced with web development and cloud native approaches might be more productive with semi-structured formats due to JSON's ubiquity in modern web development.

Implementing Evolution and Adaptation Strategies

Data representation needs typically evolve as businesses grow, mature, and encounter new requirements. Many organizations start with structured data for core business processes, then gradually add semi-structured data as they build web applications, APIs, and mobile experiences. Unstructured data often enters the picture as organizations recognize opportunities in customer feedback analysis, content management, and advanced analytics.

Azure's flexible architecture enables organizations to experiment with different approaches and evolve their data representation strategies over time without major disruptions. The platform's diverse storage and processing options allow organizations to start with one approach and gradually incorporate others as needs change, skills develop, and new opportunities emerge.

Migration strategies should consider both current requirements and future growth. Starting with overly rigid structured approaches can constrain future flexibility, while beginning with overly flexible unstructured approaches might create performance and consistency challenges as requirements mature.

Exam Tip

For success on the DP-900 exam, focus on understanding the trade-offs between different data representation approaches rather than memorizing specific service details. Be prepared to analyze scenarios and recommend appropriate approaches based on business requirements, technical constraints, and organizational capabilities.

Summary

The journey from traditional data management to modern cloud-based solutions represents more than just a technological upgrade. It's a fundamental shift in how we conceptualize, organize, and leverage information. Understanding data representation is the cornerstone of making informed decisions in Azure's data platform, where the right choice can dramatically impact performance, cost, and functionality.

Throughout this chapter, we explored how data exists on a spectrum rather than in rigid categories, and how each type serves specific business needs:

Structured data

Provides the reliability and consistency needed for core business operations, offering strong ACID properties and powerful querying capabilities for scenarios requiring predictable formats and complex relationships.

Semi-structured data

Bridges the gap between rigidity and flexibility, enabling rapid development and adaptation while maintaining enough organization for meaningful analysis and integration.

Unstructured data

Captures the full richness of real-world information, preserving context and nuance that would be lost in more restrictive formats.

Exam Tip

The DP-900 exam frequently presents scenarios requiring you to choose between data representation approaches. Focus on understanding the trade-offs: structured data offers consistency and performance for well-defined requirements, semi-structured provides flexibility for evolving needs, and unstructured preserves complete context for complex content.

The evolution from simple spreadsheets to today's complex digital ecosystems reflects how modern organizations must handle diverse data types simultaneously. A CRM system might store contact information as structured data for consistency, communication preferences as semi-structured data for flexibility, and email attachments as unstructured data for complete context preservation—all within the same business process.

Understanding these data representation concepts is crucial because they form the foundation for all subsequent Azure data services we'll explore in later chapters. Whether you're implementing relational databases, NoSQL solutions, or analytics platforms, the principles learned here will guide your architectural decisions and help you optimize for your specific requirements.

Exam Essentials

For success on the DP-900 exam, focus on these key areas:

- Understanding the data spectrum:
  - Know that data representation exists on a continuum, not in rigid categories.
  - Understand when rigidity benefits your solution versus when flexibility is paramount.
  - Recognize that real-world scenarios often require hybrid approaches using multiple data types.
- Structured data fundamentals:
  - Understand schema enforcement and ACID properties.
  - Know the benefits of strong consistency and complex querying capabilities.
  - Recognize scenarios requiring predictable formats and relational integrity.
  - Identify when structured data's limitations outweigh its benefits.
- Semi-structured data characteristics:
  - Understand self-describing data with embedded schema information.
  - Know the flexibility benefits for modern application development.
  - Recognize JSON, XML, and YAML as common semi-structured formats.
  - Identify scenarios where schema flexibility provides business value.
- Unstructured data concepts:
  - Understand the lack of predefined schema and rich contextual information.
  - Know the processing requirements for extracting insights from unstructured content.
  - Recognize scenarios where preserving complete context is crucial.
  - Identify when specialized tools and techniques are needed for analysis.

The key insight from this chapter is that successful data strategies don't force all information into a single representation model. Instead, they strategically combine different approaches, choosing the right format for each specific use case. This hybrid thinking prepares you for the sophisticated Azure data services we'll explore next, where understanding these fundamental concepts becomes essential for designing effective, scalable, and cost-efficient solutions.

As we move forward to explore specific Azure data services in subsequent chapters, remember that these data representation principles will guide every architectural decision. The structured data concepts prepare you for relational databases and data warehousing, semi-structured understanding enables success with NoSQL and document databases, and unstructured data principles become crucial for analytics and AI scenarios.

Beyond the Exam

While the DP-900 exam provides an excellent foundation for understanding data representation, real-world implementation often involves additional complexity and nuance that extends beyond certification requirements. Drawing from my experience helping organizations navigate these choices, let me share some practical insights that will serve you well beyond the exam room.

Common Misconceptions About Data Types and When to Use Each

One of the most persistent misconceptions I encounter is the belief that organizations must choose one data representation approach and stick with it throughout their systems. In reality, the most successful implementations use different approaches for original use cases within the same organization—sometimes even within the same application. A CRM system might store contact information as structured data for consistency and query performance, product interaction history as semi-structured data for flexibility, and customer communications as unstructured data for complete context preservation.

Another frequent misunderstanding involves the relationship between data representation and storage costs. Many organizations assume that structured data is always the most cost-effective because it's more compact, but this ignores processing costs and development time. Semi-structured approaches might use more storage, but they reduce development complexity and time-to-market so significantly that the total cost of ownership is actually lower.

The notion that newer formats are inherently better than traditional approaches represents another common misconception. While semi-structured and unstructured approaches enable capabilities that weren't feasible with traditional methods, structured data remains the best choice for many scenarios requiring strong consistency, optimal query performance, and mature tooling support.

Real-World Examples of Data Type Decisions Gone Wrong

I've worked with organizations that attempted to force all their data into structured formats, only to discover that the rigidity made it impossible to adapt to changing business requirements or integrate with modern web-based systems. One manufacturing client tried to capture all IoT sensor data in a traditional relational database, including variable sensor readings, device configurations, and maintenance notes. The result was a system so complex and rigid that adding new sensor types required months of database schema changes and application updates.

Conversely, I've seen organizations go too far in the opposite direction, storing everything as unstructured data without considering the performance and consistency implications. A financial services client adopted JSON document storage for all their data, including core transaction records, only to discover that regulatory reporting requirements were nearly impossible to meet efficiently without structured data representations and the strong consistency guarantees they provide.

Perhaps most commonly, I've seen organizations underestimate the importance of data quality and governance when working with flexible data formats. Without proper governance frameworks, semi-structured and unstructured data can quickly become inconsistent, unreliable, and difficult to use for meaningful analysis.

Practical Tips for Evaluating Data Structure Needs

When evaluating data representation needs for Azure implementations, start by understanding your query patterns and performance requirements. If you need complex analytical queries with joins across multiple data entities, structured data will probably serve you better. If you need flexibility to adapt to changing requirements or integrate with external APIs, semi-structured approaches might be more appropriate.

Weigh your consistency requirements, but don't assume you need the same level of consistency for all data. Customer financial information requires immediate consistency, but product catalog updates might work perfectly well with eventual consistency models that enable greater flexibility and scalability.

Evaluate your development team's skills and preferred tools honestly. Teams comfortable with SQL and traditional database tools might achieve better results with structured data initially, while teams experienced with web development and APIs might be more productive with semi-structured approaches from the start.

Think about your data's lifecycle and access patterns. Data that's frequently updated and queried might benefit from structured approaches optimized for these operations, while data that's primarily written once and occasionally analyzed might work well with more flexible formats optimized for storage efficiency and analytical processing.

Don't ignore the total cost of ownership in your evaluation. While structured data might have higher licensing costs, it could provide better performance that reduces processing costs and development time. Similarly, while unstructured data might be cheaper to store, the processing costs for extracting insights could be significant and should be factored into decision making.

How to Future-Proof Your Data Representation Choices

The data landscape continues to evolve rapidly, with new formats, processing approaches, and analytical techniques emerging regularly. When making data representation decisions, consider how your choices will adapt to future requirements and technological developments.

Cloud native formats and processing approaches are becoming increasingly important as organizations embrace cloud-first strategies. Understanding how your data representation choices align with cloud native principles—like microservices architectures, API-first designs, and event-driven processing—will help ensure that your solutions remain relevant and efficient as your organization's cloud maturity grows.

AI and machine learning are becoming integral to many business processes, and different data representations have varying levels of compatibility with AI and machine learning workflows. Some formats are more suitable for machine learning tasks than others and considering these future applications during initial design can prevent costly rearchitecture later.

Consider the ecosystem of tools and services that work with different data representations. Structured data benefits from decades of tool development and standardization, while newer formats are rapidly gaining tool support but may have gaps in specific areas. Understanding these tool ecosystems helps inform decisions about long-term maintainability and feature availability.

CHAPTER 2

Data Storage Fundamentals

This chapter explores data storage fundamentals and their implementation in Azure services. Key Azure services covered include Azure Blob Storage for unstructured data, Azure SQL Database for structured data, Azure Cosmos DB for semi-structured data, Azure Data Lake Storage Gen2 for big data scenarios, and Azure Synapse Analytics for data warehousing.

Coverage of Curriculum Objectives

This chapter addresses the following DP-900 exam objectives:

- Understand common data file formats and their characteristics.
- Identify different databases and their use cases.
- Understand the difference between cloud and on-premises storage approaches.
- Recognize appropriate storage solutions for different data scenarios.

Imagine walking into your local coffee shop and placing your usual order. The barista pulls up your loyalty account on their tablet, checks your purchase history, snaps a photo of your custom latte art to post on social media, and processes your payment—all in under a minute. This simple transaction demonstrates the three fundamental challenges every modern organization faces: where to store your structured customer data (loyalty account), how to handle your semi-structured purchase patterns (varying order details), and what to do with unstructured content like photos and social media posts.

Just 20 years ago, that same coffee shop might have used a simple cash register and a paper loyalty punch card. Today's digital-first world has fundamentally transformed not just how we interact with businesses but how organizations must think about storing and managing the explosion of data that these interactions create. The choices you make about data storage impact everything from how quickly customers can complete transactions to how much you spend on technology infrastructure to whether you can extract meaningful business insights from your data.

The evolution of data storage reflects a broader transformation in how businesses operate. That coffee shop's journey from cash registers to cloud-connected point-of-sale systems mirrors what's happening across every industry. A decade ago, most business data fit neatly into spreadsheets and simple databases. Today, the same businesses must handle customer reviews, social media interactions, mobile app usage data, IoT sensor readings, video content, and real-time location information—often all at the same time.

Think about your own daily digital footprint. When you stream a video, you're accessing unstructured multimedia content stored somewhere in the cloud. When you check your bank balance, you're querying structured data that must be absolutely accurate and immediately consistent. When you update your social media profile, you're modifying semi-structured data that needs to be flexible enough to accommodate new features but organized enough for the platform to function. Each of these interactions requires different storage approaches, and understanding these differences is crucial for success in Azure's data platform.

Real-World Insight

I've worked with organizations that struggled for months with performance issues and cost overruns simply because they chose the wrong storage approach for their data types. Understanding these fundamentals can save both time and money while enabling capabilities that wouldn't be possible with mismatched storage solutions.

Data File Format Essentials

Just as different types of content require different containers—you wouldn't ship fragile electronics in an envelope or mail a letter in a shipping crate—different types of data benefit from different file formats. File formats determine how data is encoded, compressed, and organized within files, which directly impacts storage efficiency, processing performance, and compatibility with different tools and systems. A critical distinction exists between row-based formats (optimized for transactional processing where entire records are accessed) and columnar formats (optimized for analytical workloads where specific columns are queried across many records).

The choice of file format often makes the difference between a system that scales efficiently and one that becomes prohibitively expensive as data volumes grow. A social media company storing billions of user photos needs very different file format characteristics than a financial institution processing millions of daily transactions, yet both might use cloud storage—just with different formats optimized for their specific needs.

Figure 2-1 shows the fundamental trade-offs between different file formats. Some formats, like CSV, prioritize human readability and universal compatibility, while others, like Parquet, optimize for storage efficiency and analytical query performance. Understanding these trade-offs helps you make informed decisions about how to store your data for both current and future needs.

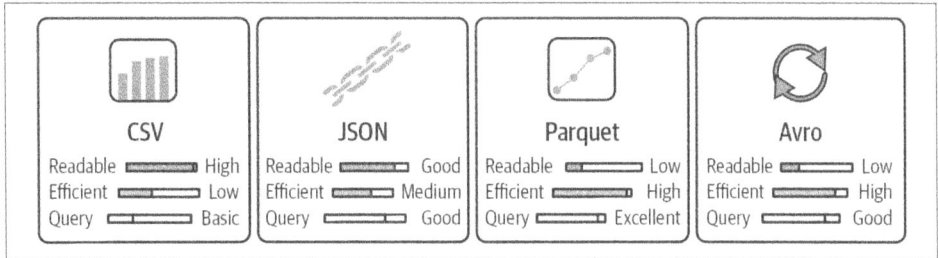

CSV	JSON	Parquet	Avro
Readable — High	Readable — Good	Readable — Low	Readable — Low
Efficient — Low	Efficient — Medium	Efficient — High	Efficient — High
Query — Basic	Query — Good	Query — Excellent	Query — Good

Figure 2-1. Common data file formats and their trade-offs, illustrating how different formats optimize for human readability, storage efficiency, or query performance

Beyond CSV and Parquet, JSON serves as the de facto standard for semi-structured data in web APIs and document databases like Azure Cosmos DB. For streaming scenarios, Apache Avro provides a compact binary format with schema evolution capabilities, making it ideal for use with Azure Event Hubs and Azure Stream Analytics.

In this section, we'll explore the fundamental file formats used in modern data platforms. We'll examine how different formats optimize for specific use cases, from simple data exchange to complex analytical workloads, and understand their trade-offs in terms of storage efficiency, processing performance, and compatibility.

CSV: The Universal Translator

CSV, commonly stored in Azure Blob Storage or Azure Data Lake Storage Gen2, represents one of the most enduring and universally supported data file formats ever created, and there's a good reason it has survived in our increasingly complex digital world. Despite its apparent simplicity—or perhaps because of it—CSV, which stands for *comma-separated values*, remains the go-to choice for data exchange, reporting, and initial data storage across virtually every industry and application domain.

Think of CSV as the common language that almost every system can understand. Whether you're working with Excel, importing data into a database, feeding information to a machine learning algorithm, or sharing data with a business partner who uses completely different software, CSV files provide a reliable bridge between different technologies and organizations.

Strengths of the CSV format

The universality of CSV support represents perhaps its greatest strength. Virtually every database system, analytical tool, spreadsheet application, and programming language can work with CSV files. This makes CSV an excellent choice for data exchange between different systems, providing data to users who might use various tools for analysis, or creating data exports that can be consumed by virtually any downstream system.

Human readability makes CSV files accessible to nontechnical users who can open and understand the data using familiar tools like Excel or Google Sheets. This accessibility enables business users to review, validate, and even modify data without requiring specialized technical tools or expertise—a capability that becomes invaluable during data validation and business review processes.

Simplicity and lightweight nature mean that CSV files are easy to generate, process, and transmit. The format has minimal overhead—no complex headers, metadata, or formatting information—making it efficient for simple data exchange scenarios where you need to move information quickly and reliably.

Limitations that matter in practice

However, CSV files have significant limitations that become apparent in modern data scenarios. Its lack of native data type support means everything is stored as text and must be interpreted by the consuming application. A date might be stored as 2023-12-25, but it's just text until an application interprets it as a date, which can lead to inconsistencies and errors when different systems interpret the same data differently.

Poor handling of complex data structures represents another major limitation. CSV cannot naturally represent nested or hierarchical data, arrays, or complex relationships. Any complex data must be flattened or stored in separate files, which can lead to data integrity challenges and complex processing requirements.

While CSV files cannot represent complex nested structures, alternatives like JSON excel at representing hierarchical data with nested objects and arrays. For analytical workloads requiring better compression and query performance, Parquet format offers columnar storage that can achieve 10x better compression ratios than CSV while enabling efficient column-specific queries.

> **Warning**
>
> Don't assume CSV is always the simplest solution. While CSV files appear simple, the lack of data type information and schema validation can create hidden complexity when systems interpret the same data differently.

When to choose CSV

CSV excels in scenarios involving data exchange between different organizations or systems where universal compatibility is more important than advanced features. It's also ideal for initial data exploration and prototyping where you need to quickly examine data without setting up complex infrastructure.

Business reporting and manual data review scenarios often benefit from CSV's human readability, allowing business users to validate and understand data using familiar spreadsheet tools. However, for production systems requiring data type validation, complex relationships, or high-performance processing, other formats typically provide better long-term solutions.

JSON: The Modern Standard

JSON, natively supported by Azure Cosmos DB and Azure Functions, has emerged as the dominant format for data exchange in modern web applications, APIs, and cloud services. Originally developed for web browsers to communicate with servers, JSON has transcended its JavaScript origins to become the universal language of modern software development, cloud computing, and API integration.

What makes JSON special is its ability to represent complex, nested data structures while remaining both human readable and machine parseable. Unlike CSV, which forces everything into a flat table structure, JSON can naturally represent the way we think about real-world entities with their relationships, attributes, and hierarchical organization.

The power of a flexible structure

JSON's native support for hierarchical data allows it to represent complex real-world entities naturally without requiring the flattening or normalization needed for tabular formats. A customer record can include embedded address information, arrays of order history, and nested preference objects all within a single JSON document.

Consider this example of customer data that would require multiple CSV files or database tables to represent completely:

```
{
  "customerId": "CUST-12345",
  "personalInfo": {
    "name": "Sarah Johnson",
    "email": "sarah.johnson@email.com",
    "memberSince": "2019-03-15"
  },
  "addresses": [
    {
      "type": "billing",
      "street": "123 Main Street",
```

```
      "city": "Seattle",
      "state": "WA",
      "postalCode": "98101"
    },
    {
      "type": "shipping",
      "street": "456 Oak Avenue",
      "city": "Portland",
      "state": "OR",
      "postalCode": "97201"
    }
  ],
  "preferences": {
    "newsletter": true,
    "notifications": "email",
    "language": "en-US"
  }
}
```

This single JSON document contains information that would require at least three separate CSV files or database tables to represent in a normalized structure. JSON's flexibility eliminates the complexity of managing relationships between separate files while preserving the natural organization of the information.

Real-world applications

API communication represents JSON's most common use case, as virtually every modern web service and cloud API uses JSON for both input and output. This ubiquity makes JSON a natural choice for applications that integrate with cloud services, web APIs, or modern software platforms.

Configuration files and settings often use JSON because it can represent complex configuration hierarchies while remaining readable for both humans and software. Many Azure services use JSON for configuration templates, deployment scripts, and service definitions.

Exam Tip

The DP-900 exam frequently tests understanding of when JSON's flexibility provides business value versus when structured data's consistency is more important. Focus on scenarios where data structures vary or evolve frequently.

Trade-offs to consider

JSON offers compelling advantages for modern applications, but like all approaches, it involves trade-offs that must be carefully considered.

Larger file sizes compared to optimized binary formats result from JSON's text-based nature and embedded schema information. However, the flexibility and tool support often justify this overhead for applications prioritizing development speed and system integration over pure storage efficiency.

Processing overhead can be higher than binary formats since JSON requires parsing text into data structures, though modern JSON processing libraries have minimized this impact for most applications. The key is understanding when this trade-off makes sense for your specific use case.

Parquet: The Analytics Powerhouse

Parquet, optimized for Azure Synapse Analytics and Azure Databricks, represents a specialized but increasingly important file format designed specifically for analytical workloads and big data processing. Unlike CSV and JSON, which prioritize readability and interoperability, Parquet optimizes ruthlessly for storage efficiency and query performance in scenarios involving large datasets and analytical processing.

The secret to Parquet's effectiveness lies in its columnar storage approach, which organizes data by columns rather than rows. This organization provides significant advantages for analytical queries that typically operate on subsets of columns across many rows—exactly the pattern common in business intelligence, data warehousing, and analytical reporting scenarios.

Why columnar storage matters

Imagine you're analyzing sales data for a retail chain with millions of transactions. A typical business intelligence query might ask: "What were the total sales by region for the last quarter?" This query needs to read the sales amount and region columns from millions of records while completely ignoring customer names, product descriptions, transaction IDs, and dozens of other fields.

With traditional row-based storage (like CSV), the system must read entire records—including all the irrelevant columns—to access the sales amounts and regions it actually needs. With Parquet's columnar storage, the system can read only the specific columns required for the query, dramatically reducing the amount of data that must be transferred from storage and processed.

Exceptional performance benefits

Compression ratios in Parquet often exceed what's possible with row-based formats because similar data types stored together compress much more efficiently. Columns containing repetitive values (like status codes, country names, or product categories) can achieve compression ratios of 10:1 or better, significantly reducing storage costs and improving query performance.

Query performance optimization comes from the ability to skip irrelevant data entirely. Parquet files include metadata that allows query engines to determine whether specific sections of data contain relevant information before reading them. If you're looking for sales data from January 2024, Parquet can skip entire chunks of data from other time periods without reading them.

When Parquet excels

Data warehousing and business intelligence scenarios represent Parquet's sweet spot. When you need to analyze large volumes of historical data, calculate complex aggregations, or generate reports that examine specific dimensions across millions of records, Parquet's optimizations can improve query performance by orders of magnitude compared to row-based formats.

Big data analytics and machine learning workflows often use Parquet because it can handle massive datasets efficiently while providing the performance needed for iterative analysis and model training. The format's optimization for reading specific columns makes it ideal for feature extraction and data exploration in machine learning pipelines.

> **Note**
>
> Parquet files require specialized tools for viewing and editing, making them less accessible for manual review compared to text-based formats like CSV. However, the performance benefits for analytical workloads often justify this trade-off.

Considerations for implementation

When implementing Parquet, there are several factors to consider.

Parquet files are *not human readable*, which means they require specialized tools for viewing and editing, making them less suitable for scenarios requiring manual data review or debugging. You'll need appropriate tools and skills to work with Parquet effectively, though most modern analytics platforms provide excellent Parquet support.

Optimized for read-heavy workloads rather than frequent updates, Parquet is excellent for analytical scenarios but less suitable for transactional systems that require frequent data modifications. Understanding your access patterns is crucial for determining whether Parquet's benefits align with your requirements.

Avro: The Evolution Engine

Avro occupies a unique position among data formats by providing *schema evolution capabilities* and compact binary encoding while maintaining cross-language compatibility. Originally developed for big data processing systems, Avro has found particular applications in streaming data scenarios and systems requiring schema evolution over time.

The key innovation in Avro is its approach to schema management. Unlike JSON, where schema information is repeated for every record, Avro stores the schema once per file and references it for all records. This provides the benefits of self-describing data while minimizing storage overhead and enabling sophisticated schema evolution capabilities.

Schema evolution in practice

Schema evolution in Avro allows controlled changes to data structure over time while maintaining compatibility with existing data and applications. You can add new fields, change field types (with appropriate conversions), and modify schemas while ensuring that older applications can still read newer data and vice versa.

This capability becomes crucial in environments where data structures evolve frequently but compatibility with existing systems and historical data must be maintained. Streaming systems, event-driven architectures, and long-term data archival scenarios particularly benefit from Avro's evolution capabilities.

Optimal use cases

Event streaming and messaging scenarios, with data processed by Azure Stream Analytics with Azure Event Hubs, benefit from Avro's ability to handle schema evolution gracefully, allowing systems to evolve independently while maintaining compatibility. When you have producers and consumers of data that might update their schemas at different times, Avro provides the flexibility needed to prevent integration breakdowns.

Data archival and long-term storage, such as Azure Archive Storage, leverage Avro's self-describing nature and schema evolution to ensure that data remains accessible even as systems and requirements change over time. The format's ability to maintain compatibility across schema versions makes it ideal for scenarios requiring long-term data preservation.

How to Choose the Right Format for Your Scenario

The key to success with file formats lies in understanding that each one optimizes for different priorities, and the "best" choice depends entirely on your specific requirements and constraints.

For data exchange and initial prototyping, CSV's simplicity and universal support make it an excellent choice, despite its limitations with complex data structures and data types. When you need to quickly share data with business users or integrate with unknown downstream systems, CSV's universality often outweighs its technical limitations.

For modern application development and API integration, JSON excels in scenarios requiring flexibility, rapid development, and integration with web-based systems. Its native support for hierarchical data and wide tool support make it ideal for cloud native applications and services.

For analytical workloads and data warehousing, Parquet provides unmatched performance when query efficiency and storage optimization are paramount. Its columnar structure and compression capabilities make it the preferred choice for scenarios involving large datasets and complex analytical queries.

For streaming and event-driven architectures, Avro provides the best balance of performance and schema evolution capabilities, particularly in scenarios where data structures change over time and system compatibility is crucial.

Types of Databases: Choosing Your Data Foundation

Understanding different database types is like understanding different types of vehicles—each one is optimized for specific use cases, terrain, and performance requirements. Just as you wouldn't use a sports car to haul construction materials or a dump truck for a family road trip, different database types excel in different scenarios. The choice between database types significantly impacts application performance, development complexity, operational costs, and your ability to scale and adapt to changing requirements.

The database landscape has evolved dramatically with cloud computing, reflecting the reality that no single database type can optimally serve all possible requirements. Traditional relational databases remain critically important for many scenarios, but new database types have emerged to address limitations of relational models in handling modern application patterns, data volumes, and development practices.

Figure 2-2 illustrates how different database types optimize for different priorities. Relational databases prioritize consistency and complex relationships, NoSQL databases emphasize flexibility and scale, and specialized databases optimize for specific workloads like analytics or time-series data.

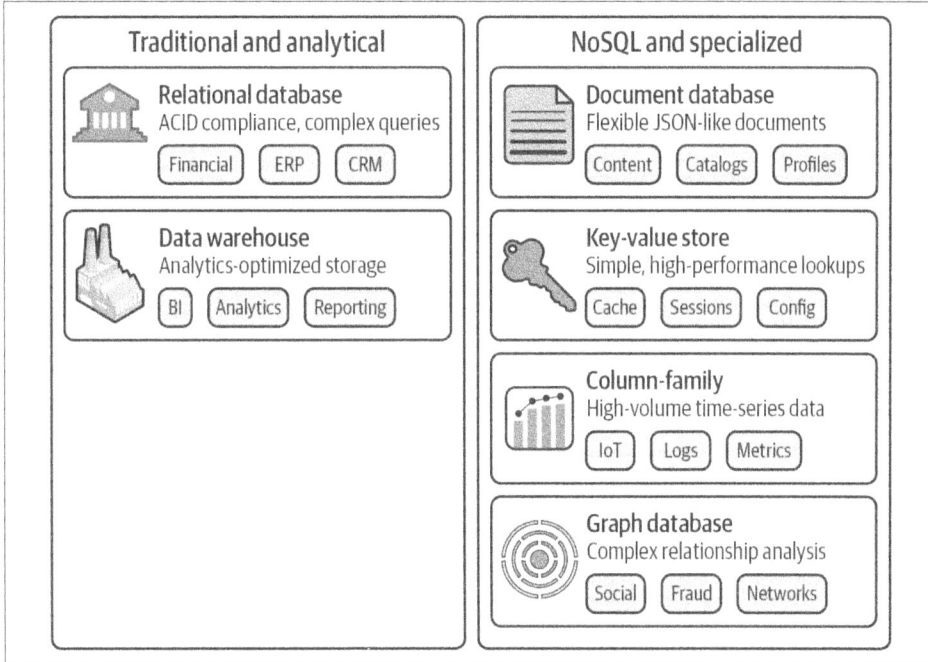

Figure 2-2. Database types and their optimal use cases, showing how different database types serve different needs, from transactional consistency to flexible schemas to massive scale

Relational Databases: The Reliable Foundation

Relational databases represent the most mature and widely understood database technology, built on decades of research, development, and real-world application. Based on mathematical principles of relational algebra, these databases organize data into tables with defined relationships between them, providing strong consistency guarantees and powerful querying capabilities through SQL.

Think of relational databases as the foundation of a well-built house—solid, reliable, and designed to support complex structures built on top of them. The core strength of relational databases lies in their ability to maintain data integrity through constraints, transactions, and normalized data structures, making them ideal for applications where data consistency is absolutely paramount.

The ACID foundation

ACID properties ensure that database transactions are processed reliably, making relational databases ideal for applications where data integrity is paramount. When you transfer money between bank accounts, relational databases guarantee the money is never lost, duplicated, or left in an inconsistent state, even if thousands of other transactions are happening simultaneously or if a power failure occurs mid-transaction.

Atomicity ensures that transactions either complete entirely or fail entirely—there's no middle ground where part of a transaction succeeds while another part fails. This all-or-nothing approach prevents data corruption and maintains system integrity.

Consistency guarantees that all database rules, constraints, and relationships are maintained after every transaction. If your business rules state that customer orders must have valid customer IDs, the database will reject any transaction that would violate this rule.

Isolation ensures that concurrent transactions don't interfere with each other, even when accessing the same data simultaneously. If two customers try to buy the last item in stock at the same time, isolation ensures that only one transaction succeeds, preventing the item from being oversold.

Durability means that once a transaction is committed, it will persist even if system failures occur immediately afterward. If you successfully transfer money between accounts, that transaction remains permanent even if the bank's computer system crashes seconds later.

Powerful query capabilities

SQL's sophisticated querying capabilities enable complex analysis and reporting that would be difficult or impossible with other database types. The predictable table structure allows for operations like joining data from multiple tables, calculating complex aggregations, and performing statistical analysis across different dimensions of your data.

Consider a retail company analyzing customer purchasing patterns. With relational databases, you can easily join customer information, order history, product details, and inventory data to answer complex questions, like "Which customers who purchased winter coats in the last two years are most likely to be interested in our new spring collection, and what's their preferred communication channel?"

When relational databases shine

Financial and transactional systems benefit from the strong consistency guarantees and mature transaction processing capabilities of relational databases. Banking systems, ecommerce order processing, and accounting applications require the reliability and accuracy that relational databases provide through their ACID properties and mature transaction management.

Complex business applications with well-defined data structures and relationships leverage the ability of relational databases to maintain data integrity across multiple interconnected entities. ERP systems, CRM platforms, and human resources management systems typically rely on relational database capabilities to ensure data consistency across complex business processes.

Analytical reporting scenarios that require complex queries across multiple related data sources benefit from SQL's sophisticated querying capabilities and the performance optimizations available in modern relational database engines. The ability to join data from multiple tables and perform complex calculations makes relational databases excellent for business intelligence and reporting scenarios.

Limitations

While relational databases provide significant advantages, they also have limitations that become apparent in certain modern scenarios. *Rigid schema requirements* can make it difficult to adapt to rapidly changing business needs. Adding new fields or changing data types often requires significant planning, testing, and potentially system downtime.

Scaling challenges arise when applications need to handle massive volumes of data or extremely high transaction rates. While modern relational databases can scale significantly, they often require complex configuration and expensive hardware to handle the largest workloads effectively.

Note that in Part II of the book, these limitations will be discussed in more detail.

NoSQL Databases: The Flexibility Champions

NoSQL databases emerged to address limitations of relational databases in handling varied data structures, massive scale, and rapid development cycles that characterize modern applications. The term *NoSQL* encompasses several different database models, each optimized for specific use cases and data patterns that don't fit well within traditional relational constraints.

The fundamental philosophy behind NoSQL databases is specialization rather than generalization—optimizing for specific use cases rather than trying to provide a universal solution. This specialization enables exceptional performance and scalability for targeted scenarios while potentially sacrificing some of the general-purpose capabilities of relational databases.

Document databases: Natural data representation

Document databases store data in document format, typically using JSON or similar structures. This approach provides flexibility for applications with varied or evolving data structures while maintaining queryability and indexing capabilities that enable sophisticated searches and analysis.

Schema flexibility allows developers to add new fields or modify data structures without database migrations, enabling agile development practices that can respond quickly to changing requirements. If you need to add a new field to customer records, you can simply start including it in new documents without modifying existing records or database schemas.

Document databases excel in *content management, product catalogs, and user profile scenarios* where data structures vary between records. An ecommerce product catalog might have very different attributes for books (author, ISBN, pages) versus electronics (manufacturer, model, warranty) versus clothing (size, color, material). Document databases handle this variation naturally without requiring complex table structures or schema modifications.

Key-value databases: Simple and fast

Key-value databases provide the simplest NoSQL model, storing data as key-value pairs without any predefined schema or complex query capabilities. This simplicity enables exceptional performance and scalability for scenarios involving simple lookup operations.

Extreme scalability becomes possible with key-value databases because their simple data model eliminates many of the consistency challenges that limit other database types. When you need to store and retrieve data using known keys—like user session information, shopping cart contents, or cache data—key-value databases can provide submillisecond response times even at massive scale.

These databases excel in *session storage, caching, and simple lookup scenarios* where you need fast access to data using a known key but don't require complex querying capabilities. Web applications often use key-value databases to store user session information that needs to be retrieved quickly during each page request.

Column-family databases: Big data optimization

Column-family databases organize data into column families rather than traditional rows and columns, optimizing for scenarios requiring massive scale and high write throughput. This structure works particularly well for time-series data, logging applications, and IoT data collection where you need to store large volumes of similar data efficiently.

High write throughput capabilities make column-family databases ideal for scenarios where you're collecting large volumes of data from multiple sources simultaneously. IoT sensors, application logs, and real-time analytics scenarios often benefit from the write performance that column-family databases provide.

Graph databases: Relationship excellence

Graph databases specialize in representing and querying relationships between entities, using nodes, edges, and properties to model complex interconnected data. They excel in scenarios where understanding connections and relationships is more important than the individual data elements themselves.

Complex relationship analysis becomes efficient with graph databases in ways that would be impractical with other database types. Social networks, recommendation engines, fraud detection, and network analysis all involve traversing complex relationships and identifying patterns across connected data—exactly what graph databases are designed to handle efficiently.

Warning

Don't assume NoSQL databases are inherently better than relational databases. They're optimized for different scenarios. The key is understanding when each approach provides the best fit for your specific requirements.

NoSQL decisions

The choice between different NoSQL approaches depends on your specific data patterns and requirements. *Document databases* work well when you have complex, nested data structures that vary between records. *Key-value databases* excel for simple, high-performance lookup scenarios. *Column-family databases* optimize for high-volume write scenarios and time-series data. *Graph databases* provide the best solution for complex relationship analysis.

Understanding these distinctions helps you choose the right NoSQL approach rather than simply selecting NoSQL as a generic alternative to relational databases.

Note that in Part III of the book, these will be discussed in more detail.

Data Warehouses: The Analytics Specialists

Data warehouses represent specialized database systems optimized for analytical workloads rather than transactional processing. Unlike transactional databases that optimize for fast individual record operations, data warehouses optimize for queries that analyze large volumes of data across multiple dimensions to support business intelligence and decision-making processes.

Think of data warehouses as the difference between a corner convenience store and a massive wholesale warehouse. The convenience store (transactional database) is optimized for quick individual purchases with immediate availability. The wholesale warehouse (data warehouse) is optimized for bulk analysis and complex operations that examine large quantities of inventory across multiple categories.

Analytical architecture

Denormalized data structures in data warehouses are designed specifically for analytical queries rather than transactional consistency. Star schemas and snowflake schemas organize data into fact tables (containing measurable events like sales transactions) and dimension tables (containing descriptive attributes like customer information, product details, and time periods) to optimize for business intelligence queries.

Data warehouses *focus on historical data*, which means they excel at storing and analyzing historical information to identify trends, patterns, and relationships over time. While they may include current data, their primary value comes from providing historical context that enables businesses to understand long-term trends and make data-driven decisions.

Data processing

Data transformation processes convert operational data from various source systems into formats optimized for analytical queries. This transformation might involve cleaning data, calculating derived metrics, organizing information into analytical structures, and combining data from multiple source systems into coherent analytical datasets.

Business intelligence integration provides optimized data structures and performance for reporting tools, dashboards, and analytical applications that business users rely on for decision making. Data warehouses are specifically designed to support the types of queries that business intelligence tools generate, often involving complex aggregations across multiple dimensions.

Data warehouse use cases

Enterprise reporting and business intelligence applications rely on data warehouses for consistent, fast access to historical data organized for analytical queries. Monthly sales reports, customer segmentation analysis, and performance dashboards typically draw from data warehouse systems that can efficiently process complex analytical queries across large datasets.

Financial analysis and planning leverage data warehouses for budgeting, forecasting, and variance analysis that requires historical data and complex calculations across multiple business dimensions. The ability to quickly analyze financial performance across different time periods, business units, and product categories makes data warehouses essential for financial management.

> **Note**
>
> You will explore specific Azure database and data warehouse services in detail in later chapters. This chapter focuses on understanding the fundamental concepts and use cases that drive database selection decisions.

Note that in Part IV, the concept of warehouses and big data will be explored further.

Cloud Versus On-Premises Storage: The Strategic Choice

The choice between cloud and on-premises storage represents one of the most significant strategic decisions organizations face when developing their data strategy. This decision impacts not just where data is stored but also how it's accessed, protected, managed, scaled, and integrated with other systems. Understanding the trade-offs between these approaches is crucial for making informed storage decisions that align with both current needs and future growth plans.

Imagine two restaurants: one that owns all its equipment and handles everything in-house and another that uses shared commercial kitchen facilities and food delivery services. Both can serve excellent meals, but they've made different strategic choices about control, cost, flexibility, and capabilities. Similarly, cloud and on-premises storage represent different strategic approaches to managing your data infrastructure.

Figure 2-3 shows how cloud and on-premises storage each offer distinct advantages. Cloud storage excels in scalability, managed services, and global accessibility, while on-premises storage provides complete control, predictable costs for stable workloads, and independence from internet connectivity.

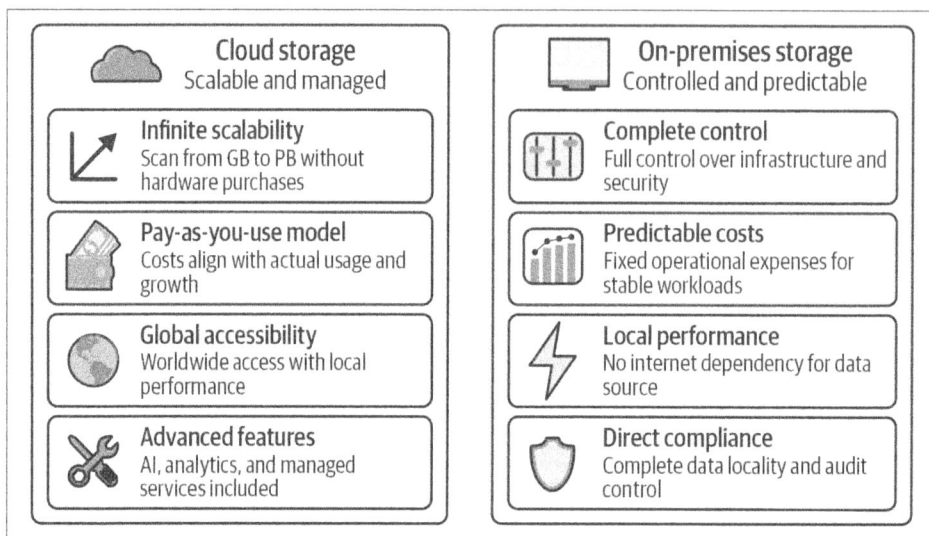

Cloud storage Scalable and managed	On-premises storage Controlled and predictable
Infinite scalability Scan from GB to PB without hardware purchases	**Complete control** Full control over infrastructure and security
Pay-as-you-use model Costs align with actual usage and growth	**Predictable costs** Fixed operational expenses for stable workloads
Global accessibility Worldwide access with local performance	**Local performance** No internet dependency for data source
Advanced features AI, analytics, and managed services included	**Direct compliance** Complete data locality and audit control

Figure 2-3. Cloud versus on-premises storage trade-offs, illustrating the different benefits and considerations for each approach

Advantages of Cloud Storage

Cloud storage provides several compelling advantages that have driven widespread adoption across industries of all sizes. These benefits often compound over time, making cloud storage increasingly attractive as organizations grow and their requirements become more sophisticated.

Scalability without limits

Cloud storage has *infinite scale potential*, which allows organizations to grow storage from gigabytes to petabytes without hardware purchases, capacity planning, or architectural changes. You can start small and scale to massive volumes as needed, paying only for what you actually use rather than having to invest in peak capacity up front.

This elasticity is particularly valuable for applications with unpredictable or seasonal demand patterns. A retail company can handle Black Friday traffic spikes without pre-purchasing infrastructure that sits idle most of the year. A startup can begin with minimal storage costs and scale seamlessly as the business grows, without the capital expenditure barriers that once limited small-business growth.

Cloud storage has *elastic scaling*, which enables storage to automatically grow and shrink based on actual usage patterns. This capability transforms storage from a constraint that requires careful planning into a flexible resource that adapts to your business needs in real time.

Cost efficiency through scale

With cloud storage, *capital expenditures are eliminated*, which means organizations can avoid up-front hardware investments and redirect capital to business-differentiating activities. The operational expense model also provides better alignment between costs and business value, with storage costs scaling proportionally to business growth rather than requiring large up-front investments.

Cloud providers achieve *economies of scale*, which result in cost efficiencies that individual organizations couldn't achieve independently. Cloud providers can invest in optimization, automation, and efficiency improvements that benefit all customers, often providing better price performance than organizations could achieve independently.

Multiple storage tiers in cloud storage enable cost optimization by automatically moving data between different performance and cost tiers based on access patterns. Frequently accessed data stays in high-performance tiers, while archival data moves to lower-cost storage automatically, optimizing costs without manual intervention.

Global capabilities

With cloud storage, *worldwide availability* enables organizations to provide fast data access from multiple geographic locations without building and managing global infrastructure. Applications can serve users worldwide with consistent performance by leveraging cloud providers' global data center networks.

Automatic replication across geographic regions provides both performance benefits through local data access and disaster recovery capabilities through geographic redundancy. This level of global distribution would be prohibitively expensive for most organizations to implement independently.

Real-World Insight

In my experience, organizations that embrace cloud storage's advanced features—not just basic storage—often see the greatest return on investment. The integration capabilities and managed services provide value beyond simple cost savings.

Built-in advanced features

There are a number of built-in advanced features to consider when using cloud storage.

Enterprise-grade security features often exceed what organizations can implement independently. Cloud providers invest heavily in security infrastructure, compliance certifications, threat detection, and incident response capabilities that would be extremely expensive for individual organizations to develop and maintain.

Automatic backup and disaster recovery capabilities provide data protection that scales with storage usage. Advanced features like point-in-time recovery, cross-region replication, and automated failover provide business continuity capabilities that would require significant investment to implement on premises.

Integration with advanced services creates opportunities for data processing, analysis, and AI capabilities that weren't feasible with traditional storage approaches. Cloud storage can trigger automated processing workflows, integrate with analytics services, and support AI and machine learning scenarios without requiring data movement.

Considerations for Cloud Storage

While cloud storage provides significant benefits, organizations must also carefully consider potential challenges and limitations to make informed decisions.

Cost management complexity

Variable costs can become unpredictable without proper monitoring and management. Data transfer costs, API call charges, and different pricing tiers for various access patterns can create unexpected expenses if not carefully planned and monitored.

Understanding the full cost model becomes crucial for success with cloud storage. While basic storage costs are usually transparent, data transfer costs, transaction fees, and access charges can add up significantly for certain usage patterns. Organizations need to design their applications and data access patterns with these cost considerations in mind.

Compliance and control considerations

When using cloud storage, you will need to factor in compliance and control considerations.

Data sovereignty requirements might constrain cloud storage options, particularly for organizations in highly regulated industries or jurisdictions with strict data residency requirements. While cloud providers offer regional data storage options, organizations must carefully evaluate these capabilities against their specific regulatory requirements.

With *reduced direct control* over infrastructure, organizations must rely on cloud providers for security, availability, and performance. While this delegation often improves outcomes, it also means organizations have less direct control over critical infrastructure and must ensure that cloud provider capabilities align with their requirements.

Advantages of On-Premises Storage

On-premises storage retains several advantages that make it appropriate for certain scenarios and organizations. Understanding these advantages helps inform decisions about when on-premises approaches might be preferable.

Complete control and customization

Infrastructure control allows organizations to customize storage configurations, security implementations, and integration approaches to meet specific requirements that might not be available through standardized cloud services. This control can be crucial for organizations with unique technical requirements or regulatory constraints that require specific configurations.

Security customization enables organizations to implement specific security controls and access patterns that might be required for regulatory compliance or organizational policies. Some organizations need to maintain complete control over their security implementation rather than relying on cloud provider security models.

Cost predictability

The *predictable operational costs* of on-premises storage can benefit organizations with stable storage requirements, as on-premises storage avoids the variable costs associated with cloud storage usage patterns. For organizations with consistent, high-volume storage needs, on-premises solutions might provide better cost predictability and potentially lower total costs over extended periods.

On-prem storage *doesn't have ongoing usage fees*, which means that once infrastructure is purchased and deployed, the ongoing costs are primarily operational (power, cooling, maintenance) rather than usage based. This can provide cost advantages for organizations with stable, predictable storage requirements that don't require frequent scaling.

Performance and latency

No internet dependency ensures that data access remains available even during internet outages or connectivity issues. This reliability can be crucial for applications requiring guaranteed data access regardless of external connectivity, particularly in mission-critical scenarios where any downtime could have significant business impact.

Optimal performance for local access can provide better performance for applications requiring very low latency access to data, particularly when processing large datasets where network transfer times would significantly impact performance. Direct attached storage can provide performance characteristics that may be difficult to achieve over internet connections.

Compliance advantages

Data locality guarantees ensure that data remains within specific geographic boundaries or under specific legal jurisdictions, which can simplify compliance with certain regulatory requirements. Some regulations require absolute certainty about data location and handling, which on-premises storage can provide more directly than cloud solutions.

Direct audit capabilities allow organizations to provide direct access to auditors and compliance officers without involving third-party cloud providers. This can simplify compliance processes and provide the level of transparency that some regulatory frameworks require.

Considerations for On-Premises Storage

On-premises storage also involves trade-offs and challenges that organizations must carefully consider.

Capital and operational requirements

Significant capital expenditures for hardware, infrastructure, and facility improvements can be substantial, particularly for organizations needing enterprise-grade storage capabilities with high availability and disaster recovery features. The up-front investment required for robust on-premises storage can be a barrier for smaller organizations or those with limited capital.

Operational complexity increases with on-premises storage, as organizations must manage hardware maintenance, software updates, security patches, capacity planning, and disaster recovery. This complexity requires specialized expertise and ongoing operational investment that many organizations underestimate.

Scalability limitations

Capacity planning challenges arise from the need to plan and purchase storage capacity in advance. Organizations risk either over-provisioning (wasting money on unused capacity) or under-provisioning (constraining growth due to storage limitations). Getting this balance right requires accurate forecasting and can be particularly challenging for growing organizations.

With *limited elasticity*, scaling storage capacity requires hardware purchases, installation, and configuration, which can take weeks or months and requires significant up-front investment. This limitation can constrain business agility and responsiveness to changing requirements.

Azure Hybrid Solutions

Recognizing that many organizations benefit from combining cloud and on-premises
storage approaches, Azure provides hybrid solutions that bridge the gap between
these models. These solutions enable organizations to keep some data on premises
while leveraging cloud capabilities for backup, archival, burst capacity, or specific use
cases.

Best of both worlds

Hybrid approaches allow organizations to maintain control over sensitive data while
leveraging cloud scalability and services for appropriate workloads. Organizations
can keep critical operational data on premises while using cloud storage for analytics,
backup, or disaster recovery, combining the advantages of both approaches
strategically.

Migration pathways enable gradual transition to cloud storage as organizational comfort and requirements evolve. Hybrid solutions often provide stepping stones that
allow organizations to gain experience with cloud storage while maintaining existing
on-premises investments, reducing the risk and complexity of cloud adoption.

Workload optimization enables different storage approaches for different types of data
and applications based on their specific requirements rather than forcing all data into
a single model. This strategic approach often provides better outcomes than trying to
use a single storage approach for all organizational needs.

Summary

The journey through data storage fundamentals reveals how the evolution from simple file cabinets to cloud-scale storage systems reflects the broader digital transformation happening across every industry. Understanding these storage concepts is crucial because they form the foundation for all Azure data services and inform every architectural decision you'll make.

Throughout this chapter, we explored how different storage approaches serve specific business needs:

File formats
> Provide the foundation for data organization, with CSV offering universal compatibility, JSON enabling flexible modern applications, Parquet optimizing analytical performance, and Avro supporting schema evolution.

Database types
> Optimize for different scenarios, with relational databases providing consistency for transactional systems, NoSQL databases offering flexibility for modern applications, and data warehouses specializing in analytical workloads.

Cloud versus on-premises storage
> Represents a strategic choice between scalability and control, with hybrid approaches often providing the best balance for real-world requirements.

The key insight from this chapter is that successful data strategies don't force all information into a single storage model. Instead, they strategically combine different approaches, choosing the right solution for each specific use case based on performance requirements, consistency needs, cost constraints, and organizational capabilities.

Exam Tip

The DP-900 exam frequently presents scenarios requiring you to choose between storage approaches. Focus on understanding the trade-offs—file formats balance readability versus efficiency, database types optimize for different workloads, and cloud versus on premises represents strategic choices about control versus scalability.

Exam Essentials

For success on the DP-900 exam, focus on these key areas:

- File format fundamentals:
  - Understand CSV's universal compatibility versus limited data type support.
  - Know JSON's flexibility for modern applications and API integration.
  - Recognize Parquet's optimization for analytical workloads.
  - Identify Avro's schema evolution capabilities for streaming scenarios.
- Database type selection:
  - Understand the ACID properties and SQL capabilities of relational databases.
  - Know the NoSQL types: document, key-value, column-family, and graph databases.
  - Recognize data warehouse optimization for analytical queries.
  - Identify scenarios where each database type provides optimal value.
- Storage strategy decisions:
  - Understand cloud storage benefits: scalability, cost efficiency, and global access.
  - Know on-premises advantages: control, predictable costs, and local performance.
  - Recognize hybrid approaches for balanced solutions.
  - Identify decision factors: performance, consistency, cost, and compliance.

Understanding these data storage fundamentals prepares you for the specific Azure data services we'll explore in subsequent chapters. The file format concepts enable success with Azure Storage services, database fundamentals guide choices between Azure SQL and Cosmos DB, and cloud storage principles inform decisions across the entire Azure data platform.

As we move forward to explore specific Azure data services, remember that these storage principles will guide every architectural decision. The structured data concepts prepare you for relational databases and data warehousing, semi-structured understanding enables success with NoSQL solutions, and unstructured data principles become crucial for analytics and AI scenarios.

Most importantly, successful Azure implementations strategically combine multiple storage approaches rather than forcing all data into a single model. This hybrid thinking—choosing the right tool for each job—represents the foundation of effective data architecture in the cloud.

Beyond the Exam

While the DP-900 exam provides excellent foundational knowledge about data storage concepts, real-world implementation often involves additional complexity and considerations that extend beyond certification requirements. Drawing from experience helping organizations navigate storage decisions, here are practical insights that will serve you well in actual Azure implementations.

Choosing the Right Storage Solution: A Practical Decision Framework

When evaluating storage options, use a systematic approach that starts with understanding the data itself and gradually incorporates business and technical constraints. This methodology helps avoid the common mistake of jumping to storage solutions before fully understanding requirements:

Start with data characterization

Is your data primarily structured, semi-structured, or unstructured? How frequently will it be accessed? Do you need real-time access, or can you tolerate some delay? What are your performance requirements for both read and write operations? These fundamental questions often eliminate many options and point toward appropriate storage approaches.

Consider access patterns

Will you be reading small amounts of data frequently or large amounts occasionally? Do you need to support many concurrent users or occasional batch processing? Understanding these patterns helps determine whether you need storage optimized for transaction processing, analytical queries, or content delivery.

Evaluate consistency requirements

Does all your data need immediate consistency, or can some data work with eventual consistency models? Financial data typically requires strong consistency, while content management might work well with eventual consistency in exchange for better performance and scalability.

Assess organizational constraints

What existing skills does your team have? What's your budget for both implementation and ongoing operations? What compliance requirements must you meet? These factors often influence storage decisions as much as technical requirements. Considering them early prevents costly redesigns later.

Identifying the Hidden Costs in Cloud Storage: What to Watch For

One of the most common surprises organizations encounter with cloud storage involves understanding the full cost model. While basic storage costs are usually transparent and predictable, several other cost factors can significantly impact your total expenses if not properly planned.

Data transfer costs represent the most frequent source of unexpected expenses. While storing data in the cloud is often very cost-effective, moving large amounts of data can be expensive, particularly for data egress (downloading data from the cloud). Organizations should carefully evaluate their data movement patterns and consider strategies to minimize unnecessary transfers.

API call costs can accumulate unexpectedly, particularly for applications that make many small requests to storage services. Each request to read, write, or list files typically incurs a small charge, but these can add up significantly for high-volume applications. Designing efficient data access patterns—like batching operations, implementing intelligent caching, or using larger file sizes—can help control these costs.

Access pattern mismatches occur when data is stored in the wrong storage tier for its actual usage pattern. Frequently accessed data stored in archival tiers incurs high access fees, while rarely accessed data in premium tiers wastes money on unnecessary performance. Understanding and monitoring actual access patterns helps optimize storage tier selection.

> **Real-World Insight**
>
> Many organizations initially focus on structured data and later realize that their unstructured data contains some of their most valuable insights. Starting with a strategy that acknowledges both types of data often leads to better long-term outcomes.

Future-Proofing Your Data Storage Choices

The storage landscape continues to evolve rapidly, with new capabilities, pricing models, and technologies emerging regularly. When making storage decisions today, it's important to consider how your choices will adapt to future requirements and technological developments.

Cloud native approaches generally provide better flexibility for adaptation to new technologies and requirements. Even if you start with traditional approaches, understanding how to evolve toward cloud native patterns can help ensure that your solutions remain relevant and efficient.

Consider emerging use cases like AI and machine learning, real-time analytics, and global applications when making storage decisions. Different storage approaches have varying levels of compatibility with these technologies, and planning for these capabilities during initial design can prevent costly re-architecture later.

Evaluate tool ecosystem evolution as storage decisions impact not just immediate capabilities but also future tool and service availability. Understanding these tool ecosystems helps inform decisions about long-term maintainability and feature availability.

CHAPTER 3

Understanding Data Workloads

The shift to cloud computing has both changed where we store data and transformed how we process it. As organizations migrate their data operations to Azure, traditional approaches to handling transactions and analytics have developed dramatically. Understanding the difference between transactional and analytical workloads—and knowing how to design systems that support each effectively—is crucial for anyone working with Azure's data platform and is essential for the DP-900 exam.

The distinction between transactional and analytical workloads is more than just academic. It drives real-world decisions about database selection, infrastructure design, application architecture, and operational procedures. For instance, Azure SQL Database excels at transactional processing, while Azure Synapse Analytics is optimized for analytical workloads. A system optimized for processing individual customer orders operates differently from one designed to analyze sales trends across millions of transactions. Getting this distinction wrong can cause poor performance, excessive costs, frustrated users, and missed business opportunities.

Coverage of Curriculum Objectives

This chapter addresses the following DP-900 exam objectives:

- Understand the characteristics of transactional workloads (OLTP).
- Understand the characteristics of analytical workloads (OLAP).
- Identify appropriate Azure solutions for different workload types.
- Understand workload considerations for system design.

Data Workloads in Everyday Terms

Figure 3-1 illustrates the fundamental distinction between transactional and analytical workloads through everyday banking interactions. When you check your bank balance on your phone, transfer money between accounts, or make a purchase online, you're interacting with *transactional workloads* that must process your request immediately and accurately. These systems handle individual transactions one at a time, ensuring that each operation is completed quickly and correctly. Your bank's computer system needs to update your account balance instantly, verify you have enough money for a purchase, and record every transaction permanently.

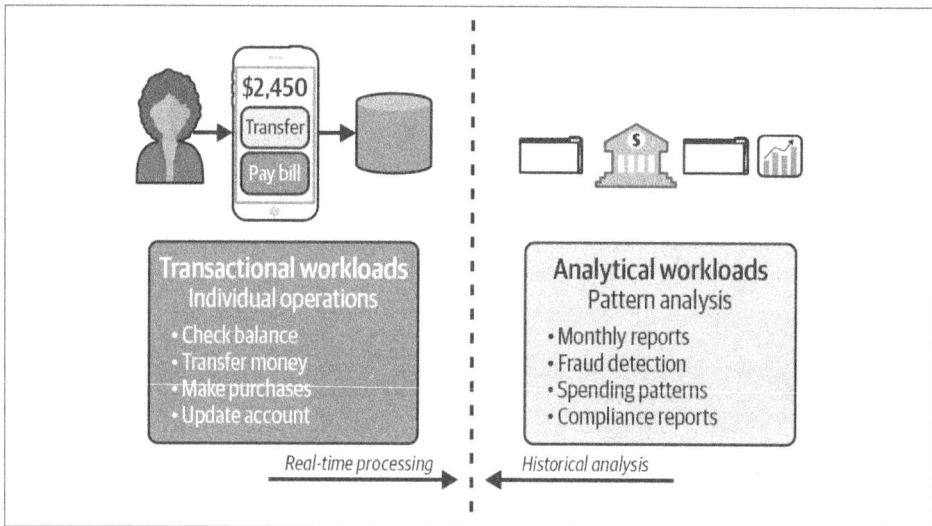

Figure 3-1. Daily digital interactions

When your bank generates monthly statements, analyzes spending patterns for fraud detection, or creates reports for regulatory compliance, it's using *analytical workloads* that examine large volumes of historical data to extract insights and patterns. These systems analyze thousands or millions of transactions simultaneously to identify trends, detect unusual behavior, and generate comprehensive reports. For example, the bank might analyze six months of credit card transactions across all customers to identify spending patterns that could show fraudulent activity.

The evolution of data workloads reflects the broader transformation of business operations in the digital age. In the early days of computing, businesses primarily dealt with transactional workloads—processing orders, managing inventory, and handling customer interactions. These systems were designed to handle the day-to-day operations that kept businesses running. As organizations grew and data volumes increased, the need for analytical workloads became apparent for competitive advantage, regulatory compliance, and operational optimization.

Today's modern businesses require both capabilities, often operating them simultaneously and integrating insights from analytical systems back into transactional processes in real time. A modern retail company, for example, uses transactional systems to process customer purchases while simultaneously using analytical systems to analyze buying patterns and adjust inventory levels or pricing strategies.

Exam Tip

The DP-900 exam emphasizes understanding workload characteristics and appropriate Azure solutions rather than specific technical implementation details. Focus on when and why you would choose different approaches, as these concepts will be foundational when we explore specific Azure services in later chapters.

The Workload Spectrum

Figure 3-2 illustrates how data workloads span a spectrum from pure transactional processing to pure analytical processing, with many hybrid scenarios in between. Understanding this spectrum helps you make informed decisions about system architecture and service selection.

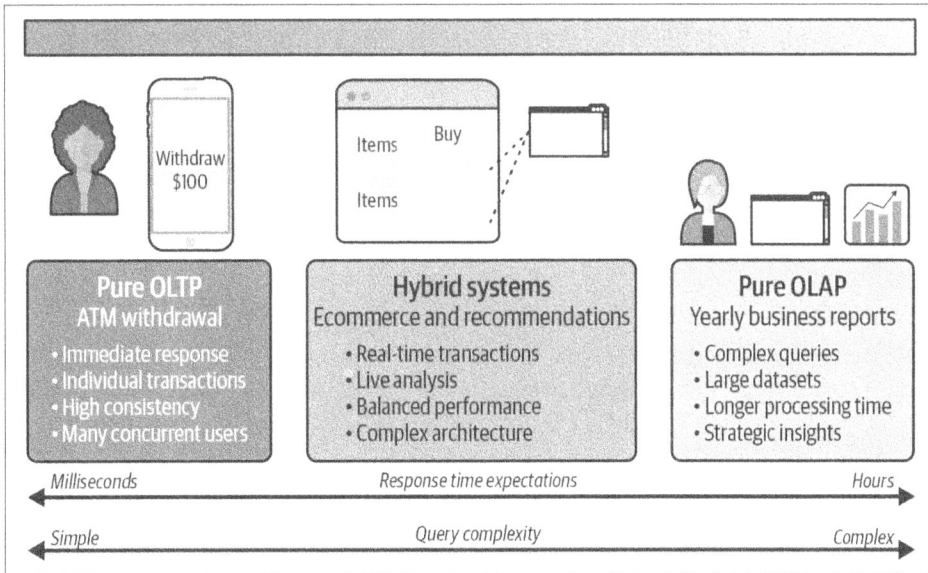

Figure 3-2. The data workload spectrum

At one end of the spectrum, we have pure *OLTP* systems that focus on individual transactions with immediate consistency requirements. Think of an ATM withdrawal—it must process immediately, update your account balance instantly, ensure that the money is dispensed correctly, and guarantee the transaction is permanent. The system cannot allow any errors, delays, or inconsistencies because real money is involved.

At the other end, we have pure *OLAP (Online Analytical Processing)* systems that focus on complex analysis across large datasets. Think of a yearly business report that analyzes millions of transactions to identify trends and patterns. This report might take several minutes or even hours to generate, but it provides valuable insights that help executives make strategic decisions about the business.

Between these extremes lie hybrid scenarios that combine both transactional and analytical requirements. Consider a modern ecommerce website that needs to process customer orders immediately (transactional) while also providing real-time product recommendations based on analysis of customer behavior patterns (analytical). These hybrid systems must balance the immediate needs of operational transactions with the complex requirements of data analysis.

> **Note**
>
> Modern applications rarely fit neatly into pure OLTP or OLAP categories. Instead, they require hybrid approaches that support both transactional and analytical capabilities, often within the same system or through closely integrated systems. Understanding this spectrum helps you make better architectural decisions.

HTAP: Bridging Transactional and Analytical Worlds

Hybrid Transactional/Analytical Processing (HTAP) represents an emerging approach that attempts to handle both OLTP and OLAP workloads within a single system. While not a focus of the DP-900 exam, understanding HTAP will help you appreciate modern data architecture evolution.

HTAP systems aim to eliminate the delay between transaction processing and analytical insights by enabling real-time analytics on operational data. Azure Cosmos DB with its analytical store capability exemplifies this pattern, allowing operational transactions while simultaneously supporting analytical queries without impacting transactional performance.

The workload spectrum also reflects different performance characteristics and user expectations. OLTP systems typically serve many users simultaneously, each expecting immediate responses to their requests. OLAP systems typically serve fewer users, but those users may run complex queries that take considerable time and computing resources to complete. Understanding these differences is crucial for selecting appropriate solutions and designing effective systems.

Transactional Workloads (OLTP)

OLTP systems form the operational backbone of most businesses, handling the day-to-day transactions that keep organizations running smoothly. These systems have evolved significantly with cloud computing, but their fundamental characteristics remain the same: they must process individual transactions quickly, reliably, and consistently.

The defining characteristic of OLTP systems is their focus on processing individual transactions immediately and accurately. When a customer places an order on an ecommerce website, updates their profile information, or transfers money between bank accounts, they're interacting with OLTP systems. These interactions must be processed immediately, accurately, and consistently, regardless of how many other users are simultaneously using the system. Azure provides several services optimized for OLTP workloads, including Azure SQL Database for relational transactions and Azure Cosmos DB for globally distributed, multimodel transactional processing.

A real-world OLTP scenario

Consider the busy restaurant's point-of-sale (POS) system shown in Figure 3-3 during peak dinner hours. This scenario perfectly demonstrates OLTP characteristics and why they matter in real-world business operations.

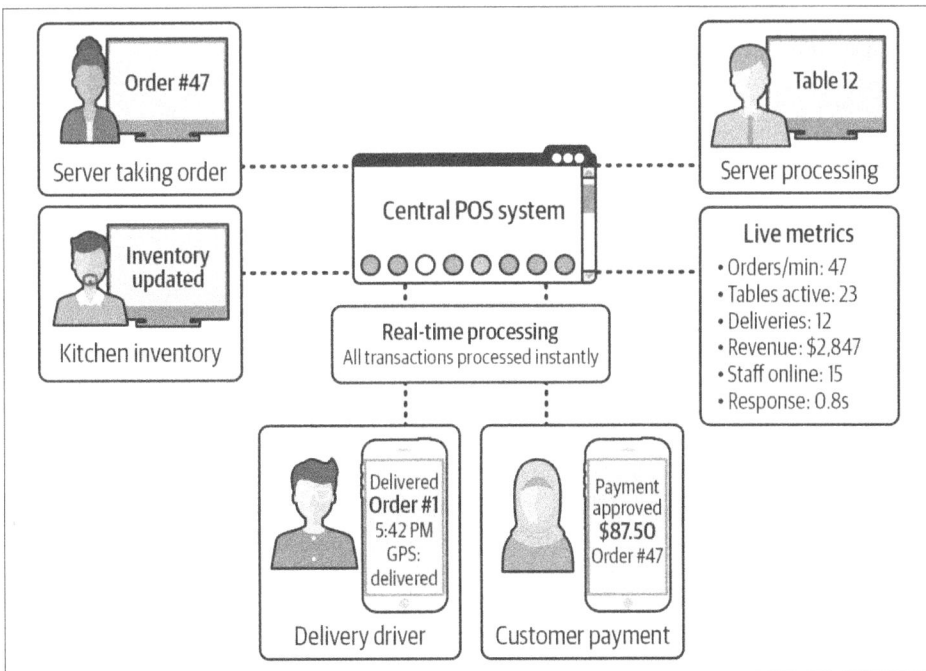

Figure 3-3. Restaurant POS system during peak hours

The rush is on. It's 7:30 p.m. on a Friday night. As shown in Figure 3-3, Sarah (the server on the left) just took an order from Table 3: two pasta dishes and a bottle of wine. She taps Send Order on her tablet, and within milliseconds, several things happen simultaneously across the restaurant's networked system.

Cascading real-time operations. The moment Sarah's order hits the central POS system (shown at the center of Figure 3-3), it triggers a cascade of immediate transactions:

- The kitchen display instantly shows "ORDER #47 – TABLE 3" in red (urgent).
- The kitchen inventory terminal (left side of the diagram) automatically updates: pasta portions drop from 85% to 83%, wine bottles from 12 to 11.
- The system reserves Table 3's seating time and updates availability forecasts.
- Cost calculations begin for profit margin tracking.
- The order appears on the live metrics dashboard (shown on the right side of the figure).

Meanwhile, as depicted throughout the diagram, other critical transactions are processing simultaneously:

At the payment counter (bottom center)
The customer shown is processing an $87.50 bill through the payment terminal, updating daily revenue totals and triggering receipt generation.

In the kitchen area
Staff mark completed orders as "READY," automatically notifying servers and updating table timing metrics.

On delivery routes (bottom left)
The delivery driver shown has confirmed delivery of Order #51, updating GPS tracking, customer notifications, and delivery performance statistics.

At the management level
The live metrics panel in the figure refreshes every few seconds, displaying the real-time data shown: 47 orders per minute, 23 active tables, and current revenue of $2,847.

Why every millisecond matters. This isn't just about speed. It's about business survival. The interconnected system shown in Figure 3-3 demonstrates why timing is critical. If Sarah's order took 30 seconds to reach the kitchen instead of 30 milliseconds, the kitchen would fall behind. If the inventory updates shown on the left lagged, the restaurant might promise dishes it can't deliver. If the payment processing depicted at bottom center hesitated, customers would grow frustrated.

Each transaction flowing through the central POS system must be:

Immediate
    Orders flow to kitchen staff without delay.

Accurate
    There are no double-charges, no lost orders, and no inventory errors.

Isolated
    One server's large order doesn't block another's simple drink request.

Durable
    Even if the system crashes, completed orders and payments remain safe.

The OLTP foundation.   The restaurant scenario illustrated in Figure 3-3 shows why OLTP systems prioritize transaction speed and reliability over analytical complexity. The system handles hundreds of small, quick transactions—taking orders (servers), updating inventory (kitchen), processing payments (customer counter)—rather than complex analytical queries about seasonal trends or customer preferences.

During peak hours, as depicted in the figure, the restaurant's survival depends on this transactional foundation working flawlessly. Analysis can wait until after closing time, but transactions cannot wait at all.

> **Warning**
>
> Don't assume that OLTP systems can't handle analytical queries or that OLAP systems can't process transactions. The distinction is about optimization and primary use cases, not absolute capabilities. Many modern systems support both workload types, but they're typically optimized for one or the other.

Key characteristics of OLTP systems

Understanding these characteristics is crucial for recognizing OLTP scenarios and making appropriate system design decisions.

High-volume, short transactions.   OLTP systems process thousands or millions of short, simple transactions throughout the day. The volume can be staggering—a large ecommerce site might process millions of transactions per day, a busy bank might handle hundreds of thousands of account inquiries per hour, and a popular mobile app might process tens of thousands of user interactions per minute.

A typical OLTP operation might involve:

Reading a customer record
Looking up account information, checking customer status, or retrieving order history

Updating an inventory quantity
Reducing available stock when someone makes a purchase or adjusting quantities after receiving new shipments

Inserting a new order record
Creating a new customer order with all associated details or generating order confirmations

Processing a payment
Charging a credit card, updating account balances, or recording payment transactions

These operations are usually focused on small amounts of data but must execute very quickly—often in milliseconds—to provide responsive user experiences. Unlike analytical queries that might examine millions of records to identify trends, OLTP transactions typically work with individual records or small sets of related records.

Strong consistency and ACID properties. As discussed in Chapter 2, OLTP systems require ACID properties to ensure reliable transaction processing. In the context of workloads, these properties become essential for scenarios like bank transfers where atomicity ensures that money isn't lost if a transaction fails midway, or ecommerce systems where isolation prevents overselling the last item in stock when multiple customers purchase simultaneously.

High concurrency requirements. OLTP systems must handle many users performing different operations simultaneously without performance degradation or data corruption. This concurrency requirement distinguishes OLTP systems from simpler applications that might serve one user at a time.

Consider these real-world concurrency scenarios:

- Ecommerce website during sales events:
  — Thousands of customers browsing products simultaneously
  — Hundreds of customers adding items to carts at the same time
  — Dozens of customers completing purchases concurrently
  — Customer service representatives processing returns and exchanges

- — Warehouse staff updating inventory levels as shipments arrive
- — Marketing team updating product descriptions and prices
- Banking system during business hours:
  - — Thousands of customers checking account balances
  - — ATM transactions happening across the city
  - — Online bill payments being processed
  - — Loan applications being submitted and reviewed
  - — Tellers processing in-branch transactions
  - — Automated systems processing scheduled transfers

The system must handle this concurrency without allowing conflicts or data corruption. This requires sophisticated mechanisms to prevent situations where concurrent operations interfere with each other.

Current, operational data focus. OLTP systems work primarily with current, operational data that represents the here-and-now of business operations. This data is characterized by:

Recency
> The data represents the current state of business operations, such as current account balances, available inventory levels, active customer orders, and real-time system status.

Volatility
> The data changes frequently throughout the day as new transactions are processed. Account balances change with every transaction, inventory levels fluctuate with sales and restocking, and customer information is updated as people move or change contact details.

Operational relevance
> The data directly supports immediate business operations rather than historical analyses. When a customer calls to check their order status, they need current information about their specific order, not historical trends about order processing times.

Common OLTP use cases

Understanding typical OLTP scenarios helps illustrate why these systems require specific characteristics and how they support different types of business operations.

Ecommerce and retail operations. Ecommerce platforms provide classic examples of OLTP workloads:

- Customer browsing product catalogs with real-time inventory checks
- Shopping cart management with instant updates
- Checkout processes requiring immediate payment verification
- Order creation with automatic inventory allocation
- Real-time inventory tracking across multiple warehouses
- Customer service interactions requiring immediate access to order information

Banking and financial services. Banking systems exemplify OLTP requirements through operations that demand the highest levels of accuracy, security, and consistency:

- Account balance inquiries requiring instant, accurate responses
- ATM withdrawals with real-time balance verification
- Online bill payments with immediate confirmation
- Credit card transaction authorization in milliseconds
- Fraud detection requiring immediate transaction analysis
- Inter-bank transfers with complex routing logic

Healthcare information systems. Healthcare systems require OLTP capabilities for operations that can literally be life-or-death situations:

- Patient record access during emergency situations
- Appointment scheduling with real-time provider availability
- Prescription management with drug interaction checking
- Laboratory result recording and physician notification
- Insurance verification and preauthorization processing

Emergency department systems must instantly access patient records, update treatment information, coordinate care across multiple providers, and maintain accurate information—all while supporting life-critical decision-making processes.

Now that we understand transactional workloads, let's explore their counterpart: analytical workloads, which serve a fundamentally different purpose in the data ecosystem.

Analytical Workloads (OLAP)

OLAP systems serve a fundamentally different purpose than OLTP systems. Instead of processing operational transactions, they focus on analyzing large volumes of data to provide insights for decision making. OLAP systems are designed for complex queries that examine large datasets, often spanning multiple years of historical data and involving sophisticated calculations and aggregations.

Unlike OLTP systems that work with individual records to process immediate business operations, OLAP queries typically process millions of records simultaneously to identify trends, patterns, and relationships that aren't apparent when looking at individual transactions.

A real-world OLAP scenario

Consider the retail chain's comprehensive analytical system shown in Figure 3-4, where executives are analyzing performance to make strategic business decisions for the upcoming year. This scenario perfectly illustrates the complexity and value of OLAP systems in contrast to the immediate transaction processing we saw in the restaurant example.

The big picture analysis. It's Monday morning at RetailCorp headquarters. Unlike the restaurant's second-by-second transaction processing, this analysis has been running for 30 minutes and will continue for another hour. As shown at the top of Figure 3-4, the system is simultaneously processing massive datasets from multiple sources:

- *500 stores* contributing three years of historical sales data
- *50,000 products* across all categories and price points
- *10 million customer transactions* with detailed behavioral patterns
- *Weather data* correlating seasonal impacts across regions
- *Economic indicators* affecting consumer spending patterns
- *Competitor intelligence* on pricing and promotional activities

Complex analytical processing. In addition to storing this data, the central data warehouse depicted in Figure 3-4 is performing incredibly complex calculations that would be impossible in a transactional system. Unlike the restaurant POS system that processes individual orders in milliseconds, this system is running queries like the following:

- "Calculate year-over-year growth rates for each product category, segmented by region and adjusted for weather patterns and economic conditions."

- "Identify seasonal demand patterns across 50,000 SKUs and predict Q4 inventory requirements."
- "Analyze customer lifetime value trends and predict churn risk by demographic segment."

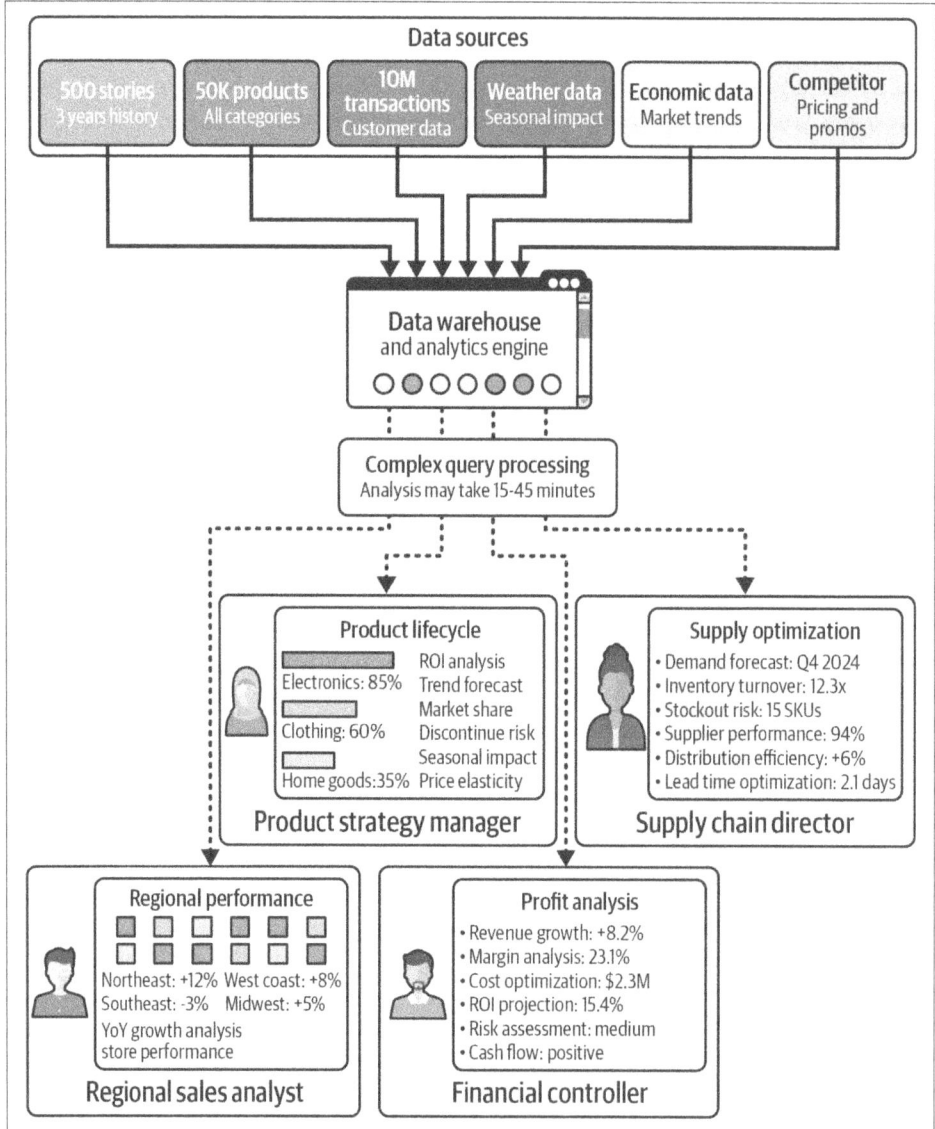

Data sources

| 500 stories 3 years history | 50K products All categories | 10M transactions Customer data | Weather data Seasonal impact | Economic data Market trends | Competitor Pricing and promos |

Data warehouse and analytics engine

Complex query processing Analysis may take 15-45 minutes

Product lifecycle
Electronics: 85% — ROI analysis, Trend forecast
Clothing: 60% — Market share, Discontinue risk
Home goods: 35% — Seasonal impact, Price elasticity
Product strategy manager

Supply optimization
- Demand forecast: Q4 2024
- Inventory turnover: 12.3x
- Stockout risk: 15 SKUs
- Supplier performance: 94%
- Distribution efficiency: +6%
- Lead time optimization: 2.1 days
Supply chain director

Regional performance
Northeast: +12% West coast: +8%
Southeast: -3% Midwest: +5%
YoY growth analysis
store performance
Regional sales analyst

Profit analysis
- Revenue growth: +8.2%
- Margin analysis: 23.1%
- Cost optimization: $2.3M
- ROI projection: 15.4%
- Risk assessment: medium
- Cash flow: positive
Financial controller

Figure 3-4. Retail chain strategic analysis

Strategic decision making. As illustrated in the bottom section of Figure 3-4, four different executives are simultaneously running complex analyses that inform million-dollar decisions:

Regional sales analyst (left)
> Examining the heat map visualization, she discovers that the Northeast region shows 12% growth while the Southeast is declining by 3%. This analysis processes millions of transactions across hundreds of stores to identify geographic patterns that would be invisible at the individual transaction level.

Product strategy manager (center-left)
> His product lifecycle analysis reveals that electronics maintain 85% profitability while home goods have dropped to 35%. The system has calculated ROI across thousands of SKUs and is now recommending which 15 products to discontinue —a decision that will affect inventory worth millions of dollars.

Financial controller (center-right)
> She's running complex profitability models that aggregate three years of cost data, revealing opportunities for $2.3M in cost optimization. Her analysis includes margin calculations that consider supplier contracts, seasonal variations, and regional economic factors.

Supply chain director (right)
> His demand forecasting model processes weather data, economic indicators, and historical patterns to predict Q4 requirements. The system recommends reallocating inventory across 500 stores and suggests closing 3 underperforming locations while opening 2 new ones.

The OLAP foundation. The strategic insights in the regional performance and profit analysis panels at the bottom of Figure 3-4 show the ultimate goal: actionable business intelligence that couldn't be obtained from individual transactions. These recommendations—expand electronics in the Northeast, discontinue underperforming SKUs, optimize Q4 inventory—result from processing millions of data points through complex analytical models.

Whereas the restaurant POS system prioritizes speed and individual transaction accuracy, this OLAP system prioritizes analytical depth and strategic insight. The queries take 15–45 minutes to complete, but they provide the foundation for decisions affecting millions in revenue and the strategic direction of the entire company.

This analysis happens overnight and during off-peak hours, using historical data that may be hours or days old. Unlike the restaurant, where every second matters for customer service, these strategic insights remain valuable whether the analysis completes at 2 a.m. or 6 a.m.

Key characteristics of OLAP systems

OLAP systems exhibit characteristics that are often quite different from OLTP systems, reflecting their different purposes and optimization priorities.

Complex queries analyzing large datasets. OLAP systems process complex queries that analyze large volumes of data to extract business insights. The complexity comes from multiple dimensions:

- Data volume complexity:
  - Queries might examine millions or billions of records simultaneously.
  - Analysis often spans multiple years of historical data.
  - Processing involves multiple large tables with complex relationships.
  - Calculations may require iterating through massive datasets multiple times.
  - Results may need to be aggregated at multiple levels of detail.
- Analytical complexity:
  - Statistical calculations like averages, medians, standard deviations, and correlations
  - Time-based analysis including seasonality, trends, and forecasting
  - Comparative analysis across different dimensions (regions, products, customer segments)
  - Complex business calculations like customer lifetime value and market basket analysis
  - What-if scenarios and sensitivity analysis for business planning

A typical OLAP query might examine five years of sales transactions to calculate monthly growth rates by product category and region, compare performance against industry benchmarks, identify seasonal patterns, and forecast future demand. This single query could involve processing hundreds of millions of records, performing thousands of calculations, and generating results that inform strategic business decisions.

Query performance over transaction consistency. OLAP systems prioritize query performance and analytical capabilities over immediate transaction consistency, though data accuracy remains critically important. This trade-off allows for optimization strategies that wouldn't be appropriate for OLTP systems:

- Acceptable data latency:
  - Business intelligence reports can often work with data that's hours or even days old.
  - Strategic analysis typically doesn't require real-time transaction data.
  - Planning and forecasting activities can use data with some latency.
  - Trend analysis remains valid even with slight delays in data updates.
- Performance optimization strategies:
  - Pre-calculated aggregations and summary tables for common queries
  - Specialized indexing strategies optimized for analytical queries
  - Data compression techniques that improve query performance
  - Specialized storage formats that optimize analytical processing
  - Caching strategies for frequently accessed analytical results

It's important to note that "performance over consistency" doesn't mean OLAP systems are inaccurate or unreliable. Rather, they optimize for different types of consistency—ensuring analytical accuracy and data quality while accepting some latency in data updates.

Fewer concurrent users, resource-intensive queries. OLAP systems typically serve fewer concurrent users than OLTP systems, but those users may run very resource-intensive queries:

- User characteristics:
  - Business analysts, data scientists, and executives typically use OLAP systems.
  - Users often run complex queries that take significant time to complete.
  - Analytical work is often iterative, with users refining queries based on results.
  - Peak usage often occurs during business planning cycles or reporting periods.
  - Users typically understand that complex analysis takes time to complete.
- Resource usage patterns:
  - Individual queries that may consume substantial CPU and memory resources
  - Long-running queries that process large amounts of data

— Intensive operations reading from large datasets

— Temporary storage requirements for intermediate query results

— Processing across multiple CPU cores or servers

A business analyst might run a complex report that examines five years of sales data across multiple dimensions—a query that could take 30 minutes to complete and consume significant system resources. While this would be unacceptable for an OLTP system serving customer transactions, it's normal and expected for OLAP systems focused on analytical insights.

Historical data focus. OLAP systems work primarily with historical, stable data that provides context for business analysis:

- Data characteristics:
  — Large volumes of historical data spanning multiple years
  — Data that remains relatively stable after initial processing, though modern Azure architectures can incorporate near-real-time updates through techniques like change data capture
  — Time-series data that shows how business metrics evolve over time
  — Reference data that provides context for historical analysis
  — Slowly changing dimensional data that tracks how business entities evolve

This historical focus enables optimization strategies such as aggressive caching of frequently accessed data, pre-calculated aggregations for common analytical operations, and specialized storage formats that optimize for read performance rather than update performance.

Common OLAP use cases

Understanding typical OLAP scenarios helps illustrate why these systems require different characteristics and optimization strategies compared to OLTP systems.

Business intelligence and reporting. Enterprise reporting and dashboards represent the most common OLAP applications:

- Executive dashboards tracking key performance indicators (KPIs)
- Monthly sales reports comparing performance across regions and product lines
- Customer segmentation analysis identifying high-value customer groups
- Financial reporting meeting regulatory requirements
- Inventory analysis optimizing stock levels and identifying slow-moving products

Financial analysis and planning.   Financial planning and analysis represent critical OLAP applications:

- Annual budget preparation incorporating historical trends and future projections
- Variance analysis comparing actual performance against budgets and forecasts
- Profitability analysis identifying the most profitable products, customers, and markets
- Cash flow forecasting predicting future liquidity needs
- Risk analysis identifying and quantifying business risks

These financial analyses are typically performed using Azure Synapse Analytics for large-scale data warehousing or Azure Analysis Services for multidimensional analytical models.

Marketing analytics and customer intelligence.   Marketing analytics represent increasingly sophisticated OLAP applications:

- Customer segmentation analysis identifying distinct customer groups
- Customer lifetime value calculations predicting long-term profitability
- Marketing campaign effectiveness measuring ROI across different channels
- Churn analysis identifying customers at risk of leaving
- Market basket analysis identifying products frequently purchased together

Analytical workloads form the intelligence layer of modern data architectures, transforming raw transactional data into strategic insights. While they operate differently from OLTP systems—accepting longer query times and some data latency—they provide the comprehensive analysis that drives informed business decisions. Understanding when to apply OLAP approaches, and how to integrate them with OLTP systems, is fundamental to designing effective data solutions.

Bringing It All Together: Modern Workload Scenarios

Most modern applications don't fit neatly into pure OLTP or OLAP categories. Instead, they require hybrid approaches that support both transactional and analytical capabilities, often within the same system or through closely integrated systems.

The Modern Data Architecture

Modern data architectures weave together both transactional and analytical capabilities to support comprehensive business requirements. At the foundation lies the transactional layer, which handles customer interactions with immediate consistency and fast response times. When customers place orders, the system must process them immediately, update inventory levels in real time, verify payments instantly, and provide customer service teams with immediate access to current information.

Above this operational foundation sits the analytical layer, which transforms accumulated transaction data into business insights. This layer analyzes customer behavior patterns to generate personalized recommendations, examines sales trends to inform inventory planning decisions, evaluates performance metrics to identify optimization opportunities, and applies predictive analytics for accurate forecasting and strategic planning.

Connecting these two layers is the integration layer, which ensures seamless communication between systems. Real-time data synchronization keeps operational and analytical systems aligned, while event-driven processes automatically trigger analytical updates whenever transactions occur. Feedback mechanisms allow analytical insights to influence operational decisions, and automated reporting systems deliver timely alerts based on analytical results.

Real-World Insight

The most successful modern implementations use multiple workload approaches strategically, choosing the right pattern for each specific use case rather than forcing all operations into a single model. This approach maximizes both performance and cost-effectiveness while meeting diverse business requirements.

A Comprehensive Real-World Example

Consider how a modern ecommerce platform illustrates the seamless integration of different workload types. When customers visit the website, OLTP systems spring into action, handling product browsing with real-time inventory checks, updating shopping carts with immediate confirmation, processing payments with instant verification, and providing order confirmation with immediate status updates.

This integration is often orchestrated through Azure Data Factory, which moves and transforms data between operational and analytical systems.

While customers navigate the site, OLAP systems work behind the scenes, analyzing browsing patterns to improve product recommendations, examining sales trends to optimize inventory levels, evaluating performance metrics to identify website optimization opportunities, and studying customer behavior to personalize the shopping experience.

The real power emerges through real-time integration, where these systems collaborate to update product recommendations based on current browsing behavior, adjust pricing according to demand analysis, trigger inventory reordering based on sales patterns, and deliver personalized offers informed by customer analysis. This orchestrated approach creates a responsive, intelligent platform that serves both immediate customer needs and long-term business objectives.

Summary

Understanding data workloads represents a fundamental skill for anyone working with data systems. The distinction between transactional (OLTP) and analytical (OLAP) workloads drives critical decisions about system architecture, service selection, performance optimization, and cost management.

OLTP systems excel at processing individual transactions quickly and consistently, making them ideal for:

- Operational systems that handle customer interactions with immediate response requirements
- Financial transactions requiring strong consistency and reliability
- Real-time business processes supporting high concurrency and availability needs
- Applications where data accuracy and immediate consistency are critical business requirements

OLAP systems excel at analyzing large volumes of data to extract business insights, making them ideal for:

- Business intelligence and reporting supporting strategic decision making
- Historical analysis and trend identification across large datasets
- Complex analytical operations involving sophisticated calculations and aggregations
- Applications where comprehensive insights are more important than immediate response times

Modern business requirements often demand hybrid approaches that combine both workload types through:

- Integrated architectures sharing data between operational and analytical systems
- Event-driven systems providing real-time insights based on operational activities
- Flexible designs supporting both immediate transactions and complex analysis
- Strategic service selection optimizing for specific business requirements

The key insight from this chapter is that successful data strategies don't force all operations into a single workload pattern. Instead, they strategically combine different approaches, choosing the right workload type for each specific business requirement while ensuring effective integration between systems. This understanding prepares you for exploring specific Azure services in subsequent chapters, where these workload concepts become essential for making informed decisions.

Beyond the Exam

While the DP-900 exam provides excellent foundational understanding of workload types, real-world implementations often involve additional complexity and considerations that extend beyond basic OLTP and OLAP concepts.

Real-World Mixed Workload Examples

Modern financial trading platforms demonstrate why academic distinctions between OLTP and OLAP quickly break down in practice. These systems must handle individual trades with submillisecond latency requirements while simultaneously analyzing portfolio risk across entire trading books. The challenge isn't just technical—it's existential. A delayed trade execution costs money immediately, but inadequate risk analysis can destroy an entire firm. The most successful implementations treat real-time integration as the primary design constraint, ensuring immediate risk calculations based on current positions while maintaining the historical analysis capabilities that support regulatory reporting and performance attribution.

Healthcare information systems reveal similar tensions with life-critical implications. Emergency room physicians need immediate access to patient records during care, but the same data must feed population health trend analysis and clinical outcome studies. The integration challenge here goes beyond performance. It requires clinical decision support that combines current patient data with historical analysis in ways that actually improve care delivery. The systems that work best in practice are those designed from the ground up to serve both immediate clinical needs and long-term analytical requirements, rather than trying to bolt analytics onto operational systems or vice versa.

Performance Considerations

OLTP performance in production environments depends heavily on connection management and pooling strategies that can handle thousands of concurrent users without degrading response times. Index design becomes critical, but not in the textbook sense. It must be optimized for the specific transaction patterns your business actually generates, not theoretical access patterns. Caching strategies for frequently accessed reference data like product catalogs can make or break user experience, while resource allocation during peak periods often determines whether your system survives events like holiday shopping surges.

OLAP performance requires a fundamentally different mindset focused on data organization and partitioning strategies for massive historical datasets. Query optimization for complex analytical operations across multiple tables becomes an art form, balancing processing efficiency with resource consumption. The real challenge lies in resource management for long-running queries that process millions of records while maintaining system availability during peak analysis periods—something that's much harder than it sounds when business users want their reports immediately.

Common Implementation Pitfalls

The single system antipattern remains the most expensive mistake organizations make. Attempting to use one system for both OLTP and OLAP requirements consistently results in poor performance for both workload types. The classic scenario involves running complex analytical queries on the same database handling customer transactions, creating slow response times for customers and delayed analytical insights. This approach fails because it ignores the fundamental reality that these workloads have opposing optimization requirements. Better approaches require dedicated systems for each workload type with carefully designed integration mechanisms that move data efficiently between operational and analytical environments.

Consistency misunderstandings create equally problematic but more subtle failures. Organizations frequently apply inappropriate consistency requirements that significantly impact both performance and cost. Requiring immediate consistency for historical reporting data used for monthly trend analysis adds unnecessary complexity and expense without delivering business value. The key insight is understanding that strong consistency matters for financial transactions, but eventual consistency works perfectly well for analytical reporting—and mixing these up costs both money and performance.

Integration complexity represents the hidden iceberg that sinks many projects. Organizations focus intensively on individual system capabilities while completely overlooking data synchronization requirements, transformation complexity, and network latency realities. The most successful implementations treat integration as the primary design challenge, planning early for data flow requirements, conducting comprehensive testing of synchronization mechanisms, and establishing clear expectations about acceptable latency between operational and analytical systems.

> **Tip**
>
> As you continue your data journey, remember that these workload concepts form the foundation for understanding more advanced topics like system architecture, service selection, and performance optimization. Master these fundamentals before diving into specific technologies and implementation details.

CHAPTER 4

Data Roles and Responsibilities in Azure

The shift to cloud computing hasn't just changed where we store data. It has fundamentally transformed how we work with it. As organizations migrate their data workloads to Azure, traditional roles have evolved and new specializations have emerged. Understanding these roles and their interactions is crucial for the DP-900 exam and for anyone working with Azure's data platform. While this chapter mentions specific Azure technologies, we'll focus primarily on how they relate to different job roles, saving detailed technical explanations for later chapters.

Coverage of Curriculum Objectives

This chapter addresses the following DP-900 exam objectives:

- Understand common data roles and responsibilities in Azure.
- Identify appropriate tools and services for different data professionals.
- Understand role interactions in Azure data environments.

Modern Data Roles

In the era of AI and the cloud, data professionals must adapt to new ways of working. As organizations embrace digital transformation, traditional roles are evolving to meet the demands of cloud native environments.

Figure 4-1 illustrates the fundamental shift in how data professionals work in the modern era. In the traditional environment, database administrators (who manage and maintain organizations' data storage systems) had to handle physical computer equipment, manual data backups, and server maintenance. For example, when a company needed more storage space for its data, a database administrator might have spent weeks going through a lengthy process: researching what computer hardware to buy, getting approval for purchases, waiting for equipment delivery, physically installing the computers in the office server room, setting up the storage drives for reliability, and installing all the necessary software systems. Similarly, data processing specialists (previously called *ETL developers*, where *ETL* stands for Extract, Transform, and Load) focused on moving and processing data in scheduled batches using software that had to be installed on computers within their building.

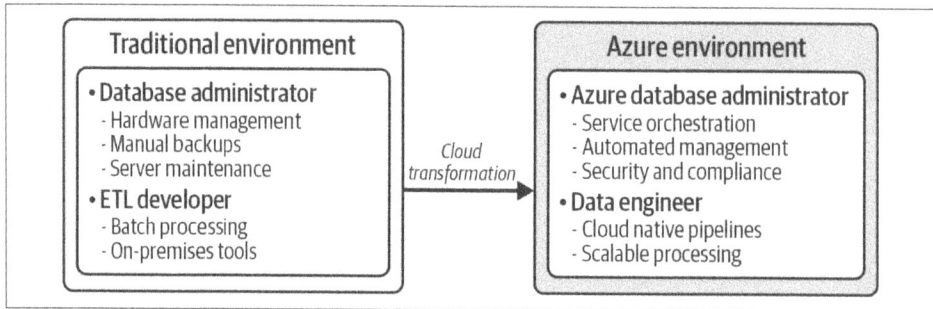

Figure 4-1. Role evolution in Azure

Through cloud transformation, these roles have evolved to meet modern demands. Azure database administrators now focus on service orchestration, automated management, and security compliance, leveraging cloud capabilities to manage databases at scale. Meanwhile, ETL developers have transformed into data engineers who build cloud native pipelines and implement scalable processing solutions.

This evolution reflects the broader shift from hands-on infrastructure management to service-oriented, automated approaches in Azure's ecosystem. The DP-900 exam validates practitioners' understanding of these evolved roles and their functions within Azure's modern data platform.

Let's start exploring each of these evolved roles in detail, beginning with database administrators.

Database Administrators

A database administrator (DBA) is an IT professional who is responsible for the installation, configuration, security, maintenance, and performance optimization of database systems that store and organize an organization's critical data. Database administration in Azure represents a significant shift from traditional on-premises database management. While the fundamental responsibility of protecting and optimizing data remains unchanged, the tools, approaches, and daily activities of a DBA have evolved considerably.

In the past, DBAs spent considerable time managing hardware, applying patches, and handling physical backups. Today's Azure DBA focuses on higher value activities like service optimization, security configuration, and automated management. Instead of worrying about storage arrays and backup tapes, they configure automated backup policies and develop geo-replication strategies, which involve creating synchronized copies of databases in different geographical locations.

Exam Tip

The DP-900 exam emphasizes how DBAs have shifted from hardware management to service orchestration. Understand this transformation from hands-on infrastructure management to strategic service configuration and optimization in the cloud environment.

Typical scenario for database administrators

Consider a typical day for an Azure DBA. Rather than walking through a data center to check physical servers, they monitor database performance through Azure Portal dashboards, configure automated scaling policies, implement security measures through Azure Active Directory (Azure AD), and optimize query performance across distributed systems.

The tools have changed as well. Where DBAs once worked primarily with SQL Server Management Studio (a desktop application for managing Microsoft SQL Server databases), they now use Azure Portal, Azure CLI, and Azure PowerShell to manage their databases. They work with fully managed services like Azure SQL Database, Azure Database for PostgreSQL, and Azure Cosmos DB. These database-as-a-service (DBaaS) offerings handle all the underlying infrastructure, freeing DBAs from managing hardware, backups, and high availability configurations. While we'll explore these technologies in depth in later chapters, for now it's important to understand that modern database administration extends beyond traditional relational databases, encompassing diverse technologies to meet varying business needs.

Core responsibilities of database administrators in Azure

Security has become a central focus for modern DBAs. They implement encryption for data both at rest and in transit, manage access controls through Azure AD, and ensure compliance with data protection regulations. This includes setting up firewalls, managing authentication, and monitoring security threats through Azure Defender for SQL.

Performance optimization takes on new dimensions in the cloud. Azure DBAs monitor database performance using built-in tools like Azure Monitor and Query Performance Insight. They can easily scale resources up or down based on demand, something that wasn't possible with physical servers. When databases experience heavy loads, DBAs can quickly adjust computing power or memory without any hardware changes.

Data backup and recovery have been transformed by Azure's automated capabilities. Instead of managing physical backup tapes, DBAs now configure automatic backup policies that store data safely in geo-redundant storage. They set up geo-replication to maintain database copies in different regions, ensuring business continuity even if an entire data center goes offline.

Cost management has become a crucial skill for Azure DBAs. They must understand Azure's pricing models and optimize database configurations to control costs while maintaining performance. This might involve choosing the right service tier, implementing auto-scaling policies, or using reserved capacity for predictable workloads.

Azure-related tools and platforms for database administrators

The Azure Portal serves as the primary interface for database management, offering a user-friendly way to monitor and manage databases. DBAs use Visual Studio Code or even traditional tools like SQL Server Management Studio (SSMS) as well as third-party tools like JetBrains' DataGrip for querying and administering databases, while Azure PowerShell and Azure CLI provide powerful automation capabilities. These tools make it possible to manage hundreds of databases efficiently.

Azure provides several database platforms to suit different needs. Azure SQL Database offers a fully managed SQL Server experience, while Azure Cosmos DB provides global scale for NoSQL workloads. Azure Database for PostgreSQL and MySQL give open source options with enterprise features. DBAs must understand these platforms' strengths to make appropriate recommendations for different scenarios.

Future evolution of database administrators in Azure

The role of the Azure DBA continues to evolve with new technological advances. AI and machine learning are being integrated into database management, helping to predict performance issues before they occur and to suggest optimization strategies. DBAs are increasingly becoming strategic advisors who help organizations make the most of their data assets while ensuring security and compliance.

Exam Tip

For success on the DP-900 exam, focus on understanding how Azure simplifies database management through automation and built-in tools, while maintaining security and performance.

Through this transformation, the fundamental goal of the DBA remains unchanged: ensuring that data is available, protected, and performing optimally. The difference lies in how these objectives are achieved, with Azure providing powerful tools and automation that allow DBAs to focus on strategic initiatives rather than routine maintenance.

Now let's explore the role of data engineers.

Data Engineers

Data engineers have perhaps seen the most dramatic evolution in their role. Where they once wrote monolithic ETL packages, they now architect flexible, scalable data pipelines using services like Azure Data Factory, Microsoft Fabric, and Azure Databricks. This transformation goes beyond just using new tools. It represents a fundamental shift in how we think about data movement and transformation.

Exam Tip

The exam particularly emphasizes understanding how data engineers use Azure-native tools rather than traditional ETL processes.

Modern data engineers in Azure work at a higher level of abstraction. Instead of writing detailed transformation logic, they often orchestrate pre-built components and managed services. A typical data engineering project in Azure might involve designing a pipeline that ingests data from multiple sources using Azure Data Factory, lands it in Azure Data Lake Storage using appropriate file formats and partitioning, transforms it using Azure Databricks or Azure Synapse Analytics, and makes it available to data analysts through Power BI datasets.

Data quality has become a key focus area for engineers. Rather than simply moving data from point A to point B, they must ensure data quality, implement proper governance controls, and maintain data lineage. The DP-900 exam often tests understanding of these broader responsibilities.

Core responsibilities of data engineers in Azure

Modern data engineers build end-to-end data solutions that span multiple Azure services. They design data lakes and data warehouses that can handle both structured and unstructured data, implementing appropriate storage tiers and file formats for optimal performance and cost efficiency. This includes understanding when to use Azure Data Lake Storage Gen2 (the latest version of Azure's data lake service, optimized for analytics) versus Azure Blob Storage, and how to organize data for efficient processing.

Data pipeline development has evolved from simple ETL processes to complex orchestrations. Engineers use Azure Data Factory to create pipelines that can handle real-time streaming data alongside traditional batch processing. They implement error handling, monitoring, and alerting to ensure reliable data delivery. The ability to design resilient, scalable pipelines is crucial in modern data engineering.

Data transformation strategies have shifted from writing custom code to leveraging powerful processing engines. Azure Databricks allows engineers to use Apache Spark for large-scale data processing, while Azure Synapse Analytics provides integrated analytics capabilities. Engineers must understand when to use each service and how to optimize their performance for different scenarios.

Security and governance have become integral to the data engineering role. Engineers implement row-level security, column-level encryption, and access controls across the data estate. They work with Microsoft Purview to maintain data catalogs and ensure compliance with data protection regulations. Understanding these aspects is crucial for success on the DP-900 exam.

Azure-related tools and platforms for data engineers

Azure provides a comprehensive toolkit for data engineers. Azure Data Factory serves as the primary orchestration tool, allowing engineers to create, schedule, and monitor data pipelines. Azure Databricks offers a collaborative environment for developing and running data transformation code, while Azure Synapse Analytics (and new tools like Microsoft Fabric) combines data warehousing with big data processing.

Data engineers must understand modern data formats and processing techniques. This includes working with Delta Lake for reliable data lakes, implementing slowly changing dimensions in data warehouses, and using streaming analytics for real-time data processing. The DP-900 exam tests basic understanding of these concepts and their implementation in Azure.

Future evolution of data engineers in Azure

This role continues to evolve with emerging technologies. Data engineers increasingly work with machine learning pipelines, implementing best practices and creating data pipelines that support AI workloads. They must understand concepts like feature stores and model serving, even if they don't directly build the models themselves.

Exam Tip

Focus on understanding how Azure services work together in data engineering scenarios. Know the basic purpose and capabilities of each service rather than deep technical details.

Collaboration has become essential in modern data engineering. Engineers work closely with data scientists to prepare data for machine learning, with analysts to ensure that data is properly modeled for business intelligence, and with database administrators to optimize data storage and access patterns. This collaborative aspect reflects the interconnected nature of modern data platforms in Azure.

The evolution of data engineering represents a shift from writing code to architecting solutions. While technical skills remain important, the ability to design scalable, maintainable data solutions using Azure's managed services has become paramount. For the DP-900 exam, understanding this architectural approach is more important than knowing specific coding details.

Building on our understanding of how data engineers prepare and process data, let's explore the role of data analysts who transform this data into actionable business insights. Their role has evolved significantly with Azure's modern analytics tools, making them crucial interpreters of data in the AI and cloud era.

Data Analysts

Data analysts represent the bridge between complex data and business understanding. In Azure, they've gained powerful new tools that have expanded their capabilities far beyond traditional spreadsheet analysis. Modern data analysts combine deep business knowledge with technical skills to deliver insights through platforms like Power BI.

Exam Tip

The exam often tests your ability to distinguish between analyst and data scientist responsibilities. While there's some overlap, analysts typically focus on descriptive analytics while data scientists handle predictive modeling.

Consider how a data analyst might approach a sales analysis project in Azure. They would start by accessing prepared data from Azure Synapse Analytics, create data models in Power BI, build interactive dashboards, and share insights through the Azure ecosystem. The role requires understanding both business needs and data technologies.

The modern data analyst must also understand data governance principles and work within established security frameworks. They need to know when to seek help from data engineers for complex data preparation and when to engage data scientists for advanced analytics needs.

Core responsibilities of data analysts in Azure

Modern data analysts spend significant time working with data modeling tools in Power BI. They create relationships between tables, design calculated columns and measures, and ensure that their models are optimized for both performance and usability. This involves understanding data modeling concepts like star schemas (a database design pattern where a central fact table connects to multiple dimension tables), slowly changing dimensions (tables that track how data changes over time), and other best practices for data modeling.

Visualization design has become increasingly sophisticated in the cloud era. Analysts must create compelling, interactive dashboards that tell stories with data. They use Power BI's advanced features to build reports that are both informative and user-friendly, incorporating features like drill-through capabilities (allowing users to move from summary to detailed data), bookmarks (saved views of report pages), and custom tooltips (enhanced pop-up information) to enhance the user experience.

Data preparation, while simplified by modern tools, remains a crucial skill. Analysts use Power Query to clean and transform data, creating repeatable processes that can be easily maintained and updated. They must understand how to handle common data quality issues, combine data from multiple sources, and create reliable data refresh processes.

Business partnership has taken on new dimensions with cloud technologies. Analysts work closely with stakeholders to understand requirements, design effective solutions, and ensure data-driven decision making. They must be able to explain complex data concepts to nontechnical audiences and translate business needs into technical specifications.

Azure-related tools and platforms for data analysts

Power BI serves as the primary tool for modern data analysts in Azure. They use Power BI Desktop for development, Power BI Service for sharing and collaboration, and Power BI Mobile for on-the-go access to insights.

Data analysts must be proficient in query languages and analytical functions. This includes writing expressions for calculations, using the Power Query M language for data transformation, and understanding fundamental SQL concepts for data retrieval. The exam tests basic understanding of these tools and when to use each one.

Azure integration knowledge has become essential. Analysts need to understand how Power BI connects with various Azure services, including Azure Synapse Analytics, Azure Analysis Services, and Azure Data Lake Storage. They should know how to establish and maintain these connections securely.

Exam Tip

While Microsoft Fabric is not explicitly covered on the DP-900 exam, understanding its role is valuable for aspiring data analysts. This unified analytics platform represents the evolution of Power BI and Azure data services, bringing together data integration, warehousing, and analytics capabilities in a seamless environment. Consider exploring Fabric after mastering the core DP-900 exam concepts.

Future evolution of data analysts in Azure

The role of data analysts continues to evolve with new technologies. AI features in Power BI, such as natural language querying and automated insights, are becoming increasingly important. Analysts need to understand how to leverage these capabilities while maintaining control over the analysis process.

Exam Tip

For success on the DP-900 exam, focus on understanding how Power BI integrates with Azure services and the basic capabilities of Power BI Desktop and Service. Detailed DAX knowledge isn't required.

Collaboration and governance have become key aspects of the analyst role. Modern analysts work within governed data environments, understanding concepts like row-level security, sensitivity labels, and certified datasets. They must balance the need for data access with security and compliance requirements.

The transformation of data analysis in Azure represents a shift from isolated analysis to integrated, collaborative insights generation. While Excel skills remain valuable, the ability to work with cloud-based tools and understand the broader data ecosystem has become essential. For the DP-900 exam, understanding this integrated approach to analysis is crucial for success.

While data analysts focus on understanding what has happened through descriptive analytics, data scientists look to what might happen next. Let's explore how these professionals use Azure's advanced analytics and machine learning capabilities to transform data into predictive insights.

Data Scientists

Data scientists apply advanced statistical methods and machine learning to solve complex business problems. In Azure, they leverage services like Azure Machine Learning and Azure Databricks to build and deploy predictive models.

This role requires a unique combination of skills: statistical knowledge, programming expertise, and business acumen. Data scientists must understand how to use Azure's machine learning tools effectively while ensuring that their solutions solve real business problems.

Exam Tip

The exam focuses on how data scientists interact with Azure services rather than the technical details of machine learning algorithms.

A typical machine learning project in Azure involves collaborating with data engineers to access and prepare training data, using Azure Machine Learning to develop and train models, and working with software engineers to deploy models into production applications.

Core responsibilities of data scientists in Azure

Modern data scientists spend considerable time in data exploration and preparation. Using tools like Azure Databricks notebooks and Azure Machine Learning studios, they analyze data patterns, handle missing values, and create feature engineering pipelines. This exploratory phase is crucial for understanding data characteristics and potential modeling approaches.

Model development has been transformed by Azure's machine learning capabilities. Data scientists use Azure Machine Learning to experiment with different algorithms, tune hyperparameters, and track model versions. They can leverage automated machine learning (AutoML, which automatically tests different machine learning algorithms and configurations) for initial model selection and optimization, while maintaining control over the modeling process.

Model deployment and monitoring have become streamlined in the cloud era. Azure provides tools for deploying models as APIs, monitoring model performance, and detecting data drift (changes in the statistical properties of data over time that might affect model accuracy).

Collaboration has become increasingly important in the data science role. Data scientists work closely with domain experts to understand business problems, with data engineers to ensure proper data preparation, and with software developers to integrate models into applications. They must effectively communicate complex technical concepts to various stakeholders.

Azure-related tools and platforms for data scientists

Azure Machine Learning serves as the primary platform for data science work. It provides notebooks for code development, experiments for model training, and deployment capabilities for productionizing models. Understanding how to navigate and use these features effectively is important for the DP-900 exam.

Azure Databricks offers a collaborative environment for large-scale data processing and machine learning. Data scientists use its distributed computing capabilities to handle big data and train complex models. The integration between Databricks and other Azure services allows for seamless workflow development.

Programming tools and frameworks are essential for modern data scientists. While the DP-900 exam doesn't test deep programming knowledge, understanding how Python (a popular general-purpose programming language) and R (a programming language specialized for statistical computing) are used within Azure's data science tools is important. This includes basic familiarity with common data science libraries and how they're supported in Azure.

Future evolution of data scientists in Azure

The field of data science continues to evolve with new technologies and approaches. Automated machine learning is making some aspects of model development more accessible, while increasing the importance of business understanding and problem formulation. Data scientists must stay current with emerging techniques while maintaining focus on delivering business value.

Exam Tip

Focus on understanding how Azure's data science tools work together rather than the technical details of machine learning algorithms. Know the basic workflow from data preparation to model deployment.

Ethical AI and responsible machine learning have become crucial considerations. Data scientists must understand concepts like model fairness, transparency, and accountability. They need to implement appropriate governance controls and ensure that their models meet ethical guidelines and regulatory requirements.

The evolution of data science in Azure represents a shift from isolated experimentation to integrated, production-ready solutions. While statistical and programming skills remain important, the ability to work within cloud-based platforms and collaborate across teams has become essential. For the DP-900 exam, understanding this integrated approach to data science and how it fits within the broader Azure ecosystem is key.

Exam Tip

While deep learning and advanced AI concepts aren't covered on theDP-900 exam, understanding how Azure supports these capabilities provides valuable context for future learning paths.

The role of the data scientist continues to evolve as Azure introduces new capabilities and automates certain aspects of the machine learning workflow. However, the fundamental skills of problem solving, statistical thinking, and business understanding remain crucial for success in this field. Those preparing for the DP-900 exam should focus on understanding how data scientists use Azure's tools to deliver value to organizations, rather than the technical details of machine learning algorithms.

As organizations mature in their data practices and face increasing regulatory pressures, a new role has emerged to bridge the gap between technical implementation and governance requirements. Let's explore the evolving role of data governors, who ensure that an organization's data assets are properly managed, protected, and utilized.

Data Governors

Data governors, also known as *data stewards* in some organizations, ensure that organizational data remains secure, compliant, and high quality. This emerging role has become increasingly critical with the introduction of data privacy regulations like GDPR (General Data Protection Regulation in Europe) and CCPA (California Consumer Privacy Act), which establish strict rules for handling personal data. In Azure, data governors use tools like Microsoft Purview to implement governance policies and maintain data catalogs.

Core responsibilities of data governors in Azure

Modern data governance extends far beyond traditional database administration or security management. Data governors serve as the bridge between business requirements, regulatory compliance, and technical implementation. They work closely with legal teams to understand compliance requirements, with business units to establish data ownership, and with technical teams to implement appropriate controls.

In the Azure ecosystem, data governors implement comprehensive data governance frameworks. They use Microsoft Purview to create and maintain data catalogs, establishing a single source of truth for data assets across the organization. This includes documenting data sources, defining business glossaries, and mapping data lineage from source to consumption.

Security and compliance have become cornerstone responsibilities. Data governors work with Azure's security features to implement appropriate access controls, data classification, and protection policies. They ensure that sensitive data is properly identified and protected, whether it resides in databases, data lakes, or analytical systems.

Data quality management has evolved into a strategic function. Data governors establish and monitor quality metrics, implement data quality rules, and work with data engineers to ensure that data pipelines maintain data integrity. They use Azure's tools to monitor data quality and implement correction procedures when issues arise.

Azure-related tools and platforms for data governors

Microsoft Purview serves as the primary tool for data governance in Azure. It provides capabilities for data discovery, classification, and lineage tracking. Data governors use Purview to create comprehensive data maps, implement sensitivity labels, and monitor data movement across the organization.

Exam Tip

The exam emphasizes Microsoft Purview's role in modern data governance. Understand its key features and use cases.

Other Azure tools, like Policy and RBAC (role-based access control), are essential for implementing governance controls. Data governors use these services to enforce compliance requirements, manage access permissions, and ensure consistent policy application across the data estate.

Integration with Azure's broader security features allows data governors to implement comprehensive data protection. This includes using Azure Information Protection for data classification, Azure Key Vault for secret management, and Azure Monitor for security monitoring.

Future evolution of data governors in Azure

As organizations continue to mature in their data practices, the data governor role is expected to become increasingly strategic. The growing importance of data privacy, the emergence of AI regulations, and the increasing complexity of data ecosystems all point to an expanding scope for this role.

The evolution of data governance in Azure represents a shift from tactical security and compliance to strategic data management. While technical skills remain important, the ability to bridge business, legal, and technical requirements has become essential. For the DP-900 exam, understanding how Azure's governance tools support this emerging role is crucial for success.

Bringing It All Together: Role Interactions in Practice

Understanding how these roles interact in real-world scenarios is crucial for success on the DP-900 exam and in actual Azure implementations. The modern data ecosystem requires seamless collaboration between all roles to deliver effective solutions. Figure 4-2 is a simplified diagram showing how these roles typically collaborate.

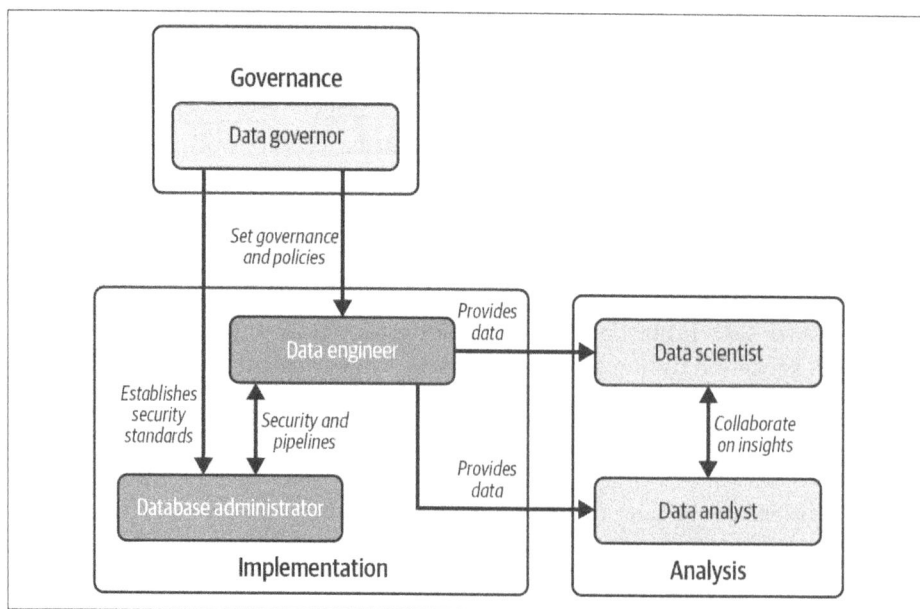

Figure 4-2. Simple data roles and their interactions

Consider a typical enterprise scenario: implementing a customer analytics solution in a retail company. This example illustrates how different roles collaborate within Azure's ecosystem.

The data governor establishes the governance framework up front, defining data classification, security requirements, and compliance standards that will guide the entire project. Using Microsoft Purview, they create the necessary data catalogs and protection policies.

Data engineers design and implement the solution within these governance guidelines, selecting appropriate Azure services and building the data pipelines. They move data from source systems through Azure Data Factory and into Azure Synapse Analytics while ensuring that the architecture aligns with business requirements.

Database administrators ensure that the underlying data platforms are optimized, secure, and properly maintained. They work with data engineers to establish proper access controls and performance benchmarks while maintaining security standards set by data governors.

Data scientists and data analysts collaborate on different aspects of insight generation. Scientists develop predictive models using Azure Machine Learning to forecast customer behavior, while analysts create Power BI dashboards for monitoring current trends and performance metrics.

Exam Tip

The DP-900 exam frequently presents scenarios requiring you to identify which roles should be involved at different project stages. Understanding these interactions is key to success.

Summary

The transition to Azure represents more than just a change in technology. It's a fundamental transformation in how data professionals work and collaborate. Each role has evolved to meet the demands of cloud-based data platforms while maintaining its core purpose:

- Data governors ensure compliance and proper data management.
- Database administrators focus on service optimization rather than hardware management.
- Data engineers architect scalable, cloud native data pipelines.
- Data analysts leverage powerful tools for insight generation.
- Data scientists build and deploy machine learning solutions at scale.

Beyond the Exam

The DP-900 certification provides an excellent foundation for understanding Azure's data platform and roles. However, the real world often presents more complex and nuanced situations than what's covered in the exam. Let's explore some key aspects of working with Azure data platforms in practice.

Real-World Role Dynamics

In my experience working with organizations adopting Azure, the most successful teams are those that maintain clear role boundaries while fostering strong collaboration. As you venture into real-world implementation, remember that the roles we've discussed aren't rigid. They're guidelines that help us work with data in an organized and effective way.

I've found that small organizations often need people to wear multiple hats, perhaps combining data engineering and analytics roles. Larger organizations might have specialized roles we haven't covered, like DataOps engineers (who focus on improving the speed and reliability of data pipelines through automation and process improvements) or machine learning engineers. The key is understanding the core responsibilities we've discussed and adapting them to your specific situation.

The career landscape in data and analytics continues to evolve, creating new opportunities and paths for professional growth that extend beyond traditional role boundaries.

Career Progression and Emerging Roles

The data professional's career journey often evolves in unexpected ways. Many data analysts progress into data science roles after developing strong statistical and programming skills. Database administrators frequently transition into data engineering or data architecture roles as they gain cloud expertise. We're also seeing new specialized roles emerge, such as DataOps engineers, machine learning engineers, and analytics engineers, reflecting the growing complexity of data platforms.

Real-World Insight

Success in data roles often depends more on soft skills like communication and problem-solving than on technical expertise alone.

As organizations mature in their data practices, the way teams work together and deliver value becomes increasingly important.

Organizational Impact

Real-world implementation often requires navigating challenges not addressed in the exam. Building effective communication channels between technical and business teams, managing technical debt, and balancing rapid delivery with governance requirements are common challenges. Success often comes from understanding how each role contributes to business value while maintaining flexibility in how these roles are implemented.

Looking ahead, the rapid pace of technological change suggests continued evolution in how we work with data in Azure.

Future Outlook

The future of data roles in Azure will likely bring even more changes as new technologies emerge. Increased automation may shift focus from implementation to strategy, while AI integration will require new skills across all roles. Privacy regulations and sustainability considerations will continue to shape how we work with data.

PART II

Relational Data on Azure

Relational data remains the backbone of many mission-critical applications because it delivers consistency, rich querying capability, and structural integrity. This part first solidifies how relational modeling works—keys, relationships, normalization intent, indexing trade-offs—and then maps those principles to Azure's spectrum of managed relational offerings and open source database services. The focus is not on memorizing SKU names; it's on understanding how responsibility shifts as you move from fully managed PaaS to infrastructure-based deployments and why that matters for cost, control, and agility.

- Chapter 5, "Relational Data Concepts", builds the conceptual toolkit: why normalization reduces anomalies, how primary and foreign keys enforce integrity, what indexing accelerates (and what it costs), and how ACID properties shape transactional guarantees.

- Chapter 6, "Azure SQL Services and Open Source Options", translates those concepts into platform choice—contrasting Azure SQL Database, SQL Managed Instance, SQL Server on Azure VMs, and managed PostgreSQL/MySQL options through lenses of compatibility, administrative overhead, scalability models, and ecosystem needs.

On completion, you should be able to justify a relational model structurally, explain when denormalization is pragmatic, and select an Azure relational deployment model aligned to control boundaries, operational burden tolerance, and workload patterns.

Common missteps addressed here include over-normalizing too early, ignoring indexing strategy until performance degrades, defaulting to virtual machines out of habit, and underestimating total cost implications of scaling modes.

Exam Alignment: These chapters reinforce DP-900 objectives around relational concepts and platform differentiation at a categorical level.

CHAPTER 5

Relational Data Concepts

In addition to changing how we store data, the shift to cloud computing has enhanced how we interact with relational databases, one of computing's most enduring and vital technologies. Whether you're working with a traditional on-premises database or a fully managed cloud service like Azure SQL Database, understanding relational fundamentals is crucial. For the DP-900 exam and for anyone working with data platforms, these concepts form the foundation of data management. While this chapter introduces core database concepts, we'll focus primarily on practical understanding rather than technical implementation details.

Coverage of Curriculum Objectives

This chapter addresses the following DP-900 exam objectives:

- Understand core relational data features and relationships.
- Implement normalization principles effectively.
- Work with fundamental SQL statements.
- Understand essential database objects and their roles.

Core Relational Concepts

In today's data landscape, we encounter both structured and unstructured data. Structured data follows a predefined schema with consistent fields and data types—perfect for transactional systems and reporting. Unstructured data, like images, videos, and documents, requires different storage approaches, often using Blob Storage or data lakes. In AI applications, structured data feeds machine learning models with clean training data, while unstructured data undergoes processing through computer vision or natural language processing before analysis. Understanding these differences helps determine the appropriate storage solution: relational databases for structured data, and object storage or NoSQL systems for unstructured content.

Despite the buzz around AI and NoSQL databases, relational databases remain important. Why? The answer lies in their unique ability to organize and manage structured data in a way that maintains consistency, reduces redundancy, and enables complex queries. Traditional spreadsheets might work for simple data storage, but when organizations need to manage thousands or millions of records with complex relationships, relational databases become essential.

Exam Tip

The DP-900 exam emphasizes practical understanding of relational concepts rather than theoretical database design. Focus on how these concepts apply in real-world scenarios.

Think about how a retail company manages its operations. It needs to track products, customers, orders, and inventory—all interconnected pieces of information. A relational database organizes this data efficiently:

- Products have prices, descriptions, and inventory levels.
- Customers have names, addresses, and order histories.
- Orders contain multiple products and belong to specific customers.
- Inventory tracks stock levels across different locations.

Note

Modern cloud platforms like Azure have streamlined how we work with relational databases, but the fundamental concepts remain unchanged.

These fundamental relationships form the backbone of how relational databases operate. To implement these relationships effectively, we need to understand the basic building blocks of relational databases, starting with their primary data structure: tables.

Understanding Tables

At their core, relational databases store information in tables—structured collections of related data. Unlike spreadsheets, which offer flexibility at the cost of consistency, database tables enforce strict rules about what kind of data can be stored and how it's organized. Think of a table as a contract with your data: every piece of information must follow specific rules to maintain order and reliability.

Columns and fields

Columns define the type of information that can be stored in a table. Each column specifies both the kind of data (like numbers, text, or dates) and rules about what values are acceptable. For instance, a `ProductID` column might require unique numbers, while a `ProductName` column stores text and cannot be left empty. `Price` columns typically use decimal numbers and must contain positive values. These specifications ensure that every piece of data fits the table's intended purpose.

Records and rows

While columns define the structure, rows contain the actual data. Each row represents one complete record in the table. For example, in a `products` table, a row might contain all the information about a single product: its ID number, name, price, and other details. Every row must follow the rules defined by the column specifications. A typical `products` table might contain rows like:

- Product #1001, "Cloud Database Basics," $29.99
- Product #1002, "Azure Fundamentals," $39.99

Primary keys

When a table needs a way to uniquely identify each row, you can use primary keys. Often implemented as automatically generated numbers, though modern approaches (especially v7 and newer) increasingly use UUIDs, which offer additional possible values, sortability, and near-zero collision risk, primary keys ensure that every record can be distinguished from all others. Primary keys are constrained by both `UNIQUE` and `NOT NULL` properties, effectively making them unique identifiers for any row. Many databases support `AUTO_INCREMENT` functionality, which automatically generates sequential values for numeric primary keys. Sometimes multiple columns work together to form a composite key. Primary keys are essential for creating relationships between tables, allowing data to be connected across the database.

To see these concepts in action, let's examine a basic example of an order management system in Figure 5-1. Before we do, however, it's important to understand foreign keys. A *foreign key* is a column in one table that references the primary key of
another table, creating a link between them. For instance, an Orders table might have
a CustomerID column that references the primary key in the Customers table, establishing which customer placed each order.

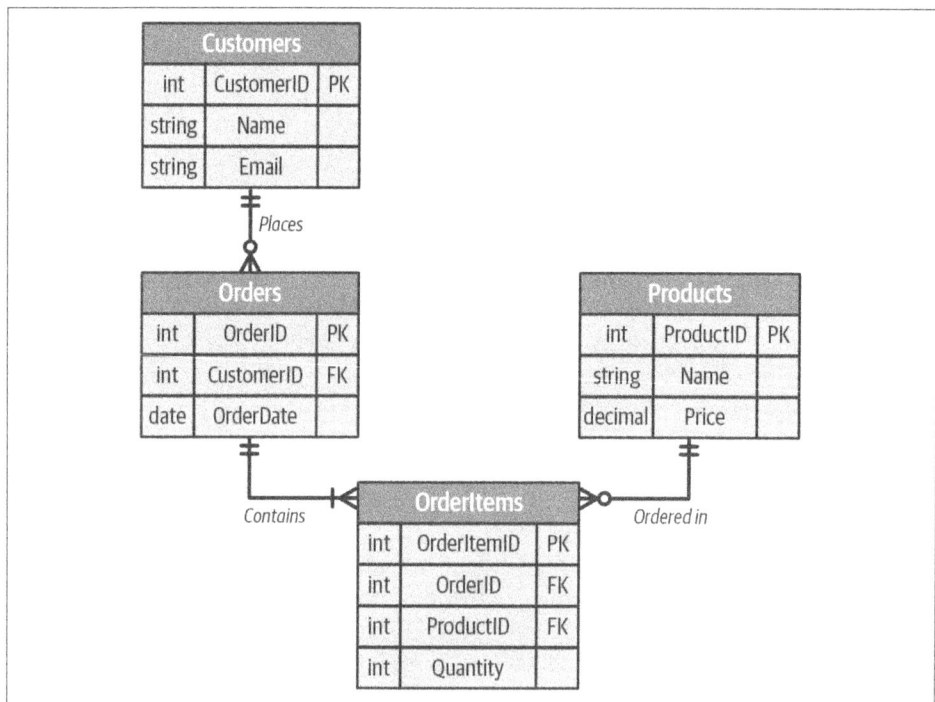

Figure 5-1. Basic order management tables

This system demonstrates how tables work together to create a complete business solution. The Customers table stores customer information, with each row representing
one customer's complete profile. The Orders table tracks when customers place
orders, linking to customer records through their unique identifiers. The Products
table maintains product details independently, while the OrderItems table serves as a
bridge, connecting orders with their products.

While tables provide the structure for our data, we need two more elements to ensure data integrity: appropriate data types and constraints. These rules act as guardians, ensuring that only valid information enters our database.

Data Types and Constraints

When designing database tables, we need to specify what kind of information each column can hold and what rules it must follow. These specifications form the foundation of data integrity in our database.

Basic data types

Every column in a database must have a specific data type that defines what kind of information it can store. Think of these as specialized containers, each designed to hold particular kinds of data efficiently and safely.

Numeric types handle all forms of numbers. Integer columns (INT) store whole numbers, perfect for IDs and counts; for example, CustomerID INT or QuantityInStock INT. Decimal types like DECIMAL(10,2) manage precise financial calculations, ensuring accuracy in prices and totals. Float types handle scientific calculations where precision requirements differ from financial calculations.

Text types manage character data with different size requirements. CHAR columns store fixed-length text, useful for codes or abbreviations that never vary in length, such as CHAR(2) for state codes. VARCHAR columns efficiently handle variable-length text like names or descriptions, such as VARCHAR(255) for product names. Text columns manage longer content such as product descriptions or comments.

Date and time types handle temporal data. DATE columns store calendar dates like birthdates, and DATETIME columns combine both, perfect for tracking when orders are placed or when inventory changes occur.

Exam Tip

While Azure databases support many advanced data types, the DP-900 exam focuses on understanding basic types and their common uses. Familiarity with INT, VARCHAR, DATE, and DECIMAL is sufficient for the exam—you don't need to know advanced or nuanced types.

Data rules with constraints

While data types specify what kind of information a column can hold, constraints define the rules that data must follow. Think of constraints as guards that protect your data's integrity.

The NOT NULL constraint ensures that essential information is always present. For example, every product needs a name, so the ProductName column would use this constraint to prevent empty values.

UNIQUE constraints prevent duplicate values where they don't make sense. Customer email addresses must be unique to avoid confusion, while product codes need to be distinct to prevent inventory mix-ups.

DEFAULT constraints provide fallback values when none are specified. When a customer places an order, the OrderDate can automatically default to the current date if not explicitly set.

Beyond Types and Rules: Building Connections

While data types and constraints help us manage individual pieces of information, real-world data rarely exists in isolation. A customer's order connects to both the customer who placed it and the products they purchased. To represent these real-world connections, we need to understand how tables can relate to each other through relationships and keys.

Understanding Relationships and Keys

In a real-world database, information rarely exists in isolation. Consider how a retail business operates: customers place orders, orders contain products, and products belong in categories. These natural connections need to be represented in our database structure. Understanding how to establish and maintain these relationships is fundamental to working with databases effectively.

Exam Tip

For the DP-900 exam, focus on identifying and understanding basic relationship types rather than complex database design principles.

Types of Table Relationships

Relational databases support three primary types of relationships, each serving a specific purpose in connecting related data.

One-to-one relationships

The simplest but least common relationship type occurs when each record in one table corresponds to exactly one record in another table. Think of an employee and their passport information. While you could store passport details in the employee

---

table, separating them might make sense for security or organizational reasons. In this case, each employee has exactly one passport record, and each passport record belongs to exactly one employee.

One-to-many relationships

The most common relationship type occurs when a record in one table can relate to multiple records in another table. The classic example is customers and their orders. A single customer can place many orders over time, but each order belongs to exactly one customer. This relationship naturally models many real-world scenarios, from departments having multiple employees to categories containing multiple products.

Many-to-many relationships

Sometimes records in both tables need to relate to multiple records in the other table. Consider products and orders: one order typically contains multiple products, and each product can appear in many different orders. This relationship requires a special junction table (sometimes called a *bridge* or *linking table*) to connect the two tables. In our example, an OrderItems table would connect Products and Orders, tracking which products appear in which orders and in what quantities.

Use of Foreign Keys to Establish Table Relationships

To implement these relationships in practice, databases use foreign keys to connect related records. A foreign key in one table references the primary key of another table, creating a link between them. For example:

- In the Orders table, a CustomerID foreign key references the Customers table's primary key, connecting each order to its customer.
- In the OrderItems table, both OrderID and ProductID foreign keys reference their respective tables, enabling the many-to-many relationship between orders and products.

Exam Tip

While you can use various column types as keys, the DP-900 exam focuses on simple numeric IDs for primary keys.

A Practical Example

To understand how these relationships work in practice, let's explore a basic scenario: an online bookstore. Consider how a bookstore needs to track customers, customers' orders, books, and book categories (Figure 5-2).

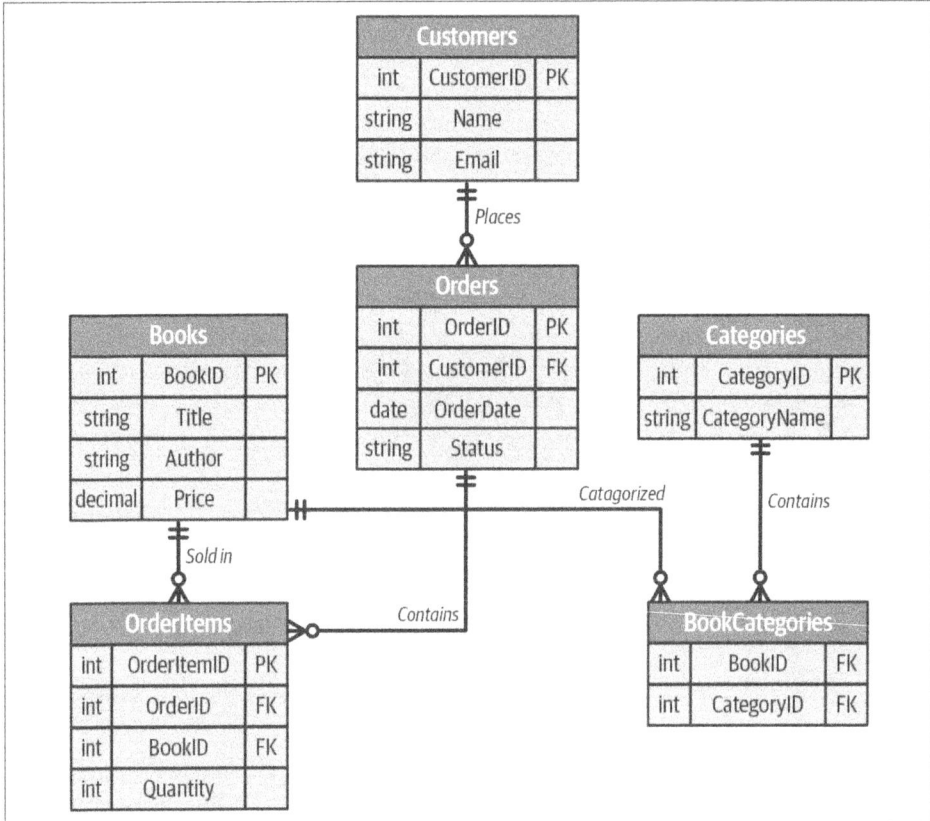

Figure 5-2. Bookstore database relationships

Our bookstore database demonstrates several key relationship types working together:

When customers place orders, we create a one-to-many relationship between the Cus tomers and Orders tables. Each customer might order multiple times throughout the year, but every order belongs to exactly one customer. The CustomerID foreign key in the Orders table makes this connection possible.

Books and categories share a more complex relationship. A book like *Cloud Computing Basics* might belong in both the "Technology" and "Professional Development" categories, and these categories naturally contain many different books. This many-to-many relationship comes to life through a junction table that tracks which books belong in which categories.

This practical example shows how relational databases mirror real-world business relationships. But how do we actually work with this connected data? That's where SQL comes in. SQL gives us the tools to extract meaningful information from our database, whether we need to find a customer's order history or generate a list of books in a specific category.

Basic SQL Queries

While the cloud has transformed how we manage databases, SQL remains the primary way to interact with relational databases. Think of SQL as a specialized language designed specifically for talking to databases—it allows you to ask questions about your data and make changes when needed. In this section, we'll explore the fundamental SQL operations you need to understand for the DP-900 exam.

SQL Language Categories

SQL statements fall into three main categories:

Data Manipulation Language (DML)
    Commands that work with data (SELECT, INSERT, UPDATE, DELETE)

Data Definition Language (DDL)
    Commands that define database structure (CREATE, ALTER, DROP)

Data Control Language (DCL)
    Commands that manage permissions (GRANT, REVOKE)

For the DP-900 exam, focus primarily on DML commands, which handle day-to-day data operations.

Exam Tip

The DP-900 exam tests basic SQL concepts rather than complex query writing. Focus on understanding what each type of query does and when to use it.

Retrieving Data with SELECT

Imagine you're managing a bookstore's database. Every day, you need to answer questions like "What books do we have by Jane Smith?" or "Which books cost more than $50?" The SELECT statement is how you ask these questions of your database. It's the most fundamental and frequently used SQL operation, allowing you to retrieve and view your data in meaningful ways.

The basic structure of a SELECT statement has three main parts: the columns you want to see (SELECT), the table you want to look in (FROM), and any conditions that must be met (WHERE). Here's the basic syntax:

```
SELECT column1, column2
FROM TableName
WHERE condition;
```

Let's put this into practice with a real example. Say a customer asks about Jane Smith's books. You would write:

```
SELECT Title, Price
FROM Books
WHERE Author = 'Jane Smith';
```

This query tells the database to look in the Books table, find all books where the author is Jane Smith, and show you the title and price of each one. It's like asking a librarian to check the shelves for all books by a specific author and tell you their titles and prices.

Filtering with WHERE

The WHERE clause is your tool for filtering data, much like how you might filter your email inbox to see only messages from a specific sender. It helps you narrow down large sets of data to just the information you need. You can use various comparison operators to create these filters:

- Equals sign (=) for exact matches
- Greater than sign (>) or less than sign (<) for numerical comparisons
- Greater than or equal to sign (>=) or less than or equal to sign (<=) for range checks

For example, if you're planning a promotion for premium books, you might want to see all books priced over $50:

```
SELECT Title, Price
FROM Books
WHERE Price > 50.00;
```

This query acts like a filter, showing you only the high-end books in your inventory. Similarly, if you need to review recent orders for your monthly report, you could find all orders placed since the start of 2024:

```
SELECT OrderID, OrderDate
FROM Orders
WHERE OrderDate >= '2024-01-01';
```

This helps you focus on just the recent orders rather than sifting through your entire order history.

Sorting with ORDER BY

Data organization is crucial for analysis and reporting. The ORDER BY clause helps you arrange your results in a meaningful sequence, much like how you might sort a spreadsheet by different columns. You can sort in ascending order (A to Z, lowest to highest) or descending order (Z to A, highest to lowest).

For instance, you could use the following query if you're preparing a display of your most expensive books:

```
SELECT Title, Price
FROM Books
ORDER BY Price DESC;
```

This query arranges books from highest to lowest price, perfect for identifying your premium inventory. Sometimes you need to sort by multiple criteria, like when reviewing orders by date and amount:

```
SELECT OrderID, OrderDate, TotalAmount
FROM Orders
ORDER BY OrderDate DESC, TotalAmount DESC;
```

This organization is particularly useful for financial reports, showing your most recent and highest value orders first, then organizing lower value orders within each date.

Exam Tip

Pay attention to how different SQL clauses work together to filter and sort data. Understanding their interaction is key to writing effective queries.

Modifying Data

While retrieving data is important, databases need to be kept up-to-date as your business operates. SQL provides three main ways to modify your data: adding new records (INSERT), changing existing records (UPDATE), and removing old records (DELETE).

Adding records with INSERT

When new books arrive at your store, you need to add them to your database. The INSERT statement handles this task. Think of it as filling out a form for each new book. You specify which information (columns) you're providing and then give the actual values:

```
INSERT INTO Books (Title, Author, Price)
VALUES ('Azure Data Fundamentals', 'Michael John Pena', 59.99);
```

This is like creating a new catalog entry for a single book. But what if you receive a shipment of multiple books? SQL allows you to add several records at once, saving time and effort:

```
INSERT INTO Books (Title, Author, Price)
VALUES
    ('Azure Data Fundamentals', 'Michael John Pena', 59.99);
    ('Azure Cosmos DB Designs and Practices', 'Mike Johnson', 44.99);
```

This bulk insert is particularly useful during inventory updates or when importing data from another system.

Modifying records with UPDATE

Prices change, errors need to be corrected, and information needs to be updated. These are all situations where the UPDATE statement comes into play. Think of UPDATE as editing an existing record in your database. It's crucial to be precise about which records you want to change, which is why the WHERE clause is so important here.

For example, to update the price of a specific book:

```
UPDATE Books
SET Price = 34.99
WHERE BookID = 1001;
```

The WHERE clause ensures that you only change the intended book's price. You can also make broader changes, like applying a storewide discount to all premium books:

```
UPDATE Books
SET Price = Price * 0.9
WHERE Price > 50.00;
```

This automatically calculates and applies a 10% discount to all books currently priced over $50, saving you from having to update each price manually.

Removing records with DELETE

Over time, databases can accumulate outdated or unnecessary records. The DELETE statement helps you clean up your database by removing records you no longer need. However, because deletion is permanent, it's crucial to be extremely careful with your WHERE clause to ensure that you only remove the intended records.

The following code removes a specific order that was canceled:

```
DELETE FROM Orders
WHERE OrderID = 5001;
```

You might also need to perform routine cleanup, like removing old orders to maintain system performance:

```
DELETE FROM Orders
WHERE OrderDate < '2023-01-01';
```

This removes all orders from 2022 and earlier but keeps your recent order history intact. Always double-check your WHERE clause before executing a DELETE statement, as recovering deleted data can be difficult or impossible.

Visualizing your SQL operations

The SQL operations we've covered—SELECT, INSERT, UPDATE, and DELETE—form the basic building blocks for interacting with your database. Each operation follows a specific pattern, making them systematic and predictable once you understand their structure.

Figure 5-3 illustrates the decision flow for each SQL operation. Starting from the top, you first choose which operation you need based on your goal:

- If you need to view data, the SELECT path guides you through choosing columns, selecting your table, adding any filtering conditions, and finally sorting your results.

- To add new data, the INSERT path shows that you'll need to specify your target table, list the columns, and provide the values.

- When changing existing data, the UPDATE path leads you through specifying the table, setting new values, and adding conditions to identify which records to update.

- For removing data, the DELETE path demonstrates the importance of specifying both the table and the WHERE clause to identify which records to remove.

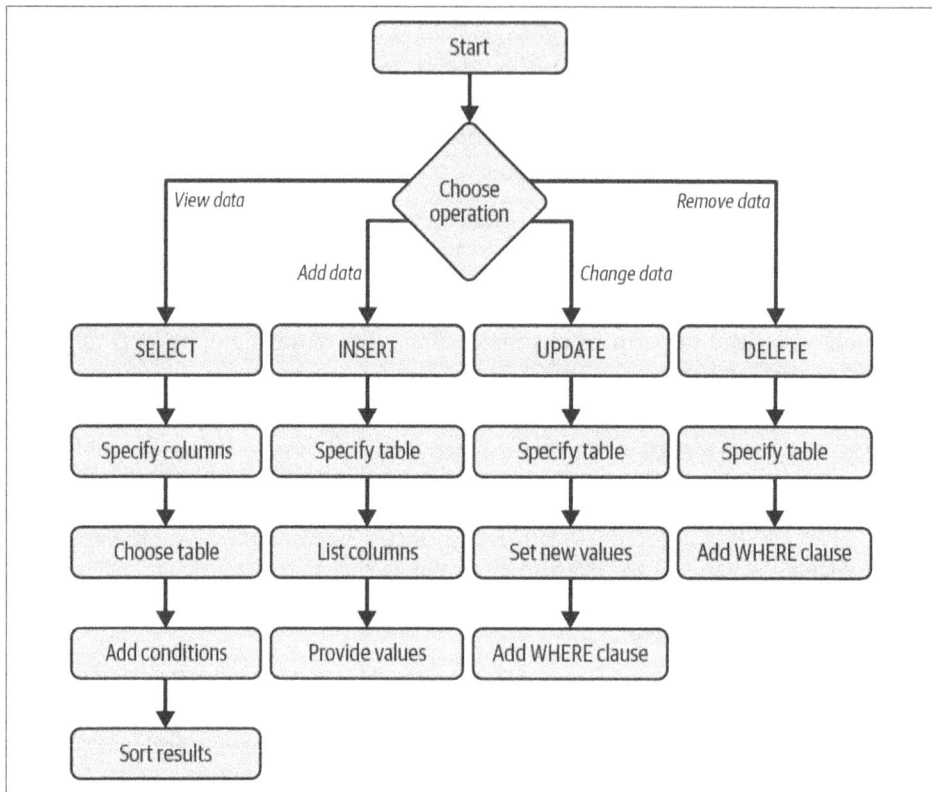

Figure 5-3. Common SQL operations

So far, we've worked with single tables in our examples. However, most real databases store related information across multiple tables. To get a complete picture of your data, you'll often need to combine information from different tables, and that's where JOIN operations come in.

Joining Tables

Most production-running databases store related information across multiple tables. This separation of data is intentional: it helps maintain data integrity and reduces redundancy. For example, instead of storing a customer's complete information with every order they make, we store customer details once in a Customers table and link it to multiple orders in an Orders table.

To get a complete picture of your data spread across these tables, you need JOIN operations. The most common types include:

INNER JOIN
: Returns only matching records from both tables.

LEFT JOIN
: Returns all records from the left table, plus matches from the right.

RIGHT JOIN
: Returns all records from the right table, plus matches from the left.

FULL OUTER JOIN
: Returns all records from both tables. For example, an INNER JOIN between Orders and Customers shows only orders with valid customers, while a LEFT JOIN would show all orders even if customer data is missing.

Think of JOIN as a way to temporarily combine tables based on their relationships. For instance, when processing orders, you might want to see both order details and customer information in a single view.

Here's how you can combine order and customer information:

```
SELECT Orders.OrderID, Customers.Name, Orders.OrderDate
FROM Orders
JOIN Customers ON Orders.CustomerID = Customers.CustomerID;
```

This query connects each order with its corresponding customer using the CustomerID that's common to both tables. The result gives you a comprehensive view showing the order ID, the customer's name, and when they placed the order—information that originally lived in separate tables.

Exam Tip

While there are several types of JOINs (INNER, LEFT, RIGHT, and FULL), the DP-900 exam focuses primarily on basic INNER JOIN operations, which only return matches found in both tables.

Understanding table relationships and joins is crucial because they reflect how data is organized in real-world business scenarios. Whether you're tracking inventory, managing customer relationships, or analyzing sales patterns, you'll often need to bring together information from multiple tables to get meaningful insights.

Common Database Objects

Tables provide the foundation for storing our data, but a modern database system relies on several additional objects to operate effectively. These objects enhance how we access, secure, and manage our data. As cloud platforms like Azure continue to evolve, understanding these fundamental building blocks becomes increasingly important for anyone working with data platforms.

> **Exam Tip**
>
> The DP-900 exam focuses on understanding what each database object does and when to use it, rather than the technical details of creating them.

Views: Simplifying Data Access

Views transform how we interact with our data by providing simplified, secure access to information spread across multiple tables. When designing a database system, we often normalize our data across many tables to reduce redundancy. However, this can make retrieving meaningful information more complex. Views solve this challenge by creating virtual tables that combine and present data in ways that make sense for different business needs.

Consider a retail database system tracking sales, products, and customers. While storing this information in separate tables makes sense for data integrity, sales managers need to see this information combined. A view can seamlessly join these tables:

```
CREATE VIEW SalesAnalysis AS
SELECT
    s.OrderDate,
    p.ProductName,
    p.UnitPrice,
    s.Quantity,
    (p.UnitPrice * s.Quantity) as Revenue,
    c.CustomerName,
    c.Region
FROM Sales s
JOIN Products p ON s.ProductID = p.ProductID
JOIN Customers c ON s.CustomerID = c.CustomerID;
```

This view provides several benefits. First, it simplifies reporting by encapsulating complex join logic. Second, it enforces consistency by ensuring that everyone uses the same calculations for metrics such as revenue. Third, it enhances security by allowing us to grant access to specific data combinations without exposing underlying tables.

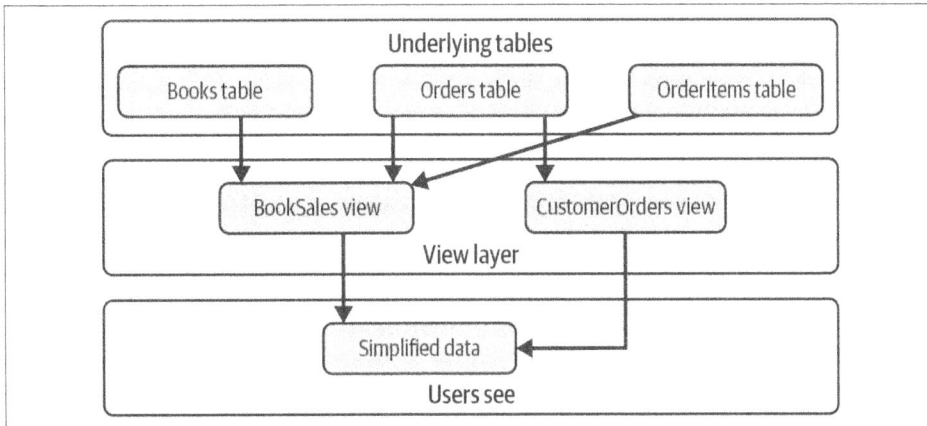

Figure 5-4. How views work

Figure 5-4 illustrates how views work in practice using a bookstore database example. At the top layer, we have our underlying tables: Books, Orders, and OrderItems, which store the raw data. In the middle layer, we see two views that have been created: BookSales and CustomerOrders. These views combine data from the underlying tables in useful ways. For instance, BookSales might combine data from Books and OrderItems to show sales metrics for each book, while CustomerOrders might join Orders with customer information to display order history.

The bottom layer shows what users actually see: simplified data that's relevant to their needs. Users don't need to understand the complex relationships between the underlying tables or write complicated join queries. Instead, they interact with these predefined views that present the data in a clear, business-focused way.

Views become particularly powerful when working with cloud databases, where different applications and teams might need varying levels of access to the same data. They act as an abstraction layer, helping us manage changes to underlying table structures without disrupting the applications that depend on them.

Views help us organize and present our data effectively, but they don't inherently speed up the data retrieval process. When we query a view, the database still needs to execute the underlying SELECT statement and process all the joined tables. This brings us to another crucial database object: indexes. While views determine what data users can see, indexes determine how quickly they can access it. In fact, proper indexing becomes even more important when working with views that join multiple tables, as these operations can become resource intensive as your data grows.

Indexes: Improving Data Retrieval

As databases grow larger, especially in cloud environments where we might be handling millions of records, finding specific data efficiently becomes crucial. Consider a customer service portal that needs to look up customer details instantly when they call. Without any optimization, the database would need to scan through every single customer record to find the right one— an approach that quickly becomes impractical as your customer base grows.

Indexes solve this performance challenge by providing optimized pathways to our data. In a customer management system, searching for customers by email address is a common operation:

```
SELECT CustomerID, Name, Region
FROM Customers
WHERE EmailAddress = 'example@company.com';
```

When this query runs on a table without an index, the database must examine every customer record to find matching email addresses, a process known as a *table scan*. For a table with millions of customers, this could take seconds or even minutes. By creating an index:

```
CREATE INDEX IX_Customers_Email ON Customers(EmailAddress);
```

the same query now completes almost instantly. The database uses the index to jump directly to the matching record, much like using a phone book's alphabetical organization to find a specific name.

Modern relational databases support several index types, each optimized for different scenarios. The *clustered index* determines the physical organization of data in the table itself. Think of it as the primary way the data is sorted, just as books in a library might be organized by their call numbers. Each table can have only one clustered index because the data can only be physically stored in one order. Most commonly, this is created on the primary key column.

Nonclustered indexes provide additional ways to locate data without reorganizing the table itself. A table can have multiple nonclustered indexes to support different query patterns. These are invaluable for columns frequently used in search conditions or join operations. However, each additional index requires extra storage space and processing time during data modifications.

A newer innovation, particularly important for data warehousing and analytics, is the *columnstore index*. Traditional indexes organize data by rows, but columnstore indexes store each column separately and compress the data. This radical change in storage structure makes them incredibly efficient for analytical queries that need to process large amounts of data, especially when calculating aggregates like sums or averages across millions of rows.

While indexes can dramatically improve query performance, they come with costs. Each index consumes additional storage space and must be updated whenever the underlying data changes. In cloud environments, where resources directly impact costs, this balance becomes even more critical. Database administrators must carefully monitor query patterns and index usage to ensure that they're providing maximum benefit without unnecessary overhead.

Index design requires careful planning to balance performance gains against maintenance costs. But optimizing data access is only part of the challenge in modern database systems. Organizations also need ways to standardize how their applications interact with data, enforce business rules consistently, and maintain security. This is where stored procedures come into play.

While we've covered the three most common index types relevant to the DP-900 exam, other specialized index types exist for specific use cases, including filtered indexes, spatial indexes, and full-text indexes.

Stored Procedures: Creating Reusable Code

In complex database applications, certain operations require multiple steps to complete correctly. Take a banking system where transferring money between accounts isn't just a simple update operation—it requires checking balances, recording transaction history, and ensuring that both accounts remain consistent. Writing this logic separately in each application that needs it introduces risks of inconsistency and makes updates difficult to manage.

Stored procedures solve this challenge by packaging database operations into reusable units of work. For example, a funds transfer procedure might look like this:

```
CREATE PROCEDURE ProcessBookOrder
    @BookID int,
    @CustomerID int,
    @Quantity int,
    @OrderStatus varchar(50) OUTPUT
AS
BEGIN
    -- Check if we have enough stock
    DECLARE @StockAvailable int;

    SELECT @StockAvailable = StockQuantity
    FROM Books
    WHERE BookID = @BookID;

    IF @StockAvailable >= @Quantity
    BEGIN
        -- Update stock level
        UPDATE Books
        SET StockQuantity = StockQuantity - @Quantity
        WHERE BookID = @BookID;
```

```
-- Create the order
INSERT INTO Orders (CustomerID, OrderDate, Status)
VALUES (@CustomerID, GETDATE(), 'Confirmed');

SET @OrderStatus = 'Order Placed Successfully';
END
ELSE
BEGIN
    SET @OrderStatus = 'Insufficient Stock';
END
END
```

When this procedure runs, it first checks if enough books are available by querying the Books table. If there's sufficient stock, it performs two critical operations: reducing the stock quantity and creating a new order record. If there isn't enough stock, it sets a status message to inform the calling application. This entire process happens as one unit of work: either all steps complete successfully or none of them do.

Exam Tip

For the DP-900 exam, understand the purpose of stored procedures rather than how to write them.

In cloud environments, stored procedures become even more valuable. They reduce network traffic by keeping processing close to the data, improve security by limiting direct table access, and help maintain consistency across different applications and services that might be running in different regions or platforms.

Modern database systems have extended stored procedures beyond simple SQL operations. Azure SQL Database, for example, allows procedures to interact with external services, process JSON data, and handle complex business rules. This flexibility makes stored procedures a crucial tool for implementing business logic consistently across all applications that access the database.

The value of stored procedures extends beyond just code organization. When applications interact with databases through stored procedures rather than direct SQL statements, database administrators can monitor and optimize these common operations more effectively. They can analyze procedure execution patterns, tune performance bottlenecks, and even modify underlying logic without requiring changes to the applications themselves.

With data integrity and consistency being paramount in modern systems, stored procedures provide the control and reliability organizations need. However, like any powerful tool, they require careful management. The next challenge organizations face is ensuring that their data stays consistent when changes occur. And this is where triggers enter the picture.

Triggers: Creating Automatic Responses

Triggers are special stored procedures that spring into action the moment specific events occur in your database. Think of them as automated responses that ensure that your data stays consistent, secure, and well managed. Let's explore how these digital guardians work through a practical example from a medical records system.

In healthcare, maintaining an accurate audit trail is crucial. Patient records are sensitive, and every change needs to be meticulously tracked. Instead of relying on individual applications to remember to log every modification, a trigger can automatically capture these changes:

```
CREATE TRIGGER PatientAudit
ON Patients
AFTER UPDATE
AS
BEGIN
    INSERT INTO AuditLog (
        PatientID,
        FieldChanged,
        OldValue,
        NewValue,
        ChangeDate,
        UserID
    )
    SELECT
        i.PatientID,
        'Status',
        d.Status,
        i.Status,
        GETDATE(),
        SYSTEM_USER
    FROM inserted i
    JOIN deleted d ON i.PatientID = d.PatientID
    WHERE i.Status <> d.Status;
END
```

This specific trigger does something powerful: whenever a patient's record is updated, it automatically creates a log entry. It captures who made the change, when it happened, and exactly what was modified.

Triggers serve various critical purposes:

Maintaining data integrity
Ensure related tables stay synchronized. When a customer is deleted, a trigger could automatically archive or delete their related orders.

Enforcing business rules
> Prevent invalid data modifications. A trigger could stop a price update if the new price is below cost.

Audit trailing
> Automatically track changes for compliance or debugging. Every modification to sensitive data can be logged with who made the change and when.

Cross-database updates
> Maintain consistency across multiple databases. A trigger could replicate certain changes to a reporting database.

Types of triggers include:

AFTER *triggers*
> Execute after the triggering action completes. Useful for audit logging or cascading updates.

INSTEAD OF *triggers*
> Replace the triggering action with custom logic. Helpful for implementing complex validation or providing updatable views.

DDL triggers
> Respond to database structure changes. Can prevent unauthorized schema modifications or document changes.

In modern cloud databases, triggers have become even more sophisticated. They can now interact with external services, process complex data formats, and implement intricate business logic across distributed systems.

While tables store data and SQL statements interact with it, triggers add an extra layer of intelligence. They automatically enforce rules, maintain consistency, and provide advanced functionality without requiring manual intervention for every specific scenario.

Bringing It All Together: The Library Database in Practice

To illustrate how the various database concepts work together, let's consider a basic banking database. This example will demonstrate the use of tables, relationships, queries, and database objects in a financial context.

Exam Tip

The DP-900 exam often presents scenarios where you need to understand how different database elements work together to solve practical problems.

Basic Banking Database Structure

Before we dive into the specifics of queries and database objects, let's take a look at the structure of our banking database (Figure 5-5).

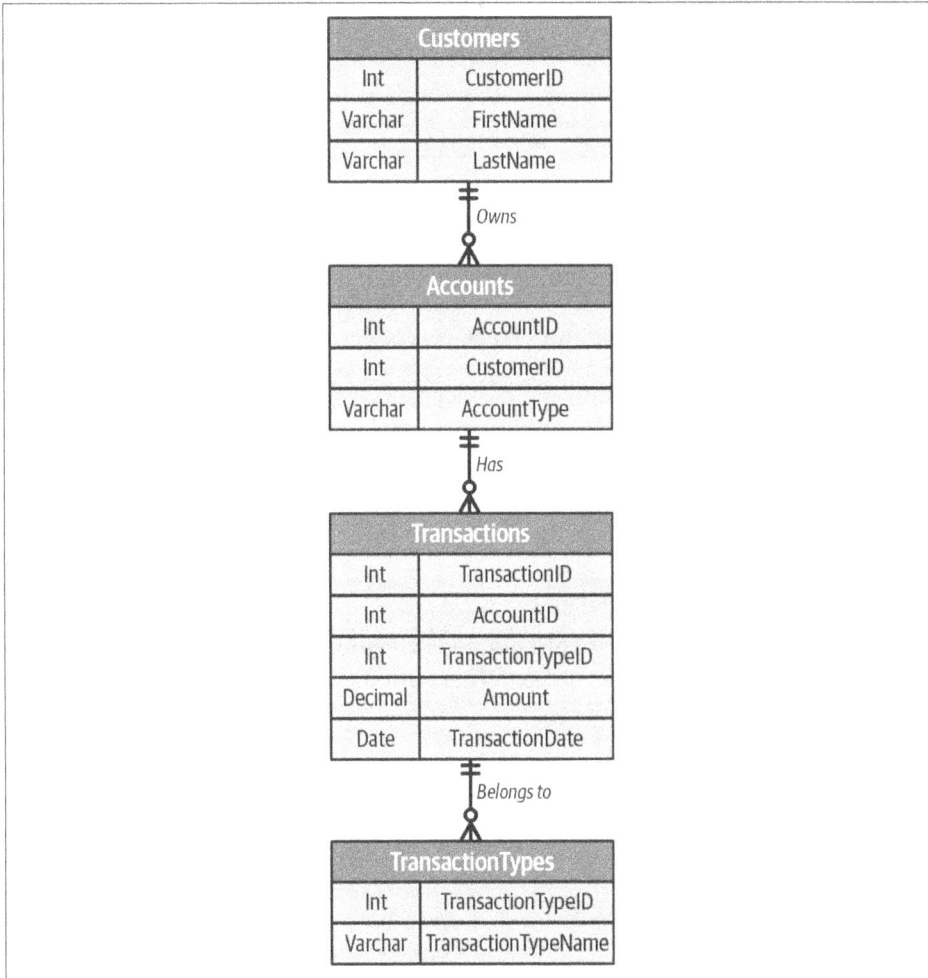

Figure 5-5. Basic banking entity relationship diagram

The ER (entity relationship) diagram in Figure 5-5 illustrates the key tables and their relationships. The lines between the tables represent the relationships, with the symbols indicating the type of relationship (one-to-many or many-to-one). This diagram provides a high-level view of how the data is organized and how the tables are connected.

This simple schema consists of four main tables:

Customers
> Stores information about each bank customer

Accounts
> Holds data about customer accounts (checking, savings, etc.)

Transactions
> Records financial transactions on accounts

TransactionTypes
> Defines types of transactions (deposit, withdrawal, transfer)

The relationships between these tables are as follows:

- Each Customer can own multiple Accounts (one-to-many).
- Each Account can have multiple Transactions (one-to-many).
- Each Transaction belongs to a TransactionType (many-to-one).

Now let's explore how we can use SQL queries and database objects to interact with this data.

Common Database Operations

In this section, we will implement common operations in our bookstore database using SQL queries and database objects. These examples demonstrate practical applications of the concepts we've covered:

Calculating account balances

To calculate the current balance for each account, we can create a view that aggregates the transactions:

```
CREATE VIEW AccountBalances AS
SELECT
    a.AccountID,
    a.CustomerID,
    a.AccountType,
    SUM(
        CASE
            WHEN t.TransactionTypeID IN (1, 3)
            THEN t.Amount
            ELSE -t.Amount
        END
    ) AS Balance
FROM Accounts a
LEFT JOIN Transactions t ON a.AccountID = t.AccountID
```

```
    GROUP BY a.AccountID, a.CustomerID, a.AccountType;

    SELECT * FROM AccountBalances;
```

This view uses a LEFT JOIN to connect accounts with their transactions and a CASE statement to add deposits and transfers while subtracting withdrawals. The SUM function calculates the total, giving us the current balance for each account.

Processing transactions

To handle the multistep process of recording a transaction and updating the account balance, we can create a stored procedure:

```
CREATE PROCEDURE ProcessTransaction
    @AccountID INT,
    @TransactionTypeID INT,
    @Amount DECIMAL(10,2)
AS
BEGIN
    INSERT INTO Transactions (
        AccountID,
        TransactionTypeID,
        Amount,
        TransactionDate
    )
    VALUES (@AccountID, @TransactionTypeID, @Amount, GETDATE());

    UPDATE Accounts
    SET Balance = Balance + CASE
        WHEN @TransactionTypeID IN (1, 3)
        THEN @Amount
        ELSE -@Amount
    END
    WHERE AccountID = @AccountID;
END;
```

This stored procedure takes in the account ID, transaction type, and amount as parameters. It first inserts a new transaction record, then updates the account balance based on the transaction type. By encapsulating this logic in a stored procedure, we ensure that these steps are always performed together as a single unit of work.

Generating monthly statements

To generate a monthly statement for a customer, we can use a stored procedure that joins the customer, account, and transaction data:

```
CREATE PROCEDURE MonthlyStatement
    @CustomerID INT,
    @Month INT,
    @Year INT
AS
```

```
BEGIN
    SELECT
        c.CustomerID,
        c.FirstName,
        c.LastName,
        a.AccountID,
        a.AccountType,
        t.TransactionID,
        t.TransactionDate,
        tt.TransactionTypeName,
        t.Amount
    FROM Customers c
    JOIN Accounts a ON c.CustomerID = a.CustomerID
    JOIN Transactions t ON a.AccountID = t.AccountID
    JOIN TransactionTypes tt ON t.TransactionTypeID = tt.TransactionTypeID
    WHERE c.CustomerID = @CustomerID
        AND MONTH(t.TransactionDate) = @Month
        AND YEAR(t.TransactionDate) = @Year
    ORDER BY t.TransactionDate;
END;
```

This procedure takes a customer ID and a month/year as parameters. It uses JOINs to bring together the customer information, account details, and transaction data for the specified period. The result is a comprehensive statement showing all activity for the customer's accounts during the given month.

A Practical Example

Let's see how these pieces work together in a typical usage scenario:

1. A customer opens a new account (insert into Accounts table).

2. They make a series of deposits and withdrawals (execute ProcessTransaction procedure for each):

   a. New Transaction records are added.

   b. The account Balance is updated.

3. At the end of the month, a statement is generated (execute MonthlyStatement procedure):

   a. The procedure queries the Customers, Accounts, Transactions, and TransactionTypes tables.

   b. Results are filtered for the specific customer and month.

   c. Transactions are ordered by date to show the activity chronologically.

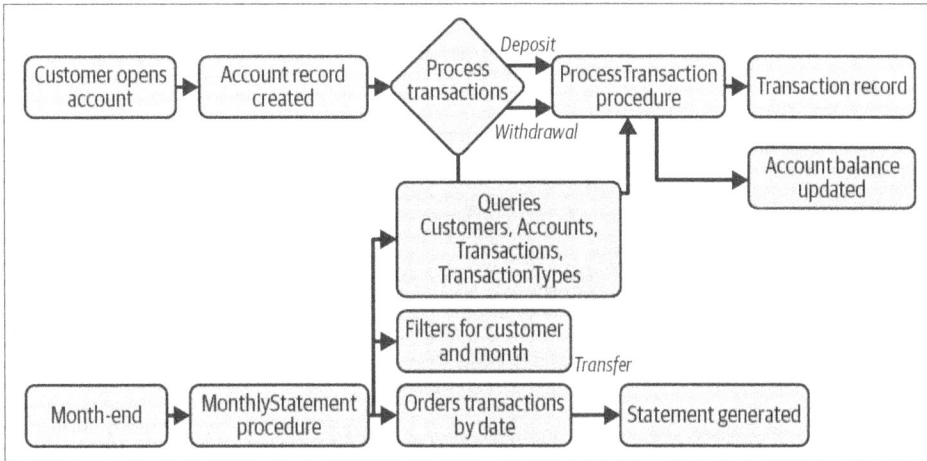

Figure 5-6. Basic banking transaction flow

The flow depicted in Figure 5-6 demonstrates how the database objects we've created—tables, views, and stored procedures—work together to support the core operations of a simple banking system. The tables provide the structure for storing data, the views simplify common queries, and the stored procedures handle complex, multistep processes.

By understanding how these components interact, you can start to see how the foundational concepts covered in the chapter—like table design, relationships, and SQL queries—come together to create a functional system. While real-world financial databases are significantly more complex, the basic principles remain the same.

As you prepare for the DP-900 exam and beyond, keep practicing with examples like this. The key is to understand not just the individual pieces but also how they fit together to support business processes and user needs. With a solid grasp of these fundamentals, you'll be well equipped to tackle more advanced database challenges in your future roles.

Summary

The transition from traditional databases to cloud platforms like Azure represents more than just a change in location. It's a fundamental shift in how we work with relational data. Throughout this chapter, we explored core concepts that remain crucial regardless of where the database runs:

Tables and relationships
    The foundation of relational databases, organizing data in a structured, efficient manner

SQL fundamentals
Basic queries and data modifications that form the language of database interaction

Database objects
Tools like views, indexes, and stored procedures that enhance database functionality

Practical implementation
How these concepts work together in real-world scenarios

Exam Essentials

For success on the DP-900 exam, focus on these key areas:

Understanding core concepts
Table structure and relationships, primary and foreign keys, basic data types and constraints

SQL fundamentals
SELECT statements for data retrieval; basic INSERT, UPDATE, and DELETE operations; simple JOIN operations

Database objects
Purpose and use of views, when to use indexes, role of stored procedures

Practical applications
How concepts work together, common database scenarios, best practices for data organization

---

Beyond the Exam

While the DP-900 exam's coverage of relational data concepts provides essential fundamentals, my years of working with production databases have shown me that real-world implementations often venture far beyond these basics. Let me share some insights that might help you bridge the gap between certification knowledge and practical application.

Modern Relational Database Evolution

Having worked with databases from the pre-cloud era through to today's modern systems, I've witnessed a remarkable transformation in how we handle relational data. Today's relational databases are far more intelligent than their predecessors. For instance, I recently worked with a system that automatically adjusted its indexing strategy based on query patterns—something we database administrators used to spend hours manually optimizing. These self-tuning capabilities represent just one way modern relational databases have evolved to meet growing data demands.

The complexity of data relationships in production environments often surprises newcomers to the field. In one recent project, what started as a simple customer-order relationship quickly evolved to include sophisticated temporal tracking, hierarchical categorizations, and complex business rules. While the DP-900 exam teaches fundamental concepts like primary and foreign keys, real-world scenarios often require more nuanced approaches to maintaining data integrity and managing relationships.

> ### Real-World Insight
>
> Don't be surprised if your first production database implementation challenges your understanding of "simple" concepts like referential integrity. What works in training environments often needs adaptation for real-world scale.

Implementation Realities

One of the most valuable lessons I've learned came from working with a major payment processing system. On paper, the relationship between transactions, accounts, and user balances seemed straightforward. However, when handling millions of real-time payment transactions during major shopping events like holiday seasons, we discovered that even well-written SQL queries could become a bottleneck.

The interesting challenge emerged when we needed to maintain real-time balance updates while simultaneously processing thousands of concurrent transactions per second. During peak periods, what seemed like a simple balance check and update operation would cascade into significant delays. The solution wasn't just about optimizing SQL queries. It required fundamentally rethinking how we structured our transaction data. We implemented a hybrid approach using an in-memory balance cache with an eventual consistency model for the main ledger database. This kind of architectural decision isn't covered on the DP-900 exam, but it demonstrates why understanding basic relational concepts is just the starting point.

The same project also revealed complex realities about data integrity in financial systems. While the certification exam teaches the importance of ACID properties and foreign key constraints, real-world financial data requires additional layers of protection. For example, we couldn't simply rely on traditional referential integrity for transaction records. We needed to implement a double-entry bookkeeping system within our database design, where every transaction required corresponding debit and credit records, along with multiple validation checkpoints. This ensured that no money could be created or lost due to race conditions or system failures—a critical requirement in financial systems that goes well beyond basic relational database concepts.

This example highlights how financial systems often push relational databases to their limits, requiring creative solutions that balance performance, accuracy, and regulatory compliance. The fundamentals you learn through DP-900 exam certification are essential, but the real world demands a deeper understanding of how these concepts apply under extreme conditions.

The Scale Challenge

As your data grows, relationships that worked perfectly in development can become performance bottlenecks in production.

We had built what I thought was an elegantly designed system tracking trading positions and their transactions. Everything worked flawlessly in development, and I remember feeling quite proud of the clean, normalized design. The relationships were textbook perfect, following every best practice I'd learned from internet articles and documentations.

Then, reality hit hard.

One month into production, our "perfect" design started showing cracks. Our parent-child relationship table grew to 50 million records, far beyond what we had tested for. Queries that used to take milliseconds now took seconds. The end-of-day reconciliation process, which had breezed through testing, started timing out. I still remember the stress of that first major slowdown, watching helplessly as the monitoring dashboards turned red.

It was a powerful lesson in humility. All those clean, theoretically perfect design patterns I'd been so proud of weren't holding up under real-world pressure. We needed help, quickly. After some difficult conversations and late nights, we worked with more experienced partners and consultants who helped us implement a practical partitioning strategy. They showed us how to balance our pristine theoretical design with real-world performance needs.

Real-World Insight

Your first production scaling challenge will likely be a humbling experience. Don't be afraid to ask for help from those who've been there before.

Looking back, that experience fundamentally changed how I approach database design. While the foundational knowledge gained through DP-900 certification is crucial, I learned that real-world data platforms require a healthy balance of theory and pragmatism. Sometimes the "theoretically perfect" solution isn't the right one for your specific situation, and that's OK.

Most importantly, I learned that it's fine not to have all the answers. In the rapidly evolving world of data platforms, we're all constantly learning, and some of the best solutions come from collaborating with colleagues and learning from their experiences.

Emerging Directions

The relational database landscape continues to evolve in exciting ways. Modern systems are beginning to blur the lines between traditional relational structures and other data models. I'm currently working with some systems that seamlessly handle JSON documents alongside traditional relational tables and others that incorporate graph relationships into standard SQL databases. These hybrid approaches maintain the robust guarantees of relational systems while offering the flexibility needed for modern applications.

The integration of AI into database management has been particularly fascinating to watch. Systems I work with now can predict performance issues before they occur and suggest optimization strategies I might have missed. While these tools don't replace the need for fundamental understanding of relational concepts, they're changing how we approach database management.

As you move beyond the DP-900 exam and into real-world database work, remember that the fundamental concepts you've learned are just the beginning. The principles of relational data remain crucial, but their practical application often requires creativity and adaptation. Stay curious, keep learning, and don't be afraid to question traditional approaches when real-world conditions demand it.

CHAPTER 6

Azure SQL Services and Open Source Options

The cloud has revolutionized how we think about and work with databases. Whether you're building a new application or migrating an existing one, understanding Azure's database offerings is crucial for success in modern data management. In this chapter, we'll explore both the Azure SQL family of products and Azure's robust support for open source database systems.

Coverage of Curriculum Objectives

This chapter addresses the following DP-900 exam objectives:

- Describe relational Azure data services, including the Azure SQL family of products: Azure SQL Database, Azure SQL Managed Instance, and SQL Server on Azure virtual machines (VMs).
- Identify Azure database services for open source database systems.

Understanding the Azure SQL Family

When organizations consider moving their databases to the cloud, they often face a crucial decision: how much control and responsibility do they want to maintain over their database infrastructure? Azure provides a spectrum of options through its SQL family of products, each designed to meet different requirements and comfort levels with cloud adoption.

Figure 6-1 illustrates the key decision points when choosing between Azure SQL services. Let's explore each option in detail to understand its unique characteristics and ideal use cases.

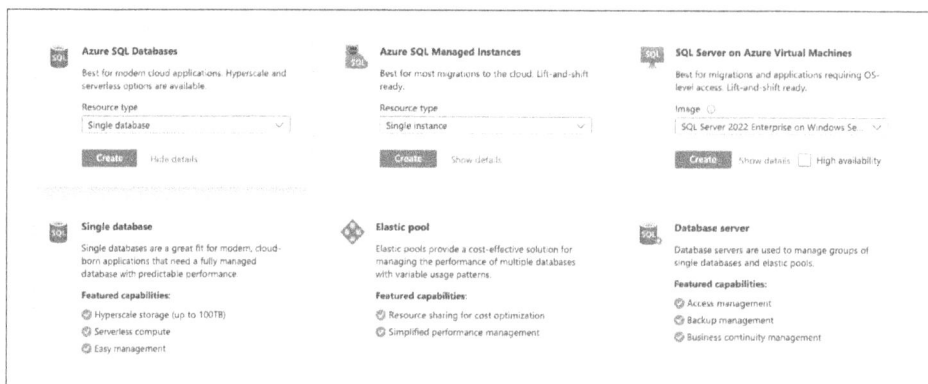

Figure 6-1. The Azure SQL family of choices

Azure SQL Database: Cloud Native Database Solution

Azure SQL Database represents Microsoft's vision of a truly cloud native database service. It takes the core capabilities of SQL Server and transforms them into a fully managed platform-as-a-service (PaaS) offering. This transformation means that while you maintain complete control over your data and access, Microsoft handles the underlying infrastructure management tasks that traditionally consume significant IT resources.

> **Note**
>
> Azure SQL Database exemplifies the DBaaS model which we discussed in Chapter 4, in which traditional database administration tasks are automated, allowing organizations to focus on data and applications rather than infrastructure management.

Features that drive cloud adoption

The appeal of Azure SQL Database lies in its ability to simplify database management while enhancing reliability and security. When you create an Azure SQL Database, you automatically get:

- *Automated maintenance* that keeps your database running smoothly without manual intervention. Think of it as having a dedicated database administrator working 24/7, handling routine tasks like patching and updates. This automation extends to performance tuning, where the service continuously monitors your workload and adjusts settings for optimal performance.

- *Built-in high availability* that becomes part of your database's DNA rather than an additional feature to configure. The service maintains multiple copies of your data and automatically fails over to a healthy copy if issues arise, typically within seconds and without requiring any application changes.

The intelligent performance monitoring system acts like a vigilant guardian, constantly watching your database's behavior. It can alert you to potential problems before they impact your applications and even provide specific recommendations for improvement.

Deployment decisions

When implementing Azure SQL Database, you'll need to choose between two primary deployment models, each suited to different scenarios.

The *single database option* deployment model provides a fully isolated database environment with dedicated resources. Unlike a full SQL Server instance, you work with individual databases rather than server-level objects. This choice is ideal for:

- Applications with predictable resource requirements
- Scenarios where guaranteed performance levels are essential
- Organizations seeking simplicity in database management while maintaining isolation

The *elastic pools* deployment model implements a shared-resource approach that pools resources across multiple databases. It's particularly beneficial for:

- Environments managing multiple databases with varying workloads
- Organizations looking to optimize costs through resource sharing
- Scenarios where databases have fluctuating resource demands and can benefit from a dynamic resource allocation model

When implementing Azure SQL Database, you'll need to carefully evaluate these deployment models based on your specific requirements and use cases. Each option offers distinct advantages that can significantly impact your database performance, cost efficiency, and management overhead.

The shared responsibility model

Azure SQL Database operates as a true PaaS offering with a clear division of responsibilities. Microsoft manages everything below the database level—the SQL Server instance, host server, storage, network infrastructure, and physical security. You manage the database itself, including your data, user access, and database-level configurations.

This shared responsibility model brings both benefits and considerations.

Microsoft manages:

- Physical infrastructure and hardware
- Operating system patching and updates
- SQL Server instance configuration
- High availability and disaster recovery infrastructure
- Physical and network security

You manage:

- Database schema and objects
- Data and access control
- Query optimization and indexing
- Database-level security settings
- Application connections

Because of this architectural design, certain server-level features available in traditional SQL Server installations aren't accessible in Azure SQL Database. For instance, SQL Server Agent jobs need to be replaced with Azure Automation or Logic Apps, and cross-database queries require different approaches using external tables or elastic queries.

Azure SQL Managed Instance: The Bridge to the Cloud

Azure SQL Managed Instance serves as a strategic middle ground in Microsoft's database portfolio. It's designed for organizations that want the benefits of a managed service but need greater compatibility with SQL Server features.

The value proposition

SQL Managed Instance provides an experience remarkably similar to traditional SQL Server but with the added benefits of cloud automation. This familiarity makes it particularly valuable for organizations with existing SQL Server deployments looking to move to the cloud.

The service maintains near-complete compatibility with on-premises SQL Server instances, supporting features like SQL Server Agent, Service Broker, and Database Mail. This compatibility extends to security features, with support for Windows authentication and Azure AD integration.

Real-world migration scenarios

The true strength of SQL Managed Instance becomes apparent in migration scenarios. Consider a company with a complex application that uses linked servers and cross-database queries. With SQL Managed Instance, the company can often move its databases to the cloud with minimal code changes, maintaining existing functionality while gaining cloud benefits.

Another common scenario involves organizations using SQL Server Agent for job scheduling and automation. Rather than redesigning these processes for Azure SQL Database, these companies can maintain their existing jobs while moving to SQL Managed Instance.

Operational considerations

Operating SQL Managed Instance requires understanding its unique characteristics. While it provides greater compatibility than Azure SQL Database, it also introduces some operational considerations:

- Network connectivity works differently, with the service deployed within your virtual network. This provides better security and isolation but requires careful network planning.
- Resource allocation follows a different model, with more granular control over compute and storage resources. This flexibility comes with the responsibility of proper capacity planning.

Success with SQL Managed Instance often depends on proper planning and understanding of its operational model. Organizations that take the time to understand these aspects typically experience smoother migrations and better long-term results.

Exam Tip

For the DP-900 exam, focus on the role of SQL Managed Instance as a bridge between on-premises SQL Server and cloud native Azure SQL Database. Understanding when to choose it over other options is crucial.

SQL Server on Azure Virtual Machines: Maximum Control and Flexibility

For organizations that need complete control over their database environment or have specific requirements that can't be met by managed services, running SQL Server on Azure VMs provides a solution that combines the familiarity of SQL Server with the benefits of cloud infrastructure.

Control and responsibility

Running SQL Server on Azure VMs means you maintain control over every aspect of your database environment, from the operating system to the SQL Server configuration. This control comes with the responsibility of managing updates, security, and performance tuning.

Consider an organization that needs to run a specific version of SQL Server with custom patches or configurations. With SQL Server on Azure VMs, the organization can maintain these requirements while still benefiting from Azure's infrastructure capabilities.

Cost and performance optimization

Azure provides several tools and features to optimize the cost and performance of SQL Server on VMs:

Azure Hybrid Benefit allows you to use existing SQL Server licenses in the cloud, potentially reducing costs significantly. The automated patching and backup features help maintain security and reliability without manual intervention.

Performance optimization tools in the Azure portal provide insights and recommendations specific to SQL Server workloads, helping you maintain optimal performance even in a self-managed environment.

Exploring Open Source Databases in Azure

The modern data landscape extends far beyond Microsoft's SQL Server ecosystem. Recognizing this, Azure provides robust support for popular open source databases through fully managed services. Let's explore these options and understand their unique characteristics.

Azure Database for MySQL: Powering Web Applications

MySQL has long been the backbone of many web applications, particularly those built on the LAMP (Linux, Apache, MySQL, PHP) stack. Azure Database for MySQL brings this popular database engine to the cloud as a fully managed service.

Service capabilities

Azure Database for MySQL maintains compatibility with community MySQL while adding enterprise-grade features. When you create a MySQL database in Azure, you get:

- Automated patching and updates that keep your database secure and up-to-date
- Built-in high availability with up to 99.99% uptime SLA

- Automated backups with point-in-time restore capabilities
- Intelligent performance recommendations
- Advanced threat protection

Deployment models

Azure Database for MySQL Flexible Server provides three distinct service tiers to meet different workload requirements.

Each tier provides flexible scaling options, with compute scaling requiring a brief 60- to 120-second restart, while storage scaling can be performed online without downtime. The service also includes automated storage management features and comprehensive backup capabilities across all tiers.

Burstable tier. Designed for workloads that don't need continuous full CPU utilization, the Burstable tier is ideal for development, testing, and nonproduction environments. It operates on a credit system where CPU performance can burst above baseline during high-demand periods. However, once credits are exhausted, the server operates at the base performance level. This tier supports storage from 20 GiB to 16 TiB but doesn't support read replicas or high availability features.

General Purpose tier. Suited for most business workloads that require balanced compute and memory resources, the General Purpose tier provides 4 GiB memory per vCore and scales from 2 to 64 vCores. This tier supports storage from 20 GiB to 16 TiB and is ideal for hosting web and mobile apps and other enterprise applications requiring consistent performance.

Business Critical tier. Optimized for high-performance database workloads, the Business Critical tier offers 8 GiB memory per vCore for most configurations and scales from 2 to 96 vCores. However, the highest tier configurations (64, 80, and 96 vCores) provide 504 GiB, 504 GiB, and 672 GiB of memory, respectively. It supports larger storage capacity up to 32 TiB with IOPS autoscaling up to 80K, and includes built-in zone resilience at no additional cost (rolled out mid-December 2024). The tier features Accelerated Logs capability that provides up to 2x throughput improvement for mission-critical workloads. This tier is particularly well suited for processing real-time transactional and analytical applications that require low latency, high concurrency, and fast failover capabilities.

Integration and development

Azure Database for MySQL integrates seamlessly with popular development tools and frameworks. Whether you're using PHP, Python, Node.js, or any other popular programming language, you'll find familiar tools and drivers that work as expected.

Azure Database for PostgreSQL: Enterprise-Grade Open Source

PostgreSQL has gained significant popularity due to its robust feature set and extensibility. Azure Database for PostgreSQL brings these capabilities to the cloud while adding enterprise-grade management and security.

Service capabilities

The service provides several unique capabilities that make it attractive for enterprise use:

- Support for complex queries and custom functions
- Rich spatial data handling through PostGIS
- Advanced data types and indexing options
- Extensive security features including data encryption and firewall rules

Deployment models

Azure Database for PostgreSQL Flexible Server offers three distinct compute tiers to meet different workload requirements.

Each tier allows flexible scaling of compute and storage resources. Compute scaling requires a brief 60- to 120-second restart, while storage scaling can be performed online without disruption.

Burstable tier.   Ideal for workloads that don't need the full CPU continuously, this tier offers variable memory per vCore and scales from 1 to 20 vCores. It provides 2 GiB to 80 GiB of memory depending on the configuration selected. Storage can scale from 32 GiB to 64 TiB. This tier is perfect for development, testing, and applications with variable workloads.

General Purpose tier.   Designed for most business workloads requiring balanced compute and memory performance, this tier provides 4 GiB memory per vCore and scales from 2 to 96 vCores. It supports storage from 32 GiB to 64 TiB and is well suited for hosting web and mobile apps and other enterprise applications requiring consistent performance.

Memory Optimized tier. Optimized for high-performance database workloads that require in-memory performance for faster transaction processing and higher concurrency, this tier provides between 6.75 GiB and 8 GiB memory per vCore and scales from 2 to 96 vCores. It supports storage up to 64 TiB. This tier is ideal for processing real-time data and high-performance transactional or analytical applications.

Extensions and ecosystem

One of PostgreSQL's strengths is its extensive ecosystem of extensions. Azure Database for PostgreSQL supports many popular extensions, allowing you to:

- Add new data types and functions.
- Implement custom indexing methods.
- Integrate with external data sources.
- Enhance security and monitoring capabilities.

The ecosystem has stood the test of time as it innovates and keeps up with the latest trends. It is particularly well suited for AI and machine learning workloads through various extensions that enable advanced capabilities. This makes PostgreSQL an excellent choice for AI-powered applications, supporting use cases such as semantic search, recommendation systems, and other vector-based machine learning operations.

Combined with Azure's AI services, Azure Database for PostgreSQL enables you to build sophisticated AI-enabled applications while keeping your vector data close to your application data.

> **Exam Tip**
>
> While PostgreSQL offers extensive AI capabilities through extensions like pgvector for vector similarity search, these features are not in scope for the DP-900 exam. Microsoft has also developed its own PostgreSQL extensions to enhance integration with Azure services, though these details are beyond the scope of the DP-900 exam.

Bringing It All Together: Choosing the Right Database Service

Choosing the right database service doesn't have to be overwhelming. Think of it like choosing a new home: just as different families have different needs when house hunting, different organizations have different requirements for their databases. Let's walk through how to make this decision in a way that makes sense for your situation.

Starting with the Basics

The first question to ask yourself is simple: how much database management do you want to handle? If you're like many organizations today, you probably want to focus on using your database rather than maintaining it. In this case, the fully managed services—Azure SQL Database or the managed open source options—are your best bet. These services are like living in a modern apartment complex where maintenance and security are handled for you.

However, if you have existing database applications that need special configurations or if you have specific requirements about how your database runs, you might want more control. This is where SQL Server on VMs comes in. It's like owning your own house where you have complete control over everything from the foundation up.

Understanding Your Workload

The next consideration is understanding what you'll be doing with your database. Let's look at some common scenarios:

If you're building a new web application, either Azure SQL Database or Azure Database for MySQL is an excellent choice. Both are designed to scale easily as your application grows, and they handle most of the maintenance work for you. It's like moving into a new home that's already equipped with modern amenities. Everything just works.

For organizations moving existing SQL Server databases to the cloud, Azure SQL Managed Instance often provides the smoothest path forward. It's like moving to a new house that's been specifically designed to feel just like your old one: most of your belongings (or in this case, your database features) will fit right in without any need for reorganization.

Thinking About Growth

One of the most important aspects of choosing a database service is thinking about the future. Your application might start small, but what happens when it grows? This is where the different service tiers come into play.

Each of Azure's database services offers different performance tiers that you can think of as different sizes of homes. The Burstable tier is like a starter home—perfect when you're beginning and you need to manage costs, but with some limitations. The General Purpose tier is like a comfortable family home—suitable for most business needs, with room to grow. The Business Critical and Memory Optimized tiers are like luxury estates—designed for organizations that need the highest levels of performance and capability.

Simplifying Cost Considerations

Understanding database costs doesn't have to be complicated. Here's what you need to know.

If you're just starting out or working on a development project, the Burstable tiers of any service can help you keep costs low while still getting the features you need. It's like renting a smaller apartment while you figure out your long-term needs.

For established applications, you can often save money by committing to longer-term use through reserved capacity pricing. This is similar to signing a longer lease on an apartment—you get better rates by committing to stay longer.

If you already have SQL Server licenses, you can use them with Azure through the Azure Hybrid Benefit program. Think of this like being able to transfer your existing home warranty to a new house—you get to keep the benefits you've already paid for.

Exam Tip

The DP-900 exam tests your ability to understand which database service best fits different scenarios. Pay attention to the distinguishing features and limitations of each service.

Summary

Azure's database services represent a fundamental shift in how organizations approach data management—moving beyond traditional infrastructure to embrace cloud native solutions. Each service tier addresses specific organizational needs while maintaining enterprise-grade capabilities:

- Azure SQL Database delivers cloud native simplicity with automated management.
- SQL Managed Instance bridges on-premises and cloud environments seamlessly.
- SQL Server on VMs provides ultimate control for specialized requirements.
- Open source options like MySQL and PostgreSQL bring enterprise features to community favorites.
- Flexible deployment models ensure that organizations can grow without compromising performance.

The choice between these services isn't just technical. It's strategic, allowing organizations to balance control, cost, and capabilities as they build their cloud future.

Beyond the Exam

While the DP-900 exam provides essential foundational knowledge, real-world database management in Azure often presents unique challenges and learning opportunities. Let's explore some practical insights from the field.

Making the Right Choice in Practice

The decision between Azure SQL Database, Managed Instance, and SQL VMs isn't always as clear-cut as exam scenarios might suggest. In my experience consulting with dozens of organizations, these decisions often involve factors beyond technical requirements:

Organizational politics
I've seen cases where technically sound choices for Azure SQL Database were overruled because certain departments weren't comfortable giving up control. Understanding and navigating these dynamics is crucial for successful implementations.

Skills transfer
One client of mine chose SQL Managed Instance despite Azure SQL Database being technically sufficient because their existing DBAs could transfer their skills more easily, reducing resistance to cloud adoption.

Navigating Cost Management

Cost management in Azure databases often reveals surprising complexities that go beyond simple service tier selection. Organizations frequently migrate their databases to Azure with a "lift and shift" mindset, matching their on-premises specifications to cloud resources. This approach typically leads to overprovisioned resources and unnecessarily high costs, as cloud databases require a different optimization strategy than on-premises systems.

Common cost optimization opportunities often emerge from right-sizing environments and implementing appropriate scaling strategies. Development and testing environments rarely need the same performance tier as production, and even production databases can often use lower tiers with burst capabilities rather than premium tiers sized for peak load. By implementing auto-scaling and choosing appropriate service tiers based on actual usage patterns rather than peak capacity, organizations can significantly reduce their monthly costs while maintaining necessary performance levels.

The most successful Azure database implementations often start with careful workload analysis and graduated scaling strategies. Using features like serverless options for varying workloads and reserved capacity pricing for stable ones helps organizations optimize costs while maintaining performance. This strategic approach to resource provisioning not only reduces costs but also provides valuable insights for long-term capacity planning.

Understanding Differences in Implementation

The exam covers features, but real-world success with open source databases in Azure often comes down to understanding subtle differences in implementation:

- A startup might initially choose Azure Database for PostgreSQL for its AI application because of its vector capabilities. However, the company might find success by carefully planning its data model to take advantage of PostgreSQL's jsonb type for flexible schema evolution.

- A media company may successfully migrate from on-premises MySQL to Azure by using read replicas strategically during its migration period, maintaining zero downtime during the transition.

Looking Ahead

The future of Azure database services continues to evolve in exciting ways. Advising with startups and small businesses recently, I witnessed firsthand how they leveraged PostgreSQL's vector capabilities for AI workloads, something that wasn't even possible a few years ago. Their experience highlighted how the lines between traditional database workloads and AI/machine learning operations are blurring.

As we look to the future, the key to success lies in understanding the technical features of Azure's database services as well as developing the judgment to apply them effectively to real-world situations. The most successful database professionals I've worked with combine deep technical knowledge with strong problem-solving skills and business acumen.

Remember, while certification knowledge provides a strong foundation, success in real-world implementations often comes from experience, adaptability, and continuous learning. The stories and experiences shared here represent just a small sample of the rich learning opportunities you'll encounter as you apply your knowledge in practice.

In the next chapter, we'll explore Azure's NoSQL and big data solutions, where you'll see how services like Cosmos DB complement the relational databases we've discussed here, providing different approaches to data storage and processing for modern applications.

PART III

Nonrelational Data on Azure

Modern applications rarely live on relational storage alone. This part broadens your perspective to the specialized storage modalities that optimize cost, scalability, and latency for unstructured content, schema-less entities, asynchronous processing, and globally distributed operational data. You'll learn how Azure Storage services provide foundational primitives and how Azure Cosmos DB delivers low-latency, globally replicated data with tunable consistency.

- Chapter 7, "Azure Storage Solutions", classifies storage services—object (Blob), table, queue, and file—explaining access characteristics, durability guarantees, and when each pattern fits (or doesn't fit). It emphasizes selecting the lightest viable abstraction rather than forcing database semantics into object stores.

- Chapter 8, "Azure Cosmos DB", examines what changes when data distribution, partitioning, consistency trade-offs, and elasticity throughout become primary design drivers. You'll see how partition key design and request unit (RU) budgeting influence both performance and spend.

After completing this part of the book, you should be able to map workload access patterns to their storage modality, articulate the consequences of a poor Cosmos DB partition strategy, and justify consistency level selection based on business tolerance for staleness versus latency.

Common mistakes surfaced here include adopting Cosmos DB without having a genuine need for global distribution, selecting a partition key that causes hot partitions, over-specifying strong consistency, and treating Blob Storage like a query engine.

Exam Alignment: Expect scenario-driven differentiation questions about storage types and high-level Cosmos DB characteristics.

CHAPTER 7

Azure Storage Solutions

The cloud has transformed how we think about storage. Gone are the days when organizations needed to predict their storage needs years in advance and purchase expensive hardware that might sit partially empty—or worse, run out of space at critical moments. Azure Storage services represent a fundamental shift in how we approach data storage, offering flexibility and scalability that wasn't possible with traditional on-premises solutions.

Think of Azure Storage as a vast, intelligent library system. Just as a modern library offers different sections for books, periodicals, and digital media—each organized in ways that make sense for that type of content—Azure provides specialized storage services optimized for different data and access patterns. Whether you're storing simple text files, large videos, structured application data, or anything in between, there's a storage service designed specifically for your needs.

For the DP-900 exam and anyone working with Azure, understanding these storage services is crucial. While Azure Storage supports several storage solutions, this chapter focuses primarily on the three most fundamental services:

- Blob Storage for unstructured data
- File Storage for shared file systems
- Table Storage for structured NoSQL data

These services form the foundation of many cloud solutions. Mastering them will prepare you for more advanced scenarios.

Coverage of Curriculum Objectives

This chapter addresses the following DP-900 exam objectives:

- Describe Azure Blob Storage capabilities, types, and use cases.
- Understand Azure File Storage features and deployment scenarios.
- Explain Azure Table Storage functionality and data modeling.

Azure Blob Storage

The journey to cloud storage often begins with a simple question: "Where do we put all our stuff?" In the cloud and AI era, organizations generate and collect massive amounts of data in various formats—from simple text documents to complex video files, from system logs to data backups. Azure Blob Storage provides the answer to this fundamental need, offering a robust, scalable solution that has revolutionized how we think about storing and managing data in the cloud.

Before diving into Blob Storage, it's important to understand the distinction between structured and unstructured data. Structured data follows a predefined schema and is typically stored in databases with rows and columns. Unstructured data, like images, videos, and documents, doesn't follow a predefined format. Azure provides different storage solutions for each: Azure SQL Database and similar services for structured data, and Azure Blob Storage for unstructured data.

The Azure Blob Storage architecture diagram in Figure 7-1 illustrates a clear hierarchical structure starting with a Storage Account at the top level. Within this Storage Account, you can see there are two main organizational components:

At the upper part of the diagram, there are two containers—Container 1 and Container 2. Container 1 holds Block Blob 1 and Page Blob 1, while Container 2 contains Append Blob 1 and Block Blob 2. This shows how blobs of different types can be organized within containers.

At the lower portion of the diagram, we see the Access Tiers section. This section displays three distinct tiers arranged horizontally: Hot Tier, Cool Tier, and Archive Tier. These tiers represent different levels of storage performance and cost options available within the Storage Account. I'll explain this throughout this section.

The entire structure is encapsulated within the Storage Account boundary, showing how all these components are unified under a single storage namespace.

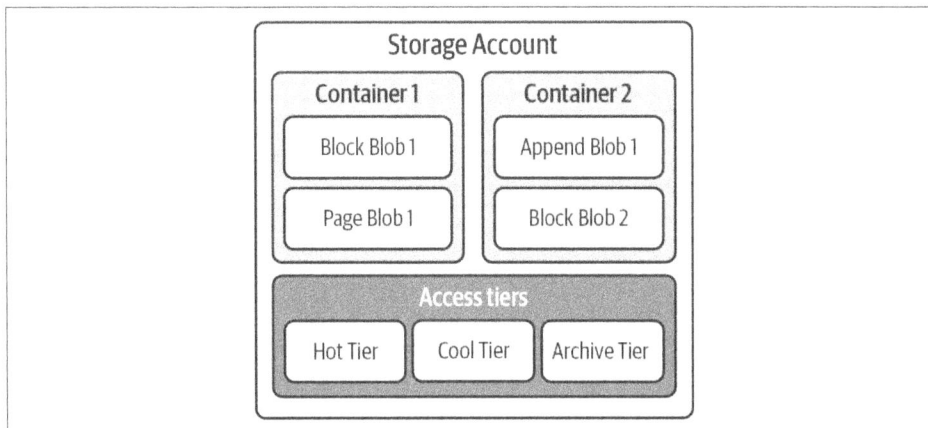

Figure 7-1. Azure Blob Storage architecture

Understanding Object Storage

The transition from traditional filesystems to cloud storage represents more than just a change in technology. It's a paradigm shift in how we organize and access data. Imagine moving from a physical filing cabinet, with its rigid structure of folders and files, to a system where physical limitations simply don't exist. This is the promise of Azure Blob Storage, where data can be stored, organized, and accessed in ways that were impossible with traditional storage systems.

In the world of blob (Binary Large OBject) storage, we think differently about data organization. Instead of folders and files, we work with containers and blobs. A container acts like a smart filing cabinet that automatically expands as needed, while blobs are the individual items stored within it. This fundamental shift in approach enables unprecedented flexibility in how we store and manage data.

The power of this system lies not just in its capacity—though storing petabytes of data is certainly impressive—but in its intelligence. Azure Blob Storage understands different types of data and can optimize how it handles each type, ensuring both efficiency and cost-effectiveness. Whether you're storing millions of small sensor readings or a handful of massive video files, the system adapts to provide optimal performance.

Exam Tip

The DP-900 exam emphasizes understanding how these different blob types serve different purposes. You won't need to know detailed technical specifications, but you should understand which type fits which scenario.

The true elegance of Blob Storage becomes apparent when we consider how it handles various real-world scenarios. A media company might use it to store and stream video content to millions of users. A healthcare organization could securely maintain patient records and medical images. A manufacturing company might collect and analyze sensor data from thousands of devices. Each scenario benefits from the unique capabilities of different blob types, which we'll explore next.

Types of Blobs

Azure's approach to blob storage demonstrates a deep understanding that not all data is created equal. Different types of data have different requirements for how they need to be written, read, and updated. This insight led to the development of three distinct blob types, each optimized for specific scenarios. Understanding these types and their appropriate use cases is crucial for designing effective storage solutions.

Block blobs: The workhorses of cloud storage

When most people think about cloud storage, they're thinking about block blobs without realizing it. These versatile storage containers handle everything from simple text files to complex multimedia content, making them the backbone of most cloud storage solutions. The genius of block blobs lies in their approach to handling large files. Instead of trying to upload or download entire files at once, they break them down into manageable chunks called *blocks*.

This block-based approach transforms how we handle large-scale data transfers. Imagine moving into a new house. Rather than attempting to move everything at once, which would be inefficient and risky, you break the task down into smaller, manageable loads. Block blobs work the same way, allowing multiple blocks to be uploaded in parallel, significantly improving performance and reliability.

The impact of this design becomes clear in real-world scenarios. Consider a video streaming service that needs to handle thousands of simultaneous uploads and downloads. Block blobs make this possible by allowing viewers to start watching a video before it's fully downloaded, while content creators can reliably upload massive files without worrying about network interruptions—if a block fails to upload, only that block needs to be retried, not the entire file.

As we wrap up our discussion of block blobs, it's worth noting that their versatility makes them the default choice for most storage scenarios. However, there are specific situations where other blob types might be more appropriate, which brings us to append blobs—a specialized storage type designed for growing datasets.

Append blobs: The digital logbook

In the world of data storage, some information grows continuously but never changes. Think of a pilot's logbook. New entries are constantly added, but previous entries remain unchanged and in chronological order. This specific pattern of data growth presents unique challenges that append blobs are specifically designed to address.

Append blobs shine in scenarios where data accumulates over time but past records must remain immutable. Consider an aircraft's flight data recorder—often called a *black box*—which continuously records flight parameters. Each new piece of data adds to the historical record, but previous entries are never modified. This pattern appears across many industries: security systems logging access attempts, IoT devices reporting sensor readings, or financial systems tracking transactions.

The beauty of append blobs lies in their simplicity and efficiency. Unlike block blobs, which might require complex coordination when multiple processes try to modify the same file, append blobs handle concurrent writes elegantly. Each write operation simply adds its data to the end of the blob, eliminating the need for complex locking mechanisms or conflict resolution.

This approach brings particular benefits in distributed systems. Imagine a large industrial facility with thousands of sensors reporting temperature readings every minute. With append blobs, each sensor can reliably write its data without worrying about interfering with data from other sensors. The result is a clean, chronological record that's perfect for later analysis or auditing.

However, there are times when sequential write operations aren't enough—sometimes we need the ability to update any part of a file at any time. This requirement brings us to our third type of blob: page blobs, which offer capabilities that neither block nor append blobs can match.

Page blobs: The virtual disk specialists

In the realm of cloud storage, some workloads require a level of flexibility that goes beyond simple file storage or sequential logging. Imagine trying to update a single sentence in the middle of a book. With traditional storage types, you'd need to rewrite everything from that point forward. Page blobs solve this challenge by breaking data into fixed-size pages that can be updated independently, much like being able to replace individual pages in a loose-leaf binder.

This unique capability makes page blobs the perfect foundation for Azure's VM disks. When you're running a VM, its operating system needs to be able to read and write data anywhere on its disk at any time. Page blobs make this possible by allowing random access to any 512-byte page within the blob, enabling the kind of rapid, random read/write operations that operating systems require.

The impact of page blobs extends beyond just VMs. Database systems that need to manage their own data pages, specialized scientific applications that work with large matrices, or any system that needs to randomly update portions of large files can benefit from this capability. However, this flexibility comes at a cost: page blobs require more overhead to maintain their 512-byte page boundaries and additional metadata, making them typically 20% to 30% more expensive than block blobs for equivalent storage.

As we conclude our exploration of blob types, it's clear that Azure has created a sophisticated ecosystem where each type serves a specific purpose. But having the right type of storage is only part of the equation. Equally important is understanding how to manage the lifecycle of your data and optimize costs through Azure's tiered storage system.

Access Tiers and Cost Management

In the early days of cloud storage, organizations faced a simple but costly choice: keep everything readily available or move it to cheaper offline storage. Azure's tiered storage system revolutionized this approach by offering a more nuanced solution that aligns storage costs with how frequently data needs to be accessed. This innovation transforms storage from a fixed cost into a dynamic resource that can be optimized based on actual usage patterns.

Hot tier: Ready for immediate access

Think of the Hot tier as your active workspace—the digital equivalent of your desk where you keep frequently accessed files within arm's reach. While this immediate accessibility comes with higher storage costs, the minimal access charges make it perfect for data that's regularly in use. Like a well-organized desk that helps you work efficiently, the Hot tier ensures that your frequently accessed data is always ready when you need it.

The impact of this tier becomes clear when we consider real-world scenarios. A news website might store current articles and images in the Hot tier, ensuring fast access for readers browsing breaking news. An ecommerce platform could keep product images and descriptions for popular items readily available during peak shopping seasons. Medical imaging systems might maintain recent patient scans for quick retrieval during follow-up appointments.

Cool tier: Balancing access and economy

Just as you might move last season's clothes to a storage closet—still accessible but not taking up prime wardrobe space—the Cool tier provides a balanced approach for data that's important but not immediately needed. This tier revolutionizes how organizations handle aging data, offering substantial storage cost savings while maintaining reasonable access times when the data is needed.

The genius of the Cool tier lies in its economics. By accepting slightly higher access costs and a minimum 30-day storage duration, organizations can significantly reduce their storage expenses. This trade-off makes perfect sense for many scenarios: quarterly financial reports that need to be kept accessible for reference but aren't accessed daily, completed project documentation that might be needed for future projects, or backup data maintained for short-term recovery scenarios.

Consider how a marketing department might use the Cool tier. After a major campaign ends, the team could move all related assets—videos, images, and documents—to Cool storage. The content remains readily available if needed for future reference or inspiration, but at a fraction of the storage cost. When the next campaign begins, any relevant assets can be quickly retrieved, with the access costs justified by the significant storage savings achieved during the interim period.

As we think about data that's accessed even less frequently, we arrive at the Archive tier—Azure's solution for long-term data retention at the lowest possible cost.

Archive tier: The digital time capsule

Every organization has data that must be kept but is rarely, if ever, accessed. Think of old tax records, completed project files from years past, or compliance documentation that must be retained for regulatory purposes. The Archive tier transforms this necessary burden into a manageable expense, offering the lowest storage costs in exchange for longer retrieval times and a minimum 180-day storage duration.

The Archive tier represents a fundamental shift in how organizations approach long-term data retention. Rather than maintaining expensive on-premises tape libraries or paying premium prices for instant access to rarely needed data, organizations can now store this information at minimal cost while maintaining the ability to retrieve it when truly necessary. This capability has particular impact in industries with strict data retention requirements, such as healthcare, finance, and legal services.

The beauty of Azure's tiered storage system lies not just in its cost savings but also in its flexibility. Data can move between tiers as its value and access patterns change. A stored video might start in the Hot tier during a marketing campaign, move to Cool storage when the campaign ends, and finally transition to the Archive tier for long-term preservation. This movement can even be automated through lifecycle management policies, ensuring optimal cost efficiency without manual intervention.

Figure 7-2 illustrates the inverse relationship between storage and transaction costs across Azure's storage tiers. The vertical arrangement shows the progression from Hot storage at the top, through Cool storage in the middle, to Archive storage at the bottom. The dollar signs ($) on the left side represent storage costs, which decrease in size as we move down through the tiers, indicating lower storage costs for cooler tiers.

Conversely, the dollar signs on the right side represent transaction costs, which increase in size as we move down through the tiers, demonstrating the higher costs associated with accessing data in cooler storage tiers. This visual representation highlights the fundamental trade-off in Azure's tiered storage system: as storage costs decrease in cooler tiers, the cost of accessing that data increases.

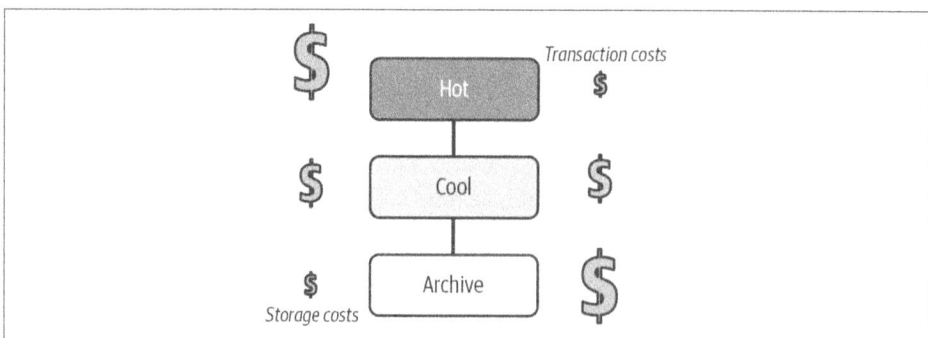

Figure 7-2. Storage and transaction cost relationships

As we conclude our exploration of storage tiers, it's clear that effective data management in the cloud requires more than just storage space. It demands a thoughtful approach to data lifecycle management. This brings us to our next topic: the advanced security features that protect your data across all tiers and access patterns.

Security Features of Blob Storage

In today's digital landscape, storing data in the cloud is just the beginning. Protecting it is equally crucial. As organizations move their most sensitive information to the cloud, security can no longer be an afterthought or a simple checkbox exercise. Azure Blob Storage approaches security as a fundamental design principle, weaving protection into every layer of the storage system.

Encryption: Protecting data at rest and in motion

The journey of data through Azure Blob Storage is like a carefully guarded secret being passed through a series of secure channels. From the moment data enters the Azure ecosystem until it's retrieved, it never exists in an unprotected state. This comprehensive protection begins with encryption at rest, a process so seamless that most users never even realize it's happening.

Storage Service Encryption (SSE) automatically encrypts every byte of data written to Azure Blob Storage using 256-bit AES encryption—one of the strongest encryption standards available. This encryption happens automatically, requiring no changes to your applications or workflows. It's like having an invisible security guard who ensures that every piece of data is secured before it's stored.

Encryption can be applied at different scopes: account-level encryption (default, applies to all data), container-level options for specific requirements, and individual blob encryption for granular control.

Organizations that need additional control over their encryption keys can choose between several options. Some prefer to let Microsoft manage the encryption keys entirely, similar to letting a bank handle the security of a safety-deposit box. Others opt for customer-managed keys through Azure Key Vault, giving them the ability to control and rotate encryption keys as needed. The most security-conscious organizations might choose to provide their own encryption keys, maintaining complete control over who can access their data.

But protection doesn't stop when data needs to move. Like an armored car protecting valuables in transit, Azure automatically encrypts all data moving to and from Blob Storage using TLS/SSL protocols. This ensures that even if someone were to intercept the data in transit, they wouldn't be able to read it.

As we secure our data both at rest and in motion, we must also consider who should have access to it. This brings us to Azure's sophisticated system for controlling access to stored data.

Role-based access control: The digital gatekeeper

In the physical world, organizations use keycards and security badges to control who can access different areas of a building. Azure's role-based access control (RBAC) brings this concept to the cloud, but with far more sophistication and granularity. Instead of simple yes/no access decisions, RBAC allows organizations to define exactly what actions each user or application can perform on specific resources.

This granular control becomes particularly powerful when integrated with Azure Active Directory. Imagine a large media company managing thousands of digital assets. Designers might need full access to their project files, while external partners should only view final deliverables. Marketing teams might need to update product images, while the legal department requires read-only access to all content for compliance reviews. RBAC makes these complex permission scenarios not just possible but also manageable.

> **Exam Tip**
>
> Understanding RBAC is crucial for the DP-900 exam, as it represents a fundamental shift from traditional file permissions to cloud native security models.

But what about scenarios where you need to grant temporary access to contractors or allow limited-time downloads for customers? This is where shared access signatures come into play.

Shared access signatures: Temporary keys to your data kingdom

Shared access signatures (SAS) solve one of the most common challenges in data sharing: how to grant limited, temporary access to specific resources without compromising security. Think of SAS like a digital hotel key card—it provides access only to specific areas, works only for a predetermined time period, and can be revoked if needed.

The flexibility of SAS becomes clear when we consider real-world scenarios. A photography studio might generate SAS URLs that allow clients to download their photos for a week after a session. A research institution could provide temporary upload access to specific containers for external collaborators. A media company might generate SAS tokens that allow its content delivery network to access video files while preventing direct public access.

As organizations implement these security features, they need tools to monitor and respond to potential threats. This brings us to Azure's advanced threat protection capabilities.

Managing the Data Lifecycle

One of Blob Storage's most powerful features is its tiered access system, as mentioned in the previous sections. Think of it like organizing your closet: frequently worn clothes stay easily accessible, seasonal items go into storage boxes, and rarely used items move to the attic. Similarly, Azure's Hot tier provides immediate access for actively used data, the Cool tier offers cost savings for infrequently accessed data, and the Archive tier provides the most economical storage for rarely needed information.

The real innovation lies in how easily data can move between these tiers. A retail company might store current product images in the Hot tier for quick website access, move last season's images to Cool storage, and archive photos of discontinued products. This automated lifecycle management ensures that you're never paying more than necessary for storage while maintaining appropriate access levels for different data types.

Having explored how Blob Storage handles unstructured data, let's turn our attention to a unique challenge: providing traditional file shares in the cloud. This is where Azure File Storage comes into play, offering familiar file sharing capabilities with cloud native advantages.

Azure File Storage

The transition to cloud storage often raises a crucial question: "How will we share files across our organization?" While Blob Storage excels at handling large-scale unstructured data, organizations still need the familiar collaborative environment that traditional file shares provide. Azure File Storage bridges this gap by bringing the well-understood world of network file shares into the cloud era, combining the familiarity of traditional file servers with the scalability and resilience of cloud computing.

Figure 7-3 shows how Azure File Storage is organized, much like a digital filing cabinet in the cloud. At the top level, we have a Storage Account, which acts as the main container for all your files. Inside this, there are two types of file-sharing spaces: an SMB File Share (which works with Windows, macOS, and Linux systems that support the SMB 3.0 protocol) and an NFS File Share (designed for Linux systems).

The SMB side contains familiar elements like Config Files and Shared Documents folders, along with a settings file. Meanwhile, the NFS side stores Linux-specific items like Linux Data and App Mounts, plus a configuration file. At the bottom of the diagram, we can see three different ways to access these files: through Windows Mount, Linux Mount, or the REST API. This setup allows users to work with their cloud files just as easily as they would with files on their local computer, regardless of which system they're using.

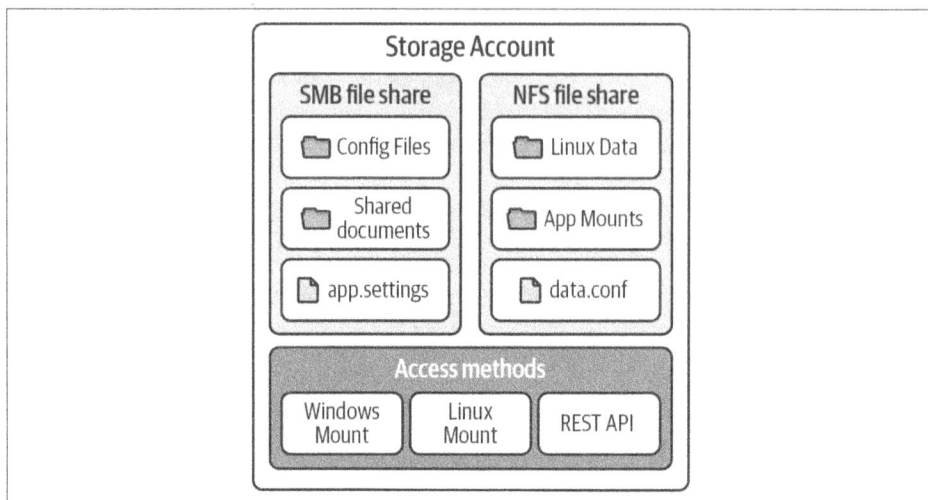

Figure 7-3. File Storage architecture

Understanding Cloud File Shares

When organizations first encounter Azure File Storage, they often see it merely as a network drive in the cloud. While this is technically accurate, it dramatically understates the transformation that occurs when file sharing moves to the cloud. Traditional file servers required careful capacity planning, regular maintenance windows, and complex backup solutions. Azure File Storage eliminates these constraints while adding capabilities that would be difficult or impossible to implement on premises.

Consider how file sharing typically works in a traditional office. You have a file server in your building, connected to your local network, with mapped drives that employees can access. This works well until you need to support remote workers, open new offices, or scale beyond your server's capacity. Azure File Storage transforms this model by making your file shares globally accessible while maintaining the simplicity of mapped network drives.

Exam Tip

For the DP-900 exam, understand that Azure File Storage isn't just a lift-and-shift of traditional file servers. It's a reimagining of file sharing for the cloud era.

SMB and NFS: Speaking Your Language

Azure File Storage's support for industry-standard protocols represents more than just technical compatibility. It's a bridge between traditional IT infrastructure and modern cloud services. The Server Message Block (SMB) protocol, familiar to

Windows users as the backbone of network file sharing, and the Network File System (NFS) protocol, beloved in the Linux world, form the foundation of this bridge.

The power of SMB integration

SMB support in Azure Files goes far beyond basic file sharing. Modern SMB features like protocol encryption, identity-based authentication, and persistent handles enable sophisticated scenarios that weren't possible with traditional file servers. For example, multiple applications can maintain open handles to the same file while Azure manages the complexity of coordinating these accesses—crucial for applications that need to maintain file locks across multiple instances.

Consider a financial services company that needs to process thousands of transaction records daily. Its Windows-based processing applications can directly access files in Azure File Storage as if they were on a local drive, while Azure handles the underlying complexity of ensuring data consistency and managing concurrent access patterns.

NFS and Linux integration

The addition of NFS support transforms Azure File Storage into a truly cross-platform solution. Linux systems can mount Azure file shares natively, enabling scenarios like hosting home directories for Linux users or sharing data between Linux-based application servers. This becomes powerful in hybrid scenarios where organizations need to maintain consistent file access across both on-premises and cloud environments.

Real-World Scenario

A media production company uses NFS shares in Azure Files to store raw footage accessible to both its on-premises editing workstations and cloud-based rendering farm. The same data is available everywhere without complex replication schemes.

Advanced Features That Transform File Sharing

Here are some of the advanced features of Azure File Storage that make it an enterprise-grade solution to most file sharing scenarios.

Snapshots: Time travel for your files

Azure File Storage's snapshot capability changes how organizations approach file protection and version control. Unlike traditional backup systems that require separate infrastructure and complex scheduling, Azure File Share snapshots provide near-instantaneous, point-in-time copies of your entire file share with minimal storage overhead.

Think of snapshots like photographs of your entire filesystem at specific moments in time. When someone accidentally deletes an important file or makes unwanted changes, recovering the previous version becomes as simple as browsing through these snapshots. This capability transforms disaster recovery from a complex IT operation into a self-service function that users can often handle themselves.

The real power of snapshots emerges in scenarios like:

- Protecting against ransomware by maintaining clean copies of files
- Supporting development and testing by providing consistent filesystem states
- Enabling file-level recovery without full share restoration
- Maintaining point-in-time copies for compliance requirements

Note that Azure File Storage supports up to 200 snapshots per share. While snapshots use incremental storage (only changed blocks consume space), consider the cumulative overhead when planning retention policies. Snapshot operations may also impact performance during creation, so schedule them during low-usage periods when possible..

Identity and access management

Security in Azure File Storage represents a sophisticated evolution of traditional file share permissions. While maintaining the familiar concepts of share- and file-level permissions, it adds cloud native capabilities that address modern security challenges.

Azure Files also preserves NTFS ACLs when used with Windows systems, maintaining familiar permission structures that IT administrators already understand.

Microsoft Entra ID integration

Integration with Azure AD transforms how organizations manage file access. Instead of maintaining separate file share credentials, users can access files using their organizational identity—the same credentials they use for Microsoft 365 or other Azure services. This integration enables:

- Single sign-on for file share access
- Conditional access policies that can restrict file share access based on device state or location
- Detailed audit logging of file access patterns
- Granular permission management through Azure AD groups

Consider how this works in practice: a global organization can implement policies that restrict sensitive file access to specific office locations or require multifactor authentication for remote access. All of this happens transparently to users, who simply see their mapped network drives as always.

Scale and performance

Azure File Storage's architecture enables scenarios that would be challenging with traditional file servers. Shares can scale to handle:

- Thousands of concurrent connections
- Petabytes of data
- Millions of files
- Global access patterns

The service automatically handles load balancing, storage optimization, and performance monitoring, allowing organizations to focus on using their file shares rather than managing infrastructure.

Exam Tip

While Azure File Storage can handle massive scale, understanding its performance tiers and limits is crucial for optimal application design. The DP-900 exam often tests understanding of when to use premium versus standard file shares.

Azure File Sync: Extending to Hybrid Scenarios

Many organizations aren't ready to completely abandon their on-premises file servers, despite the tremendous benefits of cloud storage. Perhaps they have applications that must remain local or users who need the fastest possible file access. Azure File Sync elegantly bridges this gap, creating a hybrid environment that combines the best of both worlds.

Think of Azure File Sync like having a smart replication system that keeps your on-premises file servers in sync with Azure File Storage. It is like how your smartphone keeps photos synchronized with cloud storage, but at an enterprise scale and with sophisticated caching capabilities. This synchronization happens automatically and bidirectionally, ensuring that users always have access to their files through whichever path makes the most sense for their location and needs.

Cloud tiering: Intelligence at the edge

One of File Sync's most powerful features is cloud tiering. Cloud tiering can be configured based on last access time, file age, or free space policies. Instead of simply copying all files everywhere, it intelligently manages which files are stored locally and which remain cloud only. Frequently accessed files stay cached on local servers for fast access, while rarely used files are replaced with shortcuts that point to their cloud copies. This approach dramatically reduces the storage requirements for on-premises servers while maintaining access to the full file set.

Real-World Scenario

A global engineering firm uses Azure File Sync to maintain consistent project files across offices worldwide. Each office has a local file server for fast access to current projects, while completed projects are automatically tiered to the cloud. When an old project needs review, its files are retrieved on demand, eliminating the need for massive local storage at each site.

Disaster recovery simplified

Azure File Sync transforms how organizations approach disaster recovery for file servers. Instead of maintaining complex backup systems and dealing with tape libraries, organizations can quickly restore file servers by simply installing File Sync on a new server and connecting it to their Azure file share. The system automatically pulls down the most frequently accessed files first, ensuring that critical data is available quickly while less urgent files sync in the background.

Consider how this plays out in a real disaster recovery scenario. If a file server fails, IT can:

1. Deploy a new server (physical or virtual).
2. Install the File Sync agent.
3. Connect to the existing sync group.
4. Have critical files available within minutes.

The entire process can be completed in hours rather than the days it might take to restore from traditional backups.

Managing at Scale

As organizations grow, managing file servers across multiple locations becomes increasingly complex. Azure File Sync includes centralized management capabilities that help IT teams:

- Monitor sync health across all servers.
- Track storage usage and tiering efficiency.
- Manage sync groups and cloud endpoints.
- Configure namespaces and conflict resolution policies.

This centralized control plane transforms what would traditionally be a complex distributed system into a cohesive, manageable service.

While File Storage excels at handling traditional file sharing scenarios, organizations often need different approaches for storing structured data. This brings us to Azure Table Storage, which offers a unique solution for storing large amounts of structured data without the constraints of traditional databases.

Azure Table Storage

In the world of data storage, not everything fits neatly into files or traditional databases. Consider an IoT scenario where millions of devices send temperature readings every few minutes, or a product catalog where each item might have completely different attributes. These scenarios demand a different approach—one that's both scalable and flexible. Azure Table Storage provides this alternative, offering a NoSQL data store that combines the simplicity of tables with the flexibility of schema-less design.

Figure 7-4 shows the layout of Azure Table Storage, which provides a different way to store data compared to traditional databases. Under the main Storage Account, we see two example tables shown in boxes: a Products table and an Orders table. Each table demonstrates how data is stored in a flexible format. The Products table contains information about electronics items, showing fields like PartitionKey (Electronics) and RowKey (Laptop-001), along with product details such as Name (ThinkPad X1), Price ($1299.99), and Stock (50). Similarly, the Orders table shows how order information is stored with its own PartitionKey (2024-01), RowKey (Order-12345), and relevant order details like CustomerID (C789), Total (2599.98), and Status (Shipped).

At the bottom of the diagram, we see three types of Query Patterns that can be used to access this data: Point Query, Partition Query, and Range Query. This shows how users can retrieve information from these tables in different ways depending on their needs.

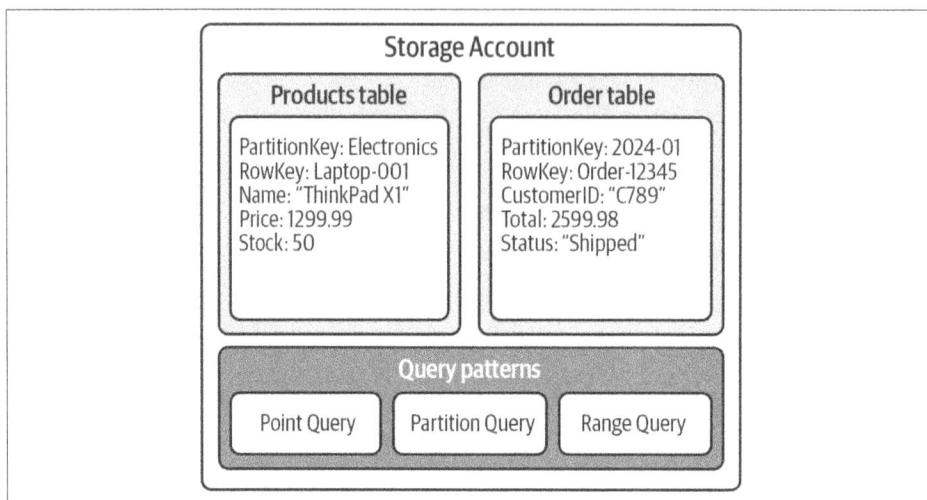

Figure 7-4. Table Storage architecture

The structure illustrates how Table Storage offers a simple yet powerful way to store different types of data without needing to define a rigid structure beforehand, making it perfect for scenarios where data might vary between entries. Now let's get into the details of how the NoSQL structure works in Azure Table Storage.

Understanding NoSQL in Azure Table Storage

Traditional relational databases require you to define your *schema*—the structure of your data—before you store anything. It's like having to decide the exact layout of a filing cabinet before you can start using it. But what if different documents need different types of folders? What if you don't know all the types of documents you'll need to store? This is where Table Storage's schema-less design shines.

Entities and Properties: A Flexible Foundation

In Table Storage, data is organized into entities (similar to rows in a traditional database) and properties (similar to columns), but with a crucial difference: each entity can have its own set of properties. This flexibility is transformative for certain types of applications.

Consider an ecommerce product catalog:

- A clothing item might need properties for size, color, and material.
- An electronic device might track voltage, dimensions, and warranty period.
- A food item might include nutritional information and expiration date.

With Table Storage, each product entity can have exactly the properties it needs—no more empty columns for irrelevant attributes, and no schema changes when new product types are added.

Partitioning Strategy: The Key to Performance

Understanding partitioning in Table Storage is like understanding how to organize a massive library. Just as a library uses categories and subcategories to make books findable, Table Storage uses partition keys and row keys to organize and locate data efficiently. This organization isn't just about keeping things tidy. It's fundamental to the performance and scalability of your solution.

The power of the partition key

Think of a partition key as the major category for your data. Just as a library might separate fiction from nonfiction, your partition key creates logical groupings of related entities. But this decision impacts more than just organization. It affects how Azure can distribute and scale your data across its infrastructure.

Exam Tip

The DP-900 exam often tests understanding of how partition keys affect performance. Remember that entities with the same partition key must reside in the same partition, which can become a bottleneck if not designed carefully.

Consider an application tracking temperature readings from sensors across different cities:

- Using the city name as the partition key groups all readings from the same location together.
- This makes queries for a specific city's data extremely efficient.
- However, if one city generates significantly more data, its partition could become a performance bottleneck.

Row keys: Ensuring uniqueness

Within each partition, the row key provides the final piece of the puzzle, ensuring that each entity can be uniquely identified and efficiently retrieved. Together, the partition key and row key form a composite key that can quickly locate any entity in your table.

For our temperature sensors example:

- The partition key is `CityName`.
- The row key is `SensorID_Timestamp`. This structure allows for efficient queries, such as:
  — All readings from a specific city (partition key)
  — Specific sensor readings in a city (partition key + partial row key)
  — Exact reading at a specific time (partition key + full row key)

Query Patterns and Performance

Understanding how to query Table Storage effectively requires a shift in thinking from traditional SQL databases. While SQL allows complex joins and arbitrary WHERE clauses, Table Storage is optimized for different access patterns.

Optimized query patterns

The most efficient queries in Table Storage are those that use the partition key and row key effectively. Think of it like having a precise address for a book in a library—if you know exactly where to look, retrieval is nearly instantaneous.

Efficient query patterns include:

- Point queries using both the partition and row keys
- Partition scans using just the partition key
- Range queries within a partition using the row key range

Example: A weather monitoring system stores millions of temperature readings daily. By using the pattern `CityName` for partition key and `YYYY_MM_DD_HH_mm` for row key, the system can efficiently:

- Retrieve all readings for a city (partition scan).
- Find specific time frame readings (row key range query).
- Get exact readings at precise moments (point query).

Advanced query capabilities

While Table Storage may seem simple at first, it supports sophisticated query capabilities when properly designed.

Filtering and projection. Just as you might want to retrieve only specific fields from a record, Table Storage allows you to:

- Select specific properties rather than entire entities.
- Filter results based on property values.
- Combine filters with partition/row key criteria.

Continuation tokens. For large result sets, Table Storage provides continuation tokens—like bookmarks that help you pick up where you left off when processing large amounts of data.

Table Storage versus Azure Cosmos DB

Azure Table Storage shares many key features with Azure Cosmos DB, particularly with its NoSQL API. As both are cloud-based NoSQL storage solutions, developers often wonder which service better suits their needs. Understanding their similarities helps establish a foundation for making an informed choice between these technologies.

While we'll explore Azure Cosmos DB in depth in the next chapter, it's important to note that the decision between these services isn't always a simple either-or choice. Many organizations successfully implement both Azure Table Storage and Cosmos DB within their architecture, leveraging each service's unique strengths for different use cases. This hybrid approach allows teams to optimize their storage solutions based on specific requirements for different parts of their application.

The decision to use Azure Table Storage versus Azure Cosmos DB typically depends on several key factors. Table Storage excels in scenarios requiring simple, cost-effective storage for large volumes of structured data with basic query needs. In contrast, Cosmos DB is better suited for applications demanding global distribution, complex queries, and guaranteed low latency. The choice ultimately comes down to balancing factors like data complexity, scalability requirements, global distribution needs, and budget constraints.

Bringing It All Together: Storage Solutions in Practice

Picture yourself as an architect designing the foundation of a modern digital enterprise. Like a well-planned city, Azure's storage services form distinct districts, each serving unique purposes while working in harmony. Let's explore how these services come together to create a robust and efficient data ecosystem.

The Modern Data Estate

Consider MJA Fashion, a rapidly growing ecommerce platform. When approaching its storage architecture, the MJA team didn't force all its data into a single solution. Instead, the team crafted a sophisticated symphony of storage services, each playing its perfect part.

The product images and marketing videos flow naturally into Blob Storage, which excels at handling large, unstructured files. Meanwhile, the development team collaborates seamlessly through File Storage, sharing configuration files and documentation as easily as if it was working with a local drive. For lightning-fast access to product metadata and user preferences, Table Storage serves as a reliable companion, delivering consistent performance at scale.

Integration Patterns in Action

The magic happens in how these services dance together. When a customer browses MJA's catalog, the system orchestrates a seamless performance: product images stream from Blob Storage through Azure CDN's global network, while Table Storage instantly retrieves pricing and availability data. Behind the scenes, the content team updates product documentation in File Storage, which synchronizes automatically across MJA's global offices.

Bridging Worlds with Hybrid Solutions

The reality of modern enterprise often requires maintaining one foot on premises while stepping confidently into the cloud. Azure's storage services embrace this reality. Through Azure File Sync, MJA's legacy file servers maintain perfect harmony with cloud storage. Its StorSimple implementation automatically moves aging data to the cloud, while frequently accessed files remain close at hand.

The Art of Cost Optimization

Perhaps the most elegant aspect of MJA Fashion's architecture is its efficiency. Like a smart power grid, Azure's storage solutions automatically adjust to demand. Frequently accessed data stays in Hot storage tiers for immediate availability, while historical records gradually transition to Cool and Archive tiers, significantly reducing costs without sacrificing accessibility.

As data flows through its lifecycle, automated policies ensure that it's always stored in the most cost-effective tier. The system continuously monitors access patterns, adjusting its strategy to maintain the perfect balance between performance and cost.

When designing your storage solution, think like a city planner. Consider the flow of data, the patterns of access, and the natural lifecycle of different types of information.

Let these patterns guide your choice of storage services rather than trying to force a one-size-fits-all approach.

Figure 7-5 illustrates how these components work together, creating a comprehensive storage solution that's greater than the sum of its parts. Each connection represents a carefully considered data flow, optimized for performance, cost, and reliability.

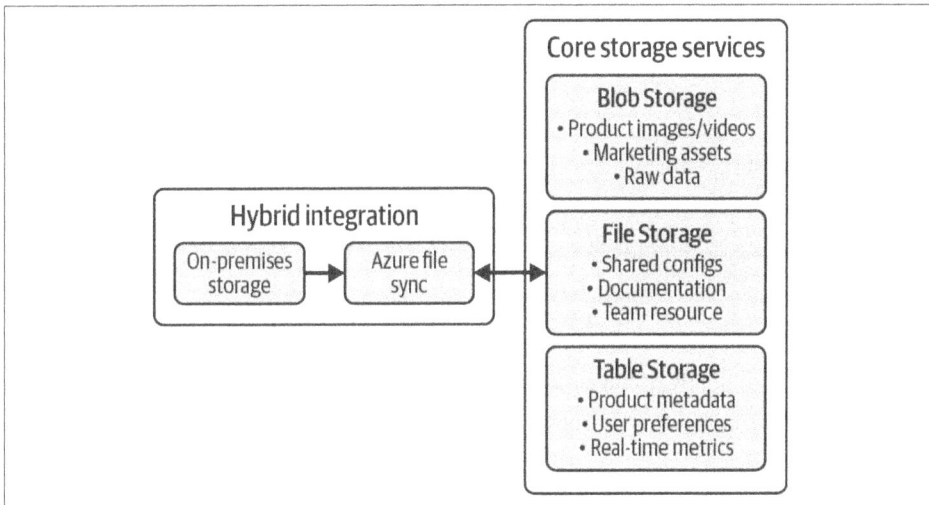

Figure 7-5. Bringing Blob, File, and Table Storage together

By understanding and leveraging the strengths of each storage service, organizations can build robust, scalable, and efficient data architectures that serve their needs today while remaining flexible enough to grow with them tomorrow.

Summary

The shift from traditional storage to Azure's cloud-based solutions represents more than just a change in technology. It's a fundamental transformation in how we think about and manage data storage. Each Azure storage service addresses specific needs while offering the flexibility and scalability that modern applications demand. Throughout this chapter, we explored how:

- Blob Storage revolutionizes unstructured data storage with its tiered access and specialized blob types.

- File Storage brings familiar file sharing to the cloud while adding enterprise-grade features.

- Table Storage offers a flexible approach to storing structured data without the constraints of traditional databases.

The DP-900 exam frequently presents scenarios where you need to choose between storage services. Focus on understanding the core strengths and typical use cases of each service, rather than memorizing technical specifications.

Exam Essentials

For success on the DP-900 exam, focus on these key areas:

- Understanding Blob Storage fundamentals
  - Know the differences between block, append, and page blobs.
  - Understand when to use each access tier (Hot, Cool, Archive).
  - Recognize how redundancy options affect availability and cost.
  - Identify scenarios for each blob type.
- Understanding File Storage fundamentals:
  - Understand SMB protocol support and authentication methods.
  - Know how file share snapshots work and their use cases.
  - Recognize hybrid scenarios involving Azure File Sync.
  - Understand file share security and access control.
- Grasping Table Storage capabilities:
  - Understand partition and row key concepts.
  - Know the differences between Table Storage and traditional databases.
  - Recognize use cases for Table Storage.
  - Understand query patterns and their performance implications.

Beyond the Exam

While the DP-900 exam's coverage of relational data concepts tests essential fundamentals, my years of working with production databases have shown me that real-world implementations often venture far beyond these basics. Let me share some insights that might help you bridge the gap between certification knowledge and practical application.

Modern Storage Evolution

Having worked with storage solutions from the pre-cloud era through to today's modern systems, I've witnessed a remarkable transformation in how we handle data. Today's storage solutions are far more intelligent than their predecessors. For instance, I recently worked with a system that automatically adjusted its storage tiers based on access patterns, something we storage administrators used to spend hours manually optimizing. These self-tuning capabilities represent just one way modern cloud storage has evolved to meet growing data demands.

The complexity of storage relationships in production environments often surprises newcomers to the field. In one recent project, what started as a simple Blob Storage implementation quickly evolved to include sophisticated lifecycle management, hierarchical access controls, and complex business rules. While DP-900 certification covers fundamental concepts like storage tiers and access controls, real-world scenarios often require more nuanced approaches to maintaining data integrity and managing relationships.

Real-World Insight

Don't be surprised if your first production storage implementation challenges your understanding of "simple" concepts like storage tiers. What works in training environments often needs adaptation for real-world scale.

Implementation Realities

One of the most valuable lessons I've learned came from working with a major ecommerce platform. On paper, the storage architecture seemed straightforward: Blob Storage for product images, file shares for internal documents, and Table Storage for product metadata. However, when handling millions of concurrent users during major shopping events, we discovered that even well-designed storage patterns could become bottlenecks.

An interesting challenge emerged when we needed to maintain high availability while simultaneously processing thousands of concurrent file operations per second. During peak periods, what seemed like a simple file access operation would cascade into significant delays. The solution wasn't just about optimizing individual storage services. It required fundamentally rethinking how we structured our storage architecture. We implemented a hybrid approach using CDN caching with an eventual consistency model for the main storage systems. This kind of architectural decision isn't covered on the DP-900 exam, but it demonstrates why understanding basic storage concepts is just the starting point.

The Scale Challenge

While DP-900 certification covers the essential fundamentals of storage concepts, my experience working with production systems has shown me that real-world implementations often extend beyond these basics. Let me share some practical insights that might help you bridge the gap between certification knowledge and actual implementation.

Emerging Directions

The storage landscape continues to evolve in practical ways. Current systems often combine different storage types with intelligent routing and caching layers. These hybrid approaches maintain reliability while providing the flexibility needed for modern applications.

I've found the integration of AI into storage management particularly useful. The systems I work with now help identify potential capacity issues early and suggest optimization opportunities. While these tools complement our fundamental understanding of storage concepts, they don't replace the need for solid architectural principles.

As you move beyond DP-900 certification and into implementing storage solutions, remember that the fundamental concepts you've learned provide a foundation for real-world work. You'll often need to adapt these principles to meet specific requirements, and that's a normal part of the process. Keep learning from each implementation, and don't hesitate to consult with colleagues who have relevant experience with similar challenges.

CHAPTER 8

Azure Cosmos DB

The landscape of data management presents an interesting paradox: while operational tasks have become more streamlined, the proliferation of available options has introduced new layers of complexity. This evolution is particularly evident in how we engage with data today. Consider how you use your favorite social media app: you expect your posts to appear instantly, your friends across the globe to see your updates immediately, and the app to work flawlessly whether you're in Tokyo or Toronto. This expectation of seamless, global data access represents a profound shift from traditional database systems. Azure Cosmos DB emerged as Microsoft's response to this new reality, offering a database service built from the ground up for the global, cloud native era.

To understand why Azure Cosmos DB represents such a significant advancement, imagine trying to build a modern social media platform using traditional database technology. You might start with separate databases in different regions, attempting to synchronize data between them. You'd quickly encounter challenges: How do you handle conflicts when users in different regions update the same data? How do you ensure that users see consistent information regardless of their location? How do you maintain performance as your user base grows globally? These are precisely the challenges that Azure Cosmos DB was designed to address, and we'll discuss them throughout this chapter.

Coverage of Curriculum Objectives

This chapter addresses the following DP-900 exam objectives:

- Describe Azure Cosmos DB APIs.
- Identify use cases for Azure Cosmos DB.

Understanding the Cosmos DB Architecture

At its core, Azure Cosmos DB reimagines what a database can be in the cloud and AI era. Rather than starting with traditional database concepts and adding cloud features, Microsoft designed Azure Cosmos DB with global distribution and massive scale as foundational principles. This approach manifests in its architecture, which differs significantly from conventional databases.

Think of Azure Cosmos DB as a global logistics network for your data. Just as a modern shipping company maintains distribution centers worldwide to ensure fast delivery, Azure Cosmos DB automatically replicates your data across multiple regions. But unlike physical goods, which can only be in one place at a time, Azure Cosmos DB allows your data to exist simultaneously in multiple locations, each copy fully functional and immediately accessible.

The Power of Global Distribution

Let's explore how this works through a real-world scenario. Imagine you're building a global gaming platform where players compete in real-time matches and maintain persistent inventories. Traditional database approaches would force you to choose between data consistency (ensuring that all players see the same game state) and performance (providing quick response times for players worldwide). Azure Cosmos DB eliminates this false choice through its sophisticated global distribution system.

Understanding Consistency Models

In the traditional database world, consistency was often a binary choice: either your data was consistent, or it wasn't. Azure Cosmos DB transforms this limitation into an opportunity by offering multiple consistency levels that can be selected based on your specific needs. Think of these consistency levels like different shipping options for a package—from expensive overnight delivery to more economical standard shipping, each with its own trade-offs between speed and guarantees.

The five consistency levels in Azure Cosmos DB represent different positions on the spectrum between strong consistency and high availability. Let's explore these through practical scenarios that demonstrate when each level makes sense.

Strong consistency

The most rigorous consistency level is strong consistency. It ensures that all readers see the most recent version of data. Imagine a banking application where a customer transfers money between accounts. Here, it's crucial that the balance shown reflects the most recent transaction, regardless of which region the customer accesses their account from. While this level provides the strongest guarantees, it comes with a performance cost as each write must be synchronized across all regions before being confirmed.

Eventual consistency

The most relaxed consistency level, eventual consistency provides the highest availability and performance but the weakest consistency guarantees. Readers might see older versions of data, but all replicas will eventually converge to the same state. This works well for scenarios like social media likes or view counts where immediate consistency isn't critical.

Consistent prefix

The consistent prefix level guarantees that readers never see out-of-order writes. If updates are made in order A, B, C, readers might see A, or A and B, but never B and C without A. This is useful for scenarios like chat applications, where message ordering matters but slight delays are acceptable.

Bounded staleness

Another flexible consistency approach is bounded staleness. The approach is done by allowing reads to lag behind writes by a bounded amount, either time or number of operations. Consider a social media platform where showing a post's Like count that's a few seconds old is acceptable. The platform might configure bounded staleness to allow reads to lag by up to five seconds, gaining better performance while still maintaining reasonably fresh data.

Session consistency

Session consistency is perhaps the most practical level for many applications, because it ensures that a single user always sees their own writes while potentially seeing older data from other users. This works particularly well for user-centric applications. Take an ecommerce platform where a customer updates their shopping cart. With session consistency, the customer always sees their current cart contents, while other users browsing the site might see slightly older product availability information.

Understanding Data Modeling in Azure Cosmos DB

Traditional relational database design often begins with creating tables and defining relationships between them. Azure Cosmos DB requires a different mindset, one that prioritizes access patterns and query performance over normalized data structures. This shift in thinking often challenges developers and database architects who are accustomed to traditional database design.

Consider how you might model a product catalog for an ecommerce platform. In a relational database, you might create separate tables for products, categories, pricing, and inventory. Each product would reference these related tables through foreign keys. In Azure Cosmos DB, a more effective approach often involves denormalization, embedding related data within a single document:

```json
{
    "id": "product_12345",
    "name": "Professional Camera XDR",
    "category": {
        "id": "electronics",
        "name": "Electronics",
        "path": "/electronics/cameras"
    },
    "pricing": {
        "basePrice": 999.99,
        "currentPrice": 899.99,
        "discounts": [
            {
                "type": "holiday_sale",
                "amount": 100.00,
                "validUntil": "2024-02-01"
            }
        ]
    },
    "inventory": {
        "totalAvailable": 157,
        "reservations": 12,
        "warehouseLocations": [
            {
                "id": "SEA-1",
                "quantity": 89
            },
            {
                "id": "NYC-4",
                "quantity": 68
            }
        ]
    }
}
```

This denormalized structure might initially seem inefficient. After all, we're storing category information with each product rather than referencing a centralized categories table. However, this design offers several crucial advantages in a distributed system. First, it eliminates the need for joins, which can be particularly expensive when data is distributed across multiple regions. Second, it ensures that all information needed to display a product is available in a single read operation, improving application performance.

Azure Cosmos DB API Types

When developers first approach Azure Cosmos DB, they often feel overwhelmed by the variety of APIs available. Think of these APIs as different languages that Azure Cosmos DB can speak, each one designed to communicate with different types of applications in their native tongue. Just as a skilled diplomat might switch between languages to better communicate with different audiences, Azure Cosmos DB adapts its communication style based on your application's needs.

At the heart of this versatile system lies the Azure Cosmos DB Core, a powerful global distribution engine surrounded by five specialized API interfaces. As shown in Figure 8-1, these interfaces—the NoSQL (Core) API, MongoDB API, Cassandra API, Table API, and Gremlin API—act as dedicated communication channels, each connecting directly to the core engine. This architecture ensures that regardless of which database "language" you prefer, you're always working with the full power of Cosmos DB's distributed capabilities.

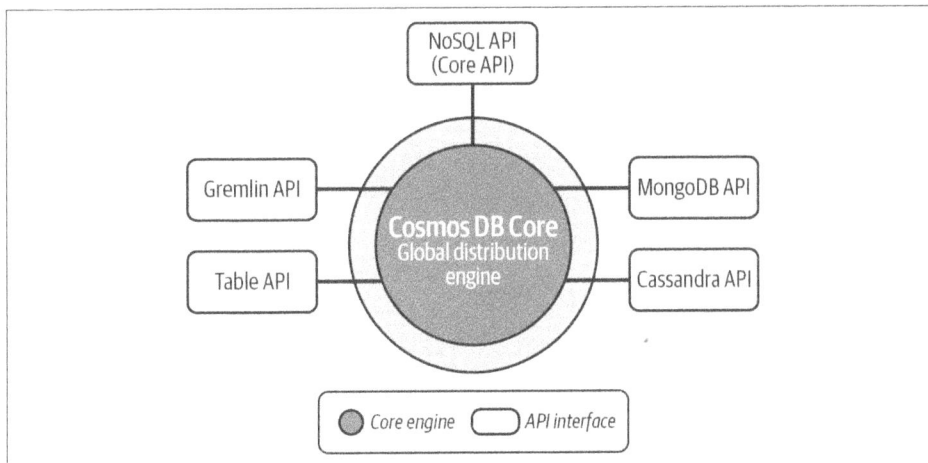

Figure 8-1. Azure Cosmos DB API architecture

Let's explore each of these APIs and understand when to use them in real-world scenarios.

NoSQL (Core) API in Azure Cosmos DB

The NoSQL API, also known as the *Core API*, is like the native language of Azure Cosmos DB. Imagine you're building a brand-new application from scratch—this would be your go-to choice. It speaks in JSON, a format that developers love for its flexibility and readability. Just as you might find it easiest to express yourself in your native language, applications built using the NoSQL API can take full advantage of everything Azure Cosmos DB has to offer without any translation layer.

Let's dive deeper into a real-world scenario to understand the power of the NoSQL API. Consider a modern social media platform that needs to handle various types of content. Initially, your posts might be simple text updates:

```
{
    "id": "post123",
    "type": "text",
    "content": "Hello world!",
    "userId": "user456",
    "timestamp": "2024-02-11T10:30:00Z"
}
```

But as your platform evolves, you might want to add support for rich media posts:

```
{
    "id": "post124",
    "type": "rich_media",
    "content": "Check out my vacation!",
    "userId": "user456",
    "timestamp": "2024-02-11T10:35:00Z",
    "location": {
        "city": "Paris",
        "country": "France",
        "coordinates": {
            "lat": 48.8566,
            "lng": 2.3522
        }
    },
    "media": [
        {
            "type": "image",
            "url": "vacation1.jpg",
            "caption": "Eiffel Tower"
        },
        {
            "type": "video",
            "url": "paris_walk.mp4",
            "duration": "00:02:30"
        }
    ],
    "mood": "excited",
```

```
"weather": {
    "condition": "sunny",
    "temperature": 22
    }
  }
}
```

The NoSQL API handles this evolution gracefully—no database schema changes required. You can even query across these different post types using SQL-like syntax:

```
SELECT p.id, p.content, p.location.city
FROM posts p
WHERE p.type = 'rich_media'
AND p.location.country = 'France'
```

Exam Tip

The DP-900 exam often tests your understanding of querying capabilities. Remember that the NoSQL API supports SQL-like syntax for querying JSON documents, combining the flexibility of NoSQL with the familiarity of SQL.

While the NoSQL API is perfect for new applications, what about organizations that have existing MongoDB applications? This brings us to our next API, which serves as a bridge between familiar MongoDB operations and Azure Cosmos DB's powerful features.

MongoDB API in Azure Cosmos DB

Have you ever moved to a new city but found a restaurant that reminds you of home? That's what the MongoDB API feels like for developers who are familiar with MongoDB. Microsoft designed this API to speak MongoDB's language fluently, allowing existing MongoDB applications to connect to Azure Cosmos DB with minimal changes to their code. It's like having a universal translator that ensures that your MongoDB applications can communicate perfectly with Azure Cosmos DB.

Let's explore this through a real-world scenario. Imagine you're working for an ecommerce company that has built its entire product catalog system using MongoDB. The system works well, but the company is expanding globally and needs better scalability and worldwide presence. Here's what its current MongoDB product document might look like:

```
{
    "_id": ObjectId("5f43b..."),
    "sku": "BIKE-123",
    "name": "Mountain Explorer Pro",
    "category": "Bikes",
    "price": {
        "amount": 1299.99,
        "currency": "USD"
```

```
    },
    "specifications": {
        "frame": "Aluminum",
        "gears": 21,
        "weight": "12.5kg"
    },
    "inventory": {
        "warehouse_1": 45,
        "warehouse_2": 32
    }
}
```

With the MongoDB API, the company can keep this exact same structure while gaining all the benefits of Azure Cosmos DB. Its existing queries continue to work:

```
db.products.find({
    "price.amount": { $lt: 1500 },
    "inventory.warehouse_1": { $gt: 0 }
})
```

Exam Tip

The DP-900 exam frequently tests your understanding of migration scenarios. Remember that the MongoDB API is ideal for existing MongoDB applications looking to leverage Azure's cloud capabilities without major code rewrites. Look for questions about minimizing application changes during cloud migration.

The beauty of this approach is that while your application continues to speak MongoDB's language, behind the scenes you're getting all of Azure Cosmos DB's enterprise features:

Automatic global distribution
    Your product catalog is automatically replicated across multiple regions, ensuring that customers worldwide get fast access to product information.

Enhanced security
    You gain Azure's comprehensive security features, including encryption at rest and in transit, without changing your application code.

Elastic scalability
    The system automatically handles traffic spikes during sales events or holiday shopping seasons.

Backup and recovery
    Enterprise-grade backup and disaster recovery capabilities protect your valuable product data.

While the MongoDB API excels at document-based workloads, some scenarios demand a different approach, particularly when dealing with massive amounts of structured data. This is where the next API comes into play, offering a solution for high-scale time-series and tabular data scenarios.

Note that while the MongoDB API provides excellent compatibility, there are some limitations to be aware of. The API supports MongoDB wire protocol version 3.6 and 4.0 features, but certain advanced features, like MongoDB transactions across shards, may have limitations. Always consult the latest documentation for feature parity details when planning migrations.

Cassandra API in Azure Cosmos DB

The Cassandra API brings the power of wide-column storage to Azure Cosmos DB. If you're familiar with Apache Cassandra, think of this API like using your favorite app that's been upgraded with premium features: all your familiar tools are there, plus some powerful new capabilities. This API is particularly valuable for scenarios involving massive amounts of structured data with predictable query patterns.

Let's explore a detailed example of how the Cassandra API excels in handling IoT data. Imagine you're building a system to track fitness data from millions of smartwatches. Each device sends regular updates about various metrics:

```
CREATE TABLE fitness_data (
    device_id uuid,
    timestamp timestamp,
    heart_rate int,
    steps int,
    calories_burned int,
    sleep_state text,
    activity_type text,
    PRIMARY KEY ((device_id), timestamp)
) WITH CLUSTERING ORDER BY (timestamp DESC);
```

This structure allows for efficient time-series queries while maintaining Cassandra's familiar syntax:

```
SELECT heart_rate, steps, calories_burned
FROM fitness_data
WHERE device_id = 123e4567-e89b-12d3-a456-426614174000
AND timestamp >= '2024-02-11 00:00:00'
AND timestamp < '2024-02-12 00:00:00';
```

Exam Warning

Watch for questions about time-series data and high write scenarios. The Cassandra API is often the correct choice for IoT telemetry, logging, and other time-series applications requiring high write throughput.

The Cassandra API particularly shines in scenarios requiring the following:

High-volume time-series data
    Perfect for IoT telemetry, system logs, or financial tick data

Write-heavy workloads
    Efficiently handles millions of writes per second across multiple regions

Complex time-based queries
    Optimized for retrieving time-sliced data efficiently

Flexible consistency levels
    Allows fine-tuned balance between consistency and performance

While the Cassandra API offers sophisticated capabilities for complex data scenarios, sometimes you need something simpler. Not every application requires the full power of document or column-family databases. This brings us to an API that proves that sometimes less is more.

Table API in Azure Cosmos DB

Sometimes simplicity is exactly what you need. The Table API enhances Azure Table Storage (discussed in Chapter 7) with Azure Cosmos DB's premium features. Think of it as upgrading from a basic bicycle to an electric bike—same simple concept but with much more power when you need it.

Let's explore how the Table API can transform a simple inventory tracking system. Consider a retail chain tracking stock levels across thousands of stores:

```
public class InventoryItem : TableEntity
{
    public string ProductId { get; set; }
    public int Quantity { get; set; }
    public string Location { get; set; }
    public DateTime LastUpdated { get; set; }
}
```

The beauty of the Table API lies in its straightforward approach to data access:

```
// Query all items in a specific store location
var items = tableClient.Query<InventoryItem>(
    filter: $"PartitionKey eq 'STORE_123'"
);
```

While the interface remains simple, you get powerful features:

Global distribution
Automatically replicate your inventory data across regions.

Automatic indexing
Benefit from faster queries without manual index management.

Enhanced scalability
Handle millions of requests without performance degradation.

Improved consistency
Choose from multiple consistency levels.

While the Table API handles straightforward data relationships effectively, modern applications often need to work with more complex, interconnected data. This leads us to our final API, which specializes in managing and analyzing relationships between data points.

Gremlin API in Azure Cosmos DB

The Gremlin API opens up the world of graph databases in Azure Cosmos DB. Imagine trying to understand how all your LinkedIn connections are related to each other—that's the kind of problem graph databases excel at solving. The Gremlin API allows you to model and traverse complex relationships naturally.

Let's dive into a fraud detection system for a financial institution. Here's how you might model transactions and relationships:

```
// Add vertices for accounts
g.addV('account').property('id', 'A1').property('owner', 'John')
g.addV('account').property('id', 'A2').property('owner', 'Jane')

// Add edges for transactions
g.addE('transfer').from('A1').to('A2')
    .property('amount', 5000)
    .property('timestamp', '2024-02-11T10:00:00Z')
```

Now you can perform sophisticated queries to detect suspicious patterns:

```
// Find all transactions over $10,000 between accounts
// that share a common connection
g.V().hasLabel('account')
    .outE('transfer')
    .has('amount', gt(10000))
    .inV()
    .path()
```

Exam Tip

The DP-900 exam may include questions about relationship-heavy data scenarios. Remember that the Gremlin API is ideal for cases where understanding connections and patterns in data is crucial.

Now that we've explored the various ways Azure Cosmos DB can speak to your applications through its APIs, you might be wondering: when should I actually use Azure Cosmos DB? Let's dive into real-world scenarios that showcase where Azure Cosmos DB truly shines. Understanding these use cases will not only help you make better architectural decisions but also prepare you for common scenario-based questions on the DP-900 exam.

Bringing It All Together: Azure Cosmos DB in Practice

Let's see how these different APIs and features come together in practice. Think of Azure Cosmos DB as a sophisticated orchestra, where different instruments (APIs) play together to create a harmonious solution. Let's explore how the fictional company GlobalTech, a rapidly growing digital platform company operating ecommerce, gaming, and financial services, orchestrates these capabilities.

Exam Tip

Pay special attention to how different APIs and features complement each other. The DP-900 exam often includes scenario-based questions where you need to identify the optimal combination of Azure Cosmos DB capabilities.

Embracing the Modern Data Platform

GlobalTech operates a diverse portfolio of digital services: a global ecommerce marketplace, a real-time multiplayer gaming platform, and a peer-to-peer payment system. Its data requirements include:

- Processing millions of transactions per second globally
- Maintaining inventory accuracy across multiple regions
- Supporting real-time gaming interactions with minimal latency
- Detecting fraudulent financial transactions in real time
- Adapting to rapidly changing product catalogs and user preferences

These requirements directly influenced GlobalTech's technical architecture choices, leading it to adopt Azure Cosmos DB with its multiple APIs and global distribution capabilities.

GlobalTech's journey with Azure Cosmos DB began with a challenge familiar to many growing companies: how to build a data platform that could serve multiple applications with different requirements while maintaining simplicity and efficiency. Its solution showcases how Azure Cosmos DB's various APIs and features can work in perfect harmony.

At the heart of its architecture lies its ecommerce platform, leveraging the NoSQL API to handle product catalogs and user profiles. The flexibility of JSON documents allows GlobalTech to adapt quickly to changing business requirements. When it added personalized recommendations, it simply extended its product documents without any schema changes:

```
{
    "id": "product_789",
    "name": "Smart Fitness Watch",
    "basePrice": 199.99,
    "categories": ["Electronics", "Fitness"],
    "recommendations": {
        "frequentlyBoughtWith": ["product_790", "product_791"],
        "similarItems": ["product_792", "product_793"],
        "personalizedScores": {
            "newCustomer": 0.85,
            "fitnessEnthusiast": 0.95,
            "techSavvy": 0.90
        }
    }
}
```

Exam Tip

Notice how the NoSQL API's flexible schema allows for easy addition of new features without disrupting existing functionality. The exam often tests your understanding of when schema flexibility provides business value.

Consider a multiplayer game where players can:

- Purchase in-game items.
- Trade with other players.
- Compete in real-time events.
- Chat with players worldwide.

Azure Cosmos DB handles these scenarios elegantly through the following:

Automatic data replication
    Player data is automatically copied to regions where it's needed.

Multiregion writes
    Players can make purchases or trades from any region.

Consistent experience
    Game state remains consistent across the globe.

Low latency
    Players experience minimal lag due to data locality.

Exam Tip

The DP-900 exam frequently tests understanding of global distribution scenarios. Pay attention to questions involving multiregion applications and data consistency requirements. Remember that Azure Cosmos DB can maintain multiple active write regions simultaneously.

While global distribution solves the challenge of worldwide data access, many modern applications face another crucial requirement: the need to process and analyze data as it arrives. This brings us to our next critical use case, where speed and real-time processing are paramount.

Harmonizing Different Data Models

As GlobalTech expanded, it acquired a logistics company specializing in supply chain optimization that had built its entire inventory management system using MongoDB. Instead of a costly rewrite, GlobalTech seamlessly integrated this system using Azure Cosmos DB's MongoDB API. The existing application continued to function without modification, while gaining the benefits of Azure's global infrastructure:

```
// Existing MongoDB queries continued to work
db.inventory.find({
    "stock.quantity": { $lt: 100 },
    "location.region": "APAC"
})
```

Meanwhile, its data science team needed to analyze vast amounts of time-series data from user interactions across all its platforms: ecommerce browsing patterns, gaming sessions, and payment transactions. The Cassandra API proved perfect for this requirement, handling millions of events per second while maintaining query performance:

- Traffic management:
    - Real-time traffic flow data
    - Signal timing adjustments
    - Accident detection and response
    - Parking availability updates
- Environmental monitoring:
    - Air quality measurements
    - Noise level tracking
    - Weather condition updates
    - Energy consumption patterns
- Public transportation:
    - Bus and train locations
    - Passenger count data
    - Schedule adherence tracking
    - Maintenance alerts

Azure Cosmos DB excels in these scenarios because it can:

- Ingest millions of data points per second.
- Process and analyze data in real time.

- Scale automatically with demand.
- Maintain performance under heavy load.

> **Exam Tip**
>
> For the exam, understand how Azure Cosmos DB's automatic indexing and partitioning strategies enable real-time data processing at scale. Questions often focus on scenarios requiring immediate data availability and processing.

Building Connections Through Graph Data

GlobalTech's payment services division implemented sophisticated fraud detection using the Gremlin API. By modeling transactions and user relationships as a graph, the company could identify suspicious patterns that would be difficult to spot using traditional database queries:

Phase 1: Basic Product Catalog

```
{
    "id": "prod123",
    "name": "Wireless Headphones",
    "price": 99.99,
    "category": "Electronics"
}
```

In Phase 1, GlobalTech started with a basic product catalog structure that captured just the essential product information. The JSON structure was intentionally simple, containing only fundamental fields like ID, name, price, and category. This minimal approach allowed the company to quickly launch its initial ecommerce platform.

Phase 2: Added Customer Reviews

```
{
    "id": "prod123",
    "name": "Wireless Headphones",
    "price": 99.99,
    "category": "Electronics",
    "reviews": [
        {
            "userId": "user789",
            "rating": 5,
            "comment": "Great sound quality!",
            "verified_purchase": true
        }
    ],
    "average_rating": 4.8
}
```

As the platform matured, Phase 2 introduced customer engagement features through a review system. The data model was enhanced to include an array of customer reviews, each containing detailed information about the reviewer, their rating, and verification status. GlobalTech also added an aggregated average rating to facilitate quick product quality assessment.

Phase 3: Personalization and Social Features

```
{
    "id": "prod123",
    "name": "Wireless Headphones",
    "price": 99.99,
    "category": "Electronics",
    "reviews": [...],
    "related_products": ["prod456", "prod789"],
    "social_shares": 1234,
    "user_segments": ["audio_enthusiast", "tech_savvy"],
    "recommendation_score": 0.89
}
```

Phase 3 marked the company's transition into a sophisticated ecommerce platform with advanced personalization. The data model expanded to include social features, product relationships, and machine learning elements. The company added fields for related products, social engagement metrics, user segmentation, and recommendation scoring. This evolution demonstrates how NoSQL's flexible schema allowed GlobalTech to iteratively add features without disrupting existing functionality.

What's particularly noteworthy about this progression is how each phase built upon the previous one without requiring any schema migrations or downtime. The document structure naturally evolved to accommodate new features while maintaining backward compatibility with existing applications.

Exam Tip

Watch for questions about schema flexibility and changing application requirements. The exam often tests your ability to identify scenarios where traditional rigid schemas would be problematic.

Implementing Cost Optimization and Performance Tuning

GlobalTech's success with Azure Cosmos DB isn't just about features. It's also about smart resource management. The company implemented several strategies to optimize its deployment:

RU management

By analyzing usage patterns, the company allocated RUs effectively across different containers.

Data distribution

> The company was able to strategically place data in regions where its customers are most active.

Consistency level selection

> The company was able to implement different consistency levels for different workloads—strong consistency for financial transactions and session consistency for product browsing.

"The beauty of Azure Cosmos DB," explains MJ Penn, GlobalTech's chief architect, "is that it grows with us. When we launched in Asia, we didn't have to redesign anything—we just enabled a new region in Azure, and Azure Cosmos DB handled the rest."

Summary

Azure Cosmos DB represents a fundamental shift in how organizations approach data management—moving beyond traditional databases to embrace globally distributed, cloud native solutions. Each feature and API addresses specific application needs while maintaining enterprise-grade capabilities:

- Global distribution and consistency models enable organizations to deliver data worldwide with configurable trade-offs between consistency and availability, supporting everything from banking transactions requiring strong consistency to social media feeds that can tolerate eventual consistency.

- Multiple API options (NoSQL, MongoDB, Cassandra, Table, and Gremlin) allow teams to work with familiar database interfaces while gaining cloud native capabilities, making it possible to modernize existing applications or build new ones without learning entirely new query languages.

- Flexible data modeling through schema-less design enables applications to evolve naturally over time, supporting use cases from simple key-value pairs to complex hierarchical documents and graph relationships, all while maintaining performance at global scale.

- Enterprise features including automatic indexing, built-in security, and comprehensive monitoring ensure that organizations can operate mission-critical applications with confidence while focusing on business logic rather than infrastructure management.

The choice of how to implement Azure Cosmos DB isn't just technical. It's strategic, allowing organizations to balance consistency, global reach, and development velocity as they build modern cloud applications.

Beyond the Exam

While DP-900 certification covers the essential fundamentals of Azure Cosmos DB, my years of implementing distributed databases for global supply chain operations have shown that real-world applications are far more complex. Let me share some insights from managing supply chain data across Australia, Singapore, the Eastern United States, and Western Europe.

The Reality of Global Distribution in the Supply Chain

Having evolved from traditional single-region warehouse management systems to globally distributed supply chain platforms, I've witnessed firsthand how theoretical concepts translate into practical challenges. I remember one particularly challenging implementation with a major logistics provider's inventory tracking system. In testing, our global distribution setup appeared flawless: inventory updates propagated smoothly, and our consistency levels seemed well tuned.

Then, we expanded operations into Singapore.

What we hadn't anticipated was the complex interplay between consistency levels and real-world supply chain operations. During peak shipping seasons, warehouses across different regions would process thousands of simultaneous inventory updates. Our chosen consistency level (Bounded Staleness) occasionally led to temporary inventory discrepancies between regions, causing fulfillment delays. While our setup followed best practices from the documentation, we hadn't fully understood how it would impact real-time operations.

The solution wasn't just about adjusting consistency levels. It required rethinking our entire approach to inventory management. We implemented a hybrid system where critical inventory counts used Strong consistency for absolute accuracy, while less critical metrics like trending data used Eventual consistency. This balanced operational accuracy with system performance.

Cost Management in Supply Chain Operations

The exam covers RUs, but managing them across a global supply chain is particularly challenging. I learned this during a major expansion of our Australian distribution centers. Our initial deployment resulted in unexpected costs because we hadn't accounted for several supply-chain-specific factors:

- Seasonal shipping patterns created massive spikes in data access.
- Cross-region queries for optimal routing calculations consumed more RUs than expected.
- Development environments replicating production data for testing consumed significant resources.

We developed the following supply-chain-specific strategies to optimize costs:

- Implemented predictive scaling based on historical shipping patterns
- Created separate containers for hot data (active shipments) and cold data (completed deliveries)
- Developed region-specific RU allocation based on warehouse operation hours
- Used data archival strategies for completed shipment data older than 90 days

Supply Chain Data Modeling Evolution

One of the most valuable lessons came from implementing a global inventory management system. Initially, we modeled our warehouse data as straightforward JSON documents. However, as operations expanded across regions, we discovered that real-world supply chain data is far more complex.

We learned to balance denormalization for performance with the need to maintain accurate inventory counts across regions. The solution involved a carefully designed system of linked documents that preserved query performance while ensuring data consistency across our global operations.

Integration Challenges in Multiregion Operations

The exam covers various APIs, but real-world supply chain integrations involve complex orchestration between multiple systems across regions. During a recent migration of our European warehouse management system to Cosmos DB's MongoDB API, we encountered several challenges:

- Legacy warehouse management systems had region-specific business logic.
- Real-time integration with customs systems required special handling.
- Cross-region reporting systems needed adaptation for different time zones.
- Disaster recovery procedures needed to account for regional compliance requirements.

The solution involved creating a comprehensive testing framework that validated not just data consistency but also regional compliance and reporting requirements.

Performance Tuning for the Global Supply Chain

Real-world performance tuning in supply chain operations goes far beyond basic optimization. In our Eastern US distribution centers, we discovered that our partitioning strategy created hot spots during certain shipping windows. The solution required us to:

- Implement a composite partition key combining warehouse ID and timestamp.
- Develop region-specific bulk import strategies for end-of-day reconciliation.
- Create custom monitoring for cross-region query patterns.
- Optimize container throughput based on regional business hours.

The Future of Global Supply Chain Technologies

As supply chain operations continue to evolve, the fundamentals you learn through DP-900 certification provide an excellent foundation for building sophisticated global solutions. The journey from managing a single warehouse to orchestrating a global supply chain network is incredibly rewarding, and Azure Cosmos DB makes this transition smoother than ever before.

What's particularly exciting is how each region adds new possibilities to your supply chain network. The Australian operation might teach you about efficient inventory management across vast distances, while the Singapore operation could show you how to optimize for incredibly high throughput. Western Europe might help you master compliance and data governance, while the Eastern US operation could demonstrate excellence in real-time analytics.

The tools and knowledge you gain through DP-900 certification are just the beginning of an exciting journey. With Azure Cosmos DB, you're well equipped to:

- Build resilient, globally distributed supply chain systems.
- Create innovative solutions for inventory tracking and management.
- Develop real-time analytics that drive business decisions.
- Implement scalable solutions that grow with your operations.

Remember, you're not just learning a database system. You're gaining the power to transform how goods move around the world. The future of global supply chain operations is bright, and with Azure Cosmos DB, you're well positioned to be part of that future. Embrace the journey ahead and get ready to make your mark on the world of global logistics!

PART IV

Analytics on Azure

Analytics bridges the gap between raw data generation and meaningful, time-appropriate insight. This part of the book traces the continuum from large-scale batch processing and data lake/lakehouse patterns, through real-time event analytics, and finally to business-oriented visualization and storytelling with Power BI. The emphasis is on how latency expectations, query shape, consumption style, and semantic modeling influence architecture.

- Chapter 9, "Large-Scale Analytics", frames layered analytical architecture—ingestion, raw/curated storage, processing engines, serving zones—and the scalability and orchestration patterns that make petabyte scale workable.

- Chapter 10, "Real-Time Analytics", shifts to continuous event streams, low-latency decision loops, and when streaming adds value over microbatch or scheduled processing.

- Chapter 11, "Data Visualization with Power BI", focuses on semantic modeling, governed datasets, measures, visualization patterns, and how self-service analytics speeds up decision cycles when properly structured.

Completion outcomes include recognizing when real time is justified versus overengineering, explaining why semantic layers reduce KPI disputes, and mapping pipeline stages to business consumption needs.

Common pitfalls include adopting streaming for vanity "real-time" claims, neglecting model design (leading to fragile reports), collapsing raw and curated data boundaries, and treating visuals as decoration rather than analytical narratives.

Exam Alignment: Expect conceptual distinctions among batch, streaming, and Power BI consumption models.

CHAPTER 9

Large-Scale Analytics

Organizations face unprecedented challenges when working with data. The volume, variety, and velocity of information have expanded exponentially, pushing traditional analytics solutions beyond their limits. Large-scale analytics represents a response to these challenges—a set of approaches, technologies, and architectures designed to extract meaningful insights from massive datasets that conventional tools simply cannot handle.

Coverage of Curriculum Objectives

This chapter addresses the following DP-900 exam objectives:

- Describe considerations for data ingestion and processing.
- Describe options for analytical data stores.
- Describe Microsoft cloud services for large-scale analytics, including Azure Databricks and Microsoft Fabric.

Figure 9-1 illustrates the key components of a large-scale analytics architecture. The flow begins with diverse data sources, moving through ingestion and storage layers, followed by processing and serving layers, and culminating with consumption. Each step contains specialized components designed to handle specific aspects of analytics.

```
┌─────────────────────────────────────────────────────────────────────┐
│              Governance and security                                 │
│  ┌──────────┐  ┌──────────┐  ┌──────────┐  ┌──────────┐  ┌──────────┐  ┌──────────┐
│  │Data sources│→│Ingestion │→│Storage   │→│Processing│→│Serving   │→│Consumption│
│  │Operational│  │Batch,stream│ │Lakes,    │  │Transform,│  │Warehouses,│ │Dashboards,│
│  │systems,  │  │processing,│  │warehouses,│ │enrich,   │  │marts,feature│ reports, │
│  │apps,external│ CDC       │  │analytical│  │modeling,ML│ │stores    │  │analytics │
│  └──────────┘  └──────────┘  │stores    │  └──────────┘  └──────────┘  └──────────┘
│              Orchestration and monitoring                            │
└─────────────────────────────────────────────────────────────────────┘
```

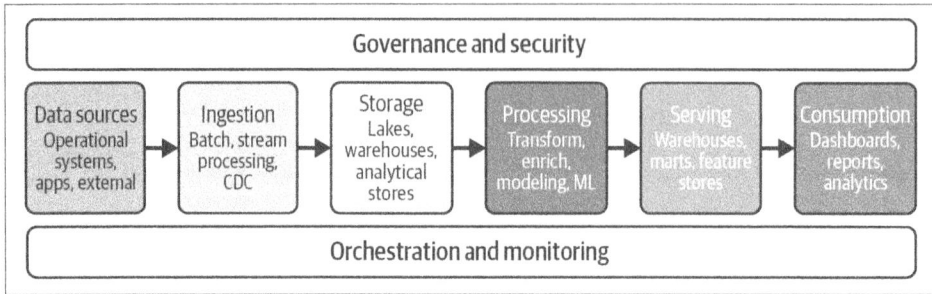

Figure 9-1. Key components of large-scale analytics

Think of large-scale analytics as the difference between crossing a small pond and crossing an ocean. The skills, tools, and planning required are fundamentally different in scale and complexity. When datasets grow from gigabytes to terabytes or even petabytes, and when data sources multiply from a handful to hundreds, traditional analytics approaches begin to falter. Large-scale analytics provides the vessel and navigation equipment needed to successfully cross these vast data oceans.

For the DP-900 exam and anyone working with Azure, understanding large-scale analytics is crucial. The cloud has revolutionized how organizations approach big data challenges, making advanced analytics capabilities accessible without massive infrastructure investments. Azure's comprehensive ecosystem of services transforms what was once possible only for the largest enterprises into capabilities available to organizations of all sizes.

Understanding Large-Scale Analytics

Your journey into large-scale analytics begins with understanding its characteristics and components. Unlike traditional analytics, which might process structured data from a single database, large-scale analytics handles diverse data from multiple sources at enormous volumes. This shift isn't simply about scaling up existing solutions. It requires completely rethinking how we collect, store, process, and analyze data.

Exam Tip

The DP-900 exam often presents scenarios asking you to identify whether a traditional database solution or a large-scale analytics approach is more appropriate. Look for clues about data volume (terabytes or petabytes), variety (multiple formats), and velocity (streaming data) that indicate large-scale analytics is needed.

The Scale Challenge

Traditional analytics infrastructure was designed for predictable, structured data flowing in at a manageable pace. Organizations would collect transaction records, customer information, and operational metrics in well-organized databases, then analyze this information using standard reporting tools. This approach worked well when data volumes grew gradually and structures remained relatively stable.

The digital transformation has shattered these comfortable constraints. Every aspect of modern business now generates data at unprecedented rates. Ecommerce platforms track every click, scroll, and view. Manufacturing equipment reports status updates every few seconds. Mobile applications generate constant streams of usage data. Social media platforms produce endless feeds of text, images, and interactions.

This digital explosion isn't just about quantity. It's also about fundamental changes in how information flows through organizations. Three major shifts define this new landscape.

First, the sheer volume of data has grown exponentially. The traditional three Vs of big data—Volume, Variety, and Velocity—have expanded to include Veracity (data quality and trustworthiness) and Value (the ability to turn data into meaningful insights).

Organizations now routinely collect and analyze petabytes of information from business transactions, sensors, social media interactions, and countless other sources. This volume quickly overwhelms traditional database systems and analytics tools designed for gigabyte-scale operations.

Second, modern data comes in remarkably diverse formats. The structured rows and columns of traditional databases now represent only a fraction of valuable information. Semi-structured data like JSON or XML files contain nested, variable information. Unstructured data includes everything from customer emails and support chat logs to product images and surveillance video. Large-scale analytics must accommodate this variety, often requiring different processing approaches for each type.

Third, the speed at which data arrives has accelerated dramatically. Many valuable data sources now generate continuous streams rather than periodic batches. Analyzing this high-velocity data requires fundamentally different approaches than traditional ETL processes designed for nightly or weekly updates.

Exam Tip

The DP-900 exam emphasizes understanding how these shifts in data volume, variety, and velocity necessitate different approaches for large-scale analytics. Focus on recognizing scenarios where traditional solutions would be insufficient.

Modern large-scale analytics addresses these challenges through specialized architectures that distribute processing across multiple computers, store diverse data types efficiently, and process information at various speeds. Rather than attempting to force all data into a single system or approach, these architectures embrace the inherent diversity of modern data landscapes.

Components of Large-Scale Analytics

While the transformation from traditional to large-scale analytics is about handling more data, it also requires rethinking the entire approach to working with information. To understand this shift, we need to examine how modern analytics systems organize the flow from raw data to business insight.

Large-scale analytics represents more than just scaled-up traditional systems. It encompasses a comprehensive approach to handling data throughout its lifecycle, from initial collection to final insight. Understanding this end-to-end process reveals why conventional tools struggle with modern data challenges.

The data flow begins with the vastly expanded universe of data sources. While traditional analytics might draw from a handful of internal databases, modern approaches incorporate information from across the digital ecosystem. Enterprise applications generate structured records of business activities. Websites and mobile apps produce detailed logs of user interactions. IoT devices report telemetry from the physical world. External sources provide market trends, social sentiment, and competitive intelligence. Each source brings unique formats, update frequencies, and quality considerations.

This diverse information flows into the organization through data ingestion processes that form the foundation of modern ELT architectures that must handle both historical information and real-time streams. Unlike traditional ETL processes that moved data on fixed schedules, modern ingestion operates continuously, adapting to varying volumes and velocities. Some data arrives in massive batches, while other information streams in constantly. Effective ingestion must handle both patterns while maintaining data integrity and tracking lineage.

After collection, the next step is storage. Traditional data warehouses excel at organizing structured information in optimized formats but struggle with the semi-structured and unstructured data due to their rigid schema requirements and inability to handle variable data structures that now dominate many landscapes. Modern analytics employs specialized storage approaches optimized for different data types and access patterns. These range from data lakes that preserve raw information in its native format to purpose-built analytical databases designed for specific query patterns.

With data properly stored, the true transformation occurs in processing, where raw information becomes analytical insight. Processing might include cleaning messy data, converting between formats, joining related datasets, aggregating for performance, or applying advanced analytics through statistical methods and machine learning. This processing often occurs in distributed systems that spread work across dozens or hundreds of computers, enabling analysis at scales impossible on single machines.

The final step in the data pipeline makes processed information available through interfaces that translate complex findings into actionable business decisions. Interactive dashboards, analytical tools, and embedded analytics within operational applications help business users derive value from the processed data.

Modern large-scale analytics connects these components into cohesive architectures that maintain data flowing from source to insight. Unlike traditional approaches that often created disconnected silos, these architectures emphasize integration while allowing specialization for different data types and analytical needs.

Data Ingestion and Processing

Now that you understand the overall components of large-scale analytics, let's examine how data begins its journey. Data ingestion forms the critical first step in any analytics pipeline—the process of collecting information from various sources and bringing it into your analytical environment. Getting this foundational step right is essential for everything that follows.

The Ingestion Challenge

In large-scale scenarios, ingestion faces challenges that require rethinking traditional approaches to data movement. Consider what happens when organizations attempt to scale up conventional data collection methods to meet modern demands.

Imagine a global retail organization collecting POS data from thousands of stores, website interactions from millions of online shoppers, inventory updates from hundreds of warehouses, and market research from dozens of third-party sources. Each data source might use different formats, update at different frequencies, and require different handling. Some provide historical data in batches, while others generate continuous streams of information.

Traditional data movement typically relied on periodic ETL processes. These would connect to source systems on a scheduled basis (perhaps nightly or weekly), extract new data, apply transformations to standardize formats, and load the results into analytics systems. This approach worked well when data sources were limited in number, relatively stable in structure, and updated on predictable schedules.

However, modern data landscapes shatter these assumptions. The number of valuable data sources has multiplied dramatically, with many organizations tracking hundreds or thousands of distinct information streams. Data structures evolve constantly as applications add features and tracking requirements change. Update frequencies have accelerated from daily batches to continuous feeds, with some sources generating thousands of records per second.

These fundamental shifts require rethinking our approach to data collection. Modern ingestion must handle both traditional batch transfers and continuous streaming data. It needs to accommodate diverse and evolving data formats without requiring extensive reconfiguration. Systems must scale dynamically to handle peak loads that might be orders of magnitude higher than average volumes. And throughout all this complexity, organizations need to maintain data quality and lineage tracking.

Real-World Scenario

A global manufacturing company previously collected production line data once daily via database extracts. After implementing sensors on equipment, data volume increased 50-fold and velocity shifted to continuous streams. The company's traditional ETL process couldn't keep up, causing data loss and delayed insights. By implementing a hybrid ingestion approach that handled both batch and streaming data, the company reduced insight latency from 24 hours to under 5 minutes while capturing 100% of critical production metrics.

Batch and Streaming Paradigms

To address diverse ingestion requirements, modern analytics leverages two complementary paradigms, each suited to different types of data sources and analytical needs.

Batch ingestion processes data in chunks, typically on a scheduled basis or when triggered by specific events. This approach resembles traditional ETL processes, but they are scaled for much larger volumes. Batch processing excels when handling historical data, performing complex transformations, or loading initial datasets. It prioritizes thoroughness and completeness over immediacy, often including comprehensive validation and quality checks.

In contrast, *streaming ingestion* processes data continuously as it's generated. This approach treats data as an endless flow rather than discrete chunks. Streaming excels at capturing time-sensitive information where immediate processing adds significant value. Examples include monitoring systems that need to detect anomalies quickly, customer experience applications that adapt to user behavior in real time, and fraud detection systems that must identify suspicious activity before transactions complete.

Most modern analytics architectures incorporate both approaches, recognizing that different data sources and analytical needs require different ingestion patterns. A retail analytics system might use streaming ingestion to capture current shopping behavior while using batch processes to load historical sales records and inventory data. These complementary approaches ensure comprehensive data availability while prioritizing timeliness for critical information flows.

I'll talk more about batch versus streaming in the next chapter.

Processing Considerations

With data flowing into our analytics environment through appropriate ingestion mechanisms, the next step is processing—transforming raw information into formats that enable effective analysis. This critical middle stage connects ingestion to storage and ultimately to business insight.

Once data enters the analytics environment, it typically requires processing before it can yield valuable insights. Processing transforms raw data into structured formats suitable for analysis, enriches it with additional information, and optimizes it for efficient querying.

Large-scale data processing faces several fundamental challenges that traditional approaches struggle to address. First, the sheer volume of data often exceeds what single machines can handle efficiently. Processing terabytes or petabytes requires distributed approaches that spread work across multiple computers. Second, diverse data formats require specialized processing techniques—text requires different handling than images or time-series data. Third, different analytical scenarios have vastly different latency requirements, from batch processes that can run overnight to interactive queries that must return results in seconds.

Modern processing technologies address these challenges through several complementary approaches. Distributed processing frameworks divide large datasets into manageable chunks, process them in parallel across multiple machines, and combine the results. Specialized processing engines optimize for particular data types and analytical patterns. Configurable execution environments balance performance against cost, scaling resources up or down based on workload demands.

Processing strategies typically fall along a spectrum from ETL to ELT. Traditional ETL transforms data before loading it into analytical stores, ensuring consistency but potentially limiting flexibility. Modern ELT approaches often load raw data first, then apply transformations as needed for specific analytical needs. This approach preserves the original information while enabling diverse processing paths for different requirements.

For example, in traditional ETL, customer data from multiple sources would be standardized to a common format with consistent field names and data types before being loaded into the warehouse. In contrast, ELT would load the raw customer data from each source into the data lake first, then transform it as needed—perhaps one way for marketing analytics and differently for financial reporting.

Analytical Data Stores

With data properly ingested and processed, we now need a place to store it that enables efficient analytics. This brings us to a crucial component of any large-scale analytics architecture: specialized data storage designed for analytical workloads.

After ingestion and processing, data must be stored in ways that support efficient analytics. Traditional transactional databases (OLTP systems) were designed to record individual business transactions quickly and reliably, not to analyze massive datasets. Large-scale analytics requires specialized data stores optimized for analytical workloads.

> **Exam Tip**
>
> Understanding the difference between transactional (OLTP) and analytical (OLAP) storage is fundamental for the DP-900 exam. OLTP systems optimize for fast recording of individual transactions, while OLAP systems optimize for complex queries across large datasets. The exam frequently tests this distinction through scenario-based questions.

The Storage Challenge

OLTP systems are designed for fast, reliable recording of business transactions, while OLAP systems optimize for complex queries across large datasets. Understanding this distinction is crucial for choosing appropriate storage solutions.

Analytical data storage presents fundamentally different requirements than transactional systems. While transactional databases optimize for quickly recording individual business activities, analytical stores must support complex queries across vast datasets. This distinction manifests in several key areas.

Query patterns differ dramatically between transactional and analytical workloads. Transactional systems typically access small amounts of data in precise locations—finding a specific customer record or updating a particular inventory item. Analytical queries often scan millions or billions of records, comparing and aggregating information across many dimensions. Stores designed for analytics optimize for these broad, scanning queries rather than precise record access.

Data volumes in analytical systems dwarf their transactional counterparts. While operational databases might manage gigabytes or terabytes, analytical stores routinely handle terabytes or petabytes. They often retain years of historical data to support trend analysis and pattern recognition. Managing these volumes requires specialized approaches to storage, indexing, and query processing.

Data diversity presents another significant challenge. Transactional systems typically work with well-defined, structured data models that change infrequently. Modern analytics incorporates structured data alongside semi-structured information like JSON documents and unstructured content like text and images. Analytical stores must accommodate this variety while still enabling efficient queries.

Concurrency patterns also differ significantly. Transactional systems handle many small, independent operations, often with strict consistency requirements. Analytical workloads might involve fewer queries, but each can consume substantial resources while scanning large datasets. Analytical stores must balance these resource-intensive operations while serving multiple users and applications simultaneously.

These differences explain why organizations maintain separate storage systems for transactional and analytical workloads, even when they contain related information. Attempting to serve both patterns from a single system inevitably compromises performance for one or both workloads.

Data Lakes

Data lakes represent a fundamental shift in how organizations store data for analytics. Unlike traditional approaches that required data to be structured and organized before storage, data lakes provide a repository for raw, unprocessed data in its native format. They serve as the foundation for many large-scale analytics architectures, particularly when organizations need to preserve data in its original form.

The concept emerged as a response to the increasing variety and volume of valuable data. Traditional data warehouses required information to be transformed into predefined structures before storage, a process that often discarded potentially valuable details and limited future analytical flexibility. Data lakes instead preserve raw information exactly as it arrives, maintaining its full fidelity and enabling diverse processing paths as analytical needs evolve.

Modern data lakes typically store information in distributed file systems like Hadoop Distributed File System (HDFS) or cloud-based object storage. Unlike simple folder structures, data lakes provide distributed processing capabilities, metadata management, query engines, and data governance features that enable analytics at scale. Files are often converted to efficient formats like Parquet or ORC that maintain all data while optimizing for analytical queries. Modern data lakes organize data into logical hierarchies that might reflect source systems, business domains, or time periods. They maintain the original format of incoming data—whether CSV files, JSON documents, images, videos, or proprietary formats—while providing tools to catalog and discover this diverse content. This approach preserves maximum analytical flexibility, allowing different teams to process the same raw data in ways that serve their specific needs.

Data lakes excel in several crucial scenarios. Organizations with changing or evolving analytical requirements benefit from preserving raw data that can be reprocessed as needs change. Data science teams value access to unfiltered information that retains all potentially valuable signals. Storage administrators appreciate the cost efficiency of maintaining a single copy of raw data rather than multiple transformed versions.

However, data lakes also present challenges. Without careful governance, they can become *data swamps*—disorganized repositories where valuable information becomes difficult to find. The flexibility of raw storage shifts transformation responsibility to data consumers, potentially creating inconsistent interpretations of the same information. Many organizations address these challenges through metadata management, data cataloging, and the creation of curated zones with processed, trusted datasets derived from the raw lake content.

Exam Tip

Data lakes store raw data in its original format, while data warehouses store processed, structured data optimized for specific analytical queries. The DP-900 exam often tests your ability to recognize when each approach is most appropriate based on scenario characteristics.

Data Warehouses

While data lakes excel at storing raw, diverse data, data warehouses take a more structured approach to analytical storage. They organize information into dimensional models specifically designed for analytical queries, enabling fast performance for business intelligence and reporting.

Data warehouses have evolved over decades as the primary platform for business analytics. They transform raw, operational data into optimized structures that support complex analytical queries. Unlike data lakes that preserve information in its original format, data warehouses impose defined schemas, relationships, and aggregations that align with how organizations analyze their business.

The core architecture of a data warehouse typically includes fact tables containing measurable business events (sales transactions, website visits, support calls) connected to dimension tables that provide context (customers, products, time periods). This star or snowflake schema design optimizes for analytical queries that aggregate measures across different dimensions—for example, calculating total sales by product category and region for each quarter.

Modern data warehouses employ several techniques to deliver performance at scale. Columnar storage organizes data by column rather than row, dramatically improving efficiency for queries that analyze specific attributes across many records. Massively parallel processing (MPP) distributes queries across many computers, enabling analysis of enormous datasets. Intelligent partitioning and indexing strategies optimize data access based on common query patterns.

Data warehouses particularly excel at supporting standardized reporting, dashboards, and business intelligence applications. Their structured approach ensures consistent results across different analyses and enables business users to work with familiar dimensions like customers, products, and time periods. The predefined nature of data warehouse models makes them ideal when analytical requirements are well understood and consistent over time.

However, data warehouses also present limitations in the modern analytics landscape. Their structured nature requires defining schemas before loading data, making them less flexible for exploratory analysis or rapidly evolving data sources. The transformation required for warehouse loading can delay data availability compared to data lakes. And the focus on structured data can make it challenging to incorporate unstructured or semi-structured information that provides valuable context.

These complementary strengths and limitations explain why many modern analytics architectures combine data lakes and data warehouses in a layered approach. Data lakes serve as the flexible foundation for storing all raw data, while data warehouses provide optimized performance for well-defined analytical workloads. This combined approach maximizes both flexibility and performance.

Analytical Databases

Beyond the broad categories of data lakes and data warehouses, the analytics landscape includes specialized databases optimized for particular analytical patterns and workloads. These purpose-built systems provide advanced capabilities for specific scenarios while maintaining familiar database interfaces.

Several specialized analytical database types have emerged to address specific needs:

In-memory analytical databases store data primarily in memory rather than on disk, delivering dramatic performance improvements for interactive analytics. They enable business users to explore data and iterate through different analytical perspectives without the delays typically associated with disk-based systems. While more expensive per terabyte than disk storage, they justify their cost through improved productivity and faster insight generation.

Columnar databases optimize storage and processing specifically for analytical workloads that typically analyze a few columns across many rows. By storing data organized by column rather than row, they minimize I/O requirements for analytical queries, often improving performance by orders of magnitude compared to traditional row-based storage. This approach directly addresses the mismatch between row-oriented transactional systems and column-oriented analytical queries.

Time-series databases specialize in handling data where time forms the primary organizing dimension. They excel at ingesting and analyzing the high-velocity streams from IoT sensors, financial markets, application monitoring, and similar sources that generate timestamp-oriented data. Their specialized indexing and storage techniques optimize for the specific patterns of time-based queries, such as identifying trends, detecting anomalies, and comparing periods.

Azure provides specialized analytical databases through services like Azure Cosmos DB, which offers multiple data models including document, key-value, graph, and column-family APIs. Each model optimizes for specific analytical patterns while maintaining the flexibility of a managed service.

Graph databases organize information based on relationships rather than tables, enabling sophisticated analysis of connections and networks. They excel at scenarios like fraud detection (identifying suspicious relationship patterns), recommendation systems (finding similar users or products), and impact analysis (understanding cascading effects through a network). Their ability to traverse relationships makes them powerful tools for analyzing complex, interconnected data.

Many organizations leverage multiple analytical store types in complementary ways. They might use data lakes for initial storage and exploration, data warehouses for structured business reporting, and specialized databases for particular analytical patterns. This multifaceted approach recognizes that no single storage technology excels at all analytical scenarios.

How to Choose the Right Analytical Store

With so many options available, selecting the appropriate analytical storage approach requires careful consideration of several key factors:

Data structure represents one of the most important considerations. Highly structured data with well-defined schemas typically works best in data warehouses, while diverse or evolving data might start in a data lake. The balance between structured and unstructured information often determines the primary storage approach, with specialized databases addressing particular segments of this spectrum.

Query patterns significantly influence storage decisions. Known, repeatable queries benefit from the optimized structure of a data warehouse, while exploratory analysis might leverage the flexibility of a data lake. The predictability and consistency of analytical needs often determine whether the up-front investment in warehouse modeling delivers appropriate returns.

Performance requirements shape both technology selection and implementation details. Time-sensitive analytics might require the speed of in-memory processing or specialized analytical databases, while batch analysis can leverage any of the options. The balance between query performance and storage cost often leads to tiered approaches where frequently accessed data resides in performance-optimized stores while historical information moves to more economical options.

Integration needs influence how analytical stores connect with existing systems, visualization tools, and other analytics components. The technological ecosystem and skill sets within an organization often guide storage decisions, favoring options that align with existing capabilities and investment.

Rather than choosing a single approach, most large-scale analytics architectures combine multiple storage technologies in a layered design. A common pattern includes the following:

Raw zone
  Lake storage that holds original, unprocessed data that will help further zones

Refined zone
  Processed data in optimized formats within Data Lake Storage

Curated zone
  Highly structured data in data warehouses or other analytical databases

Specialized zones
  Purpose-built databases for particular analytical patterns

This layered approach provides both the flexibility of a data lake and the performance of specialized analytical stores, allowing organizations to match storage characteristics to different stages of the analytical lifecycle.

Microsoft Cloud Services for Large-Scale Analytics

Having explored the core concepts and components of large-scale analytics, let's turn our attention to how Microsoft implements these capabilities in Azure. The cloud has revolutionized analytics by removing infrastructure barriers, enabling organizations of all sizes to implement sophisticated analytical capabilities without massive capital investments.

Microsoft offers a comprehensive ecosystem of services for large-scale analytics in the cloud. These services work together to provide end-to-end solutions for data ingestion, storage, processing, analysis, and visualization. Let's explore the key platforms that form the foundation of Azure's analytics capabilities.

Azure Databricks

Among Azure's analytics offerings, Databricks stands out as a specialized platform designed specifically for large-scale data processing and advanced analytics. It represents a collaborative analytics service built around Apache Spark, the popular open source distributed processing framework. Developed through a partnership between Microsoft and Databricks (founded by the creators of Spark), it provides a powerful environment for data engineering, data science, and machine learning at scale.

Databricks promotes the lakehouse architecture, combining the flexibility of data lakes with the performance and reliability of data warehouses (shown in Figure 9-2). This approach uses the medallion architecture with bronze (raw), silver (refined), and gold (curated) layers to organize data at different stages of processing.

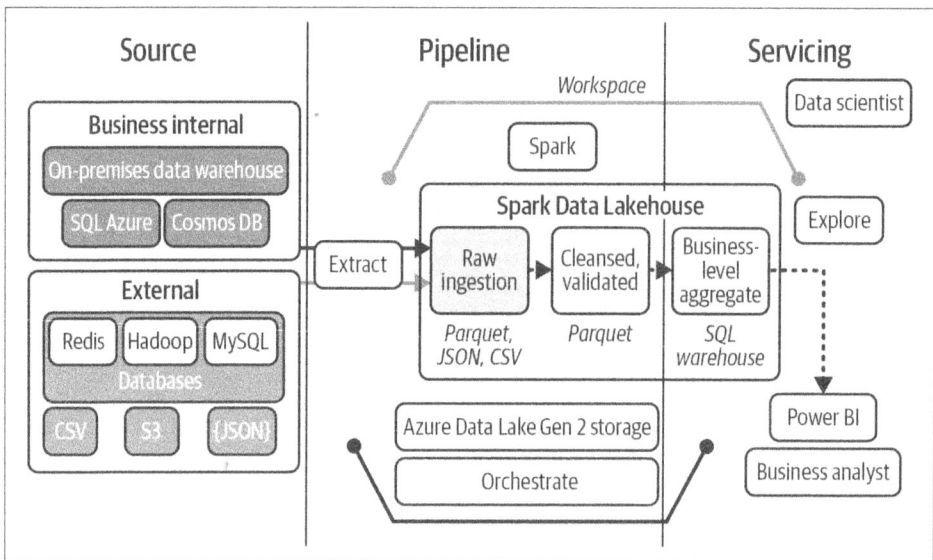

Figure 9-2. Azure Databricks common lakehouse architecture

Azure Databricks brings together several capabilities essential for modern analytics workflows. At its core lies an optimized version of Apache Spark, the distributed processing engine that enables analysis across clusters of computers rather than single machines. This foundation enables processing of enormous datasets that would overwhelm traditional tools. Surrounding this engine, Databricks provides collaborative workspaces where data professionals can develop, share, and execute analytical code and workflows.

The platform particularly excels at complex data engineering, where raw information requires substantial transformation before it yields valuable insights. Databricks includes specialized tools for defining, executing, and monitoring data pipelines that convert raw inputs into analytics-ready information. These capabilities integrate with Delta Lake, an open source storage layer that brings reliability and performance features typically associated with data warehouses to data lake environments.

Beyond data engineering, Databricks provides specialized capabilities for data science and machine learning. Its collaborative notebooks combine code, visualizations, and explanatory text, enabling data scientists to develop and share analytical approaches. The platform includes MLflow, an open source framework for managing the machine learning lifecycle from experiment tracking through model deployment. These capabilities make Databricks particularly valuable for organizations whose analytics needs extend beyond reporting into predictive and prescriptive analytics.

With its combination of powerful distributed processing and collaborative features, Databricks excels in several key scenarios.

Data engineering workflows benefit from Databricks' ability to process massive datasets, transform diverse information types, and build reliable data pipelines. The platform's integration with Delta Lake enables reliable updates to data lake content through features like ACID transactions and schema enforcement.

Data science activities leverage the collaborative nature of Databricks notebooks, which enable teams to work together on analytical approaches while providing access to the computational power needed for large-scale analysis. The ability to work interactively with enormous datasets enables more thorough exploration and insight generation.

Machine learning development takes advantage of Databricks' MLflow integration for experiment tracking, model versioning, and deployment management. The platform simplifies the path from analytical prototype to production model by providing consistent environments across development and operations.

Exam Tip

For the DP-900 exam, understand that Azure Databricks specializes in large-scale data processing and advanced analytics based on Apache Spark. Its collaborative workspace is particularly valuable for data science and machine learning scenarios where teams need to combine code development with powerful distributed processing.

Azure Synapse Analytics

While Databricks focuses on code-first advanced analytics, Azure Synapse Analytics takes a different approach by providing an integrated analytics platform that combines multiple technologies under a unified experience. It brings together enterprise data warehousing, big data processing, data integration, and analytics into a cohesive service designed to simplify end-to-end analytics development, as shown in Figure 9-3.

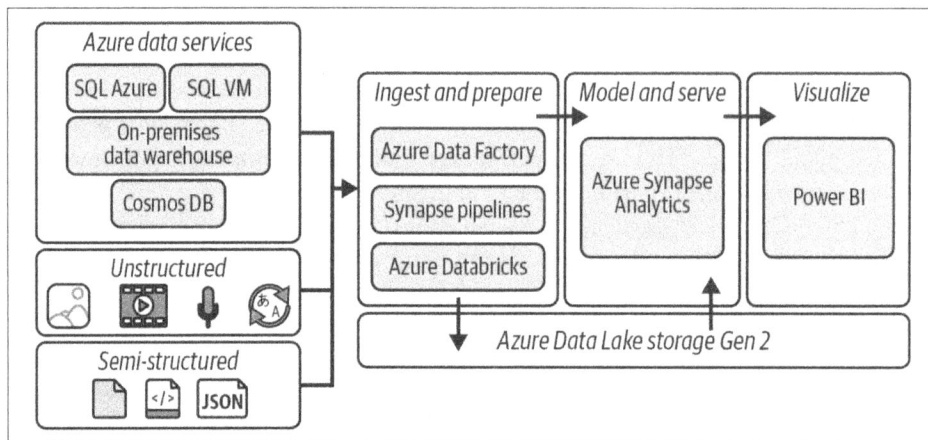

Figure 9-3. Sample large-scale analytics with Azure Synapse Analytics

Synapse Analytics evolved from Azure SQL Data Warehouse, expanding its capabilities well beyond traditional data warehousing. At its core, Synapse still provides powerful SQL-based analytics through dedicated SQL pools that leverage massively parallel processing for performance at scale. These pools excel at structured data analysis using familiar SQL syntax, making them accessible to the many data professionals with SQL expertise.

However, Synapse goes far beyond traditional SQL capabilities. It also includes Apache Spark pools that provide distributed processing for unstructured and semi-structured data, enabling code-based analytics using languages like Python, Scala, and .NET. This dual-engine approach allows organizations to handle both structured and unstructured analytics within a single service, reducing the complexity of managing multiple platforms.

Integration forms a central theme throughout Synapse Analytics. Built-in data integration capabilities enable movement and transformation across various sources without requiring separate tools. The service connects seamlessly with Azure Data Lake Storage, enabling queries directly against lake data without copying it into specialized stores. The unified Studio experience brings development, management, and monitoring together in a cohesive interface that simplifies the analytics workflow.

Synapse Analytics particularly shines in scenarios that span the spectrum from traditional data warehousing to modern big data analytics:

Enterprise Data Warehousing leverages Synapse's SQL capabilities to deliver high-performance structured analytics. The service scales from small departmental data marts to enterprise-wide warehouses, with flexible resource allocation that balances performance and cost.

Data Lake Exploration extends analytics beyond structured data, enabling organizations to gain insights from diverse information sources. Serverless SQL capabilities allow analysts to query data lake content directly using familiar SQL syntax, while Spark integration supports code-based analysis for more complex scenarios.

Integrated Data Preparation simplifies the transformation of raw data into analytics-ready formats. Synapse's data flows enable visual definition of transformations without requiring code, making data engineering more accessible to analyst personas.

Real-World Scenario

A retail organization uses Synapse Analytics to combine POS data (via SQL pools) with customer behavior from web logs (via Spark pools), creating a unified customer view for personalization and marketing analytics. Marketing analysts can use familiar SQL to analyze structured sales data, while data scientists leverage Spark notebooks to analyze browsing patterns. The unified platform ensures consistent definitions and metrics across both analysis paths.

Microsoft Fabric

Microsoft's newest addition to the analytics portfolio represents an evolution in how organizations approach analytics in the cloud. Launched in 2023, Microsoft Fabric takes integration to a new level by providing a unified software-as-a-service (SaaS) platform that brings together the entire analytics lifecycle under a single experience and data platform, as shown in Figure 9-4.

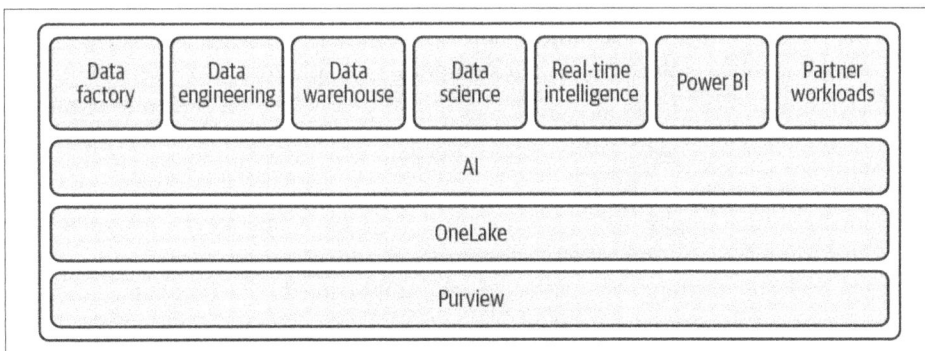

Data factory	Data engineering	Data warehouse	Data science	Real-time intelligence	Power BI	Partner workloads
AI						
OneLake						
Purview						

Figure 9-4. Microsoft Fabric unified SaaS stack approach

Fabric builds on Microsoft's analytics evolution by unifying previously separate services into an integrated experience that emphasizes simplicity and cohesion. At its foundation lies OneLake, a single data lake that serves as a unified storage layer across all analytical workloads. This approach eliminates the silos that traditionally separated different analytical tools, enabling seamless data sharing and collaboration across roles and teams.

The platform brings together multiple workload types under a consistent experience. Data engineers can build and manage pipelines that ingest and transform information. Data scientists can develop and deploy machine learning models. Data analysts can create reports and dashboards. Business users can access self-service analytics. All these personas work within a unified platform that maintains consistent data definitions and governance across activities.

Microsoft Fabric takes a fundamentally different approach to analytics infrastructure by providing a true SaaS experience. Unlike traditional analytics platforms that require significant administration and maintenance, Fabric handles the underlying infrastructure automatically. This approach dramatically reduces operational overhead, allowing organizations to focus on deriving insights rather than managing systems.

Fabric particularly excels in scenarios where simplicity and integration deliver substantial value:

End-to-end analytics
These workflows benefit from Fabric's unified approach, which eliminates the friction traditionally associated with moving data between different tools and platforms. Teams can progress smoothly from data ingestion through transformation, analysis, and visualization within a consistent environment.

Self-service analytics
This becomes more accessible when business users can access trusted data through intuitive interfaces. Fabric's emphasis on usability and integration enables nontechnical users to perform sophisticated analytics without requiring extensive technical expertise.

Governed data sharing
This becomes simpler when all analytical workloads operate on a shared data foundation. Fabric's OneLake storage provides consistent access controls and lineage tracking across analytical activities, supporting both compliance requirements and collaborative workflows.

How to Choose Between Analytics Services

With multiple powerful analytics platforms available in Azure, organizations often ask which service they should choose. Rather than thinking of these options as competing alternatives, it's more helpful to consider how they complement each other within the broader analytics ecosystem.

The selection between analytics services depends on several key factors that influence which platform best meets an organization's needs:

Existing skills often guide technology decisions, as teams naturally leverage their established expertise. Organizations with strong Spark expertise might gravitate toward Databricks, while those with SQL backgrounds might find Synapse Analytics more accessible. Fabric's unified approach appeals to organizations seeking to minimize specialized technical requirements.

Integration requirements shape platform choices, particularly for organizations with existing investments in Microsoft technologies. Synapse Analytics offers deep integration with other Azure services, while Fabric provides seamless connections across the Microsoft ecosystem. Databricks, while well integrated with Azure, also maintains compatibility with other cloud environments.

Specialized needs often determine platform selection for specific workloads. Projects requiring advanced machine learning might benefit from Databricks' comprehensive machine learning capabilities, while data warehousing workloads might favor Synapse Analytics. Fabric's simplified administration appeals to organizations seeking to minimize operational complexity.

Architectural complexity presents another important consideration. Databricks and Synapse Analytics provide specialized capabilities for particular analytics scenarios, often requiring careful architectural planning. Fabric takes a different approach by emphasizing simplification and integration over specialized optimization, potentially reducing architectural complexity at the cost of some customization options.

Many organizations adopt multiple analytics services to address different scenarios within their overall analytics strategy. They might use:

- Databricks for data science and complex processing scenarios that benefit from its advanced machine learning capabilities

- Synapse Analytics for data warehousing and structured analytics leveraging SQL expertise

- Fabric for business intelligence and self-service analytics, prioritizing simplicity and accessibility

This pragmatic approach recognizes that different analytical workloads have different requirements, with each platform offering particular strengths. Organizations often start with one platform to address their most pressing analytics needs, then add complementary services as their analytical maturity grows.

Exam Tip

The DP-900 exam frequently presents scenarios where you need to choose between analytics services. Focus on understanding the core strengths and typical use cases of each service rather than memorizing technical specifications.

Bringing It All Together: Large-Scale Analytics in Practice

Now that you've explored the concepts, components, and architectures of large-scale analytics, let's examine how these elements come together in a real-world scenario. This practical perspective helps illustrate how organizations translate technical capabilities into business value.

Consider Global Retail Inc., a fictional multinational organization with physical stores, ecommerce platforms, and mobile applications. The organization is implementing large-scale analytics in Azure to gain comprehensive insights into its business operations and customer behavior. Its journey illustrates the practical application of the concepts we've discussed throughout this chapter.

The Data Landscape

Global Retail faces classic big data challenges that exemplify why traditional analytics approaches no longer suffice. Its diverse operations generate enormous volumes of data, arriving in various formats and at different velocities:

Volume presents a significant challenge, with billions of transactions, customer interactions, and inventory movements annually. The organization's data has grown exponentially, from terabytes to petabytes as it has expanded operations and increased digital touchpoints. Traditional database systems struggled to handle this scale, particularly for analytical queries that needed to scan historical information across multiple years.

Variety complicates its analytics landscape, as information arrives in multiple formats requiring different handling approaches. Structured data from POS systems and inventory management follows well-defined schemas, while semi-structured data from web logs and mobile apps contains nested, variable information. Unstructured data includes customer reviews, support conversations, and social media mentions. No single storage or processing approach could effectively handle this diversity.

Velocity adds another dimension of complexity, with data arriving at dramatically different rates. Real-time streams flow continuously from online shopping sessions, in-store sensors, and supply chain updates. Batch updates arrive daily or weekly from operational systems and external partners. The organization's analytics architecture needed to handle both patterns while maintaining data consistency and completeness.

The Analytics Architecture

To address these challenges, Global Retail implemented a modern analytics architecture in Azure, following the layered approach we discussed earlier. Its solution integrated multiple Azure services into a cohesive ecosystem that transformed raw data into business value:

For data ingestion, Global Retail deployed a hybrid approach that accommodated both batch and streaming patterns. Azure Data Factory managed scheduled collections from operational systems, handling the extraction of sales, inventory, and customer information during off-peak hours. Azure Event Hubs captured real-time streams from websites and mobile apps, preserving every click, search, and interaction for immediate processing. Azure IoT Hub connected in-store sensors that monitored customer movement, environmental conditions, and inventory positions, bringing physical store operations into the digital analytics ecosystem.

The storage layer centered on Azure Data Lake Storage as the foundation for all analytical data. The organization organized the lake into a multitiered structure that balanced flexibility with governance. A raw zone preserved incoming data exactly as it was received, maintaining complete historical fidelity. A standardized zone applied consistent formatting and quality controls while maintaining the granular detail of original records. A curated zone contained trusted business-aligned datasets ready for self-service analytics. Throughout these zones, Global Retail implemented Delta Lake to ensure data reliability and performance at scale.

For processing and transformation, Global Retail leveraged multiple technologies optimized for different scenarios. Azure Databricks handled complex transformations and data preparation for diverse data types, using its distributed processing capabilities to process massive datasets efficiently. Azure Synapse Analytics provided SQL-based analytics accessible to the organization's large community of analysts with SQL expertise. The combination enabled both sophisticated data engineering and accessible analytical capabilities within a unified architecture.

The serving and consumption layers connected analytical insights to business value through appropriate interfaces for different roles. Data scientists accessed notebook experiences in Databricks to develop machine learning models for customer segmentation and demand forecasting. Business analysts used familiar SQL queries in Synapse Analytics to analyze sales performance and inventory metrics. Executives and store managers accessed interactive dashboards through visualization tools, delivering insights without requiring technical expertise.

Throughout this architecture, orchestration and governance ensured reliable, consistent operations. Data Factory pipelines coordinated the overall data flow, managing dependencies between processing steps and handling error conditions. Purview provided data catalog capabilities, helping users discover available datasets and understand their meaning. RBACs maintained appropriate security boundaries while enabling collaborative analytics across departments.

Implementation Approach

Rather than attempting to build this entire architecture at once, Global Retail took an incremental approach that delivered value at each stage while building toward its comprehensive vision.

It began by establishing its data lake and basic ingestion pipelines. This initial deployment focused on collecting and preserving data from its highest priority sources, including POS systems, ecommerce platforms, and inventory management. It implemented core data quality and governance processes to ensure trustworthy information, then built initial reports on these priority datasets. This approach delivered immediate value while laying the groundwork for more sophisticated capabilities.

Building on this foundation, the organization next implemented real-time analytics for its digital platforms. This phase expanded its Event Hubs implementation to capture every customer interaction on its website and mobile app, feeding this information into Stream Analytics for immediate processing. The resulting insights enabled personalized experiences for customers and real-time alerting for operational issues, delivering tangible business impact through improved conversion rates and reduced problem resolution times.

With foundational capabilities and real-time analytics in place, Global Retail progressed to advanced analytics using Databricks. This phase developed sophisticated machine learning models for customer segmentation, product recommendations, and demand forecasting. The resulting capabilities transformed how the organization approached marketing, merchandising, and supply chain management, leveraging predictive insights to optimize business decisions across the organization.

Global Retail's most recent phase expanded to IoT analytics from store sensors, integrating physical store operations into its analytical ecosystem. Sensors tracking customer movement patterns, environmental conditions, and inventory placements provided digital insights into traditionally analog operations. This information helped optimize store layouts, staffing levels, and inventory positioning, improving both operational efficiency and customer experience in physical locations.

This phased approach delivered value at each stage while building toward a comprehensive analytics ecosystem. It allowed Global Retail to learn from each phase before proceeding to the next, adjusting its implementation based on real-world experience rather than theoretical planning. It also enabled the organization to demonstrate tangible business impact early in the process, building organizational momentum and support for continued investment.

Summary

The shift from traditional storage to Azure's cloud-based solutions represents more than just a change in technology. It's a fundamental transformation in how we think about and manage data analytics. Each Azure analytics service addresses specific needs while offering the flexibility and scalability that modern applications demand.

Throughout this chapter, you explored how:

- Large-scale analytics addresses fundamental challenges of data volume, variety, and velocity.
- Modern ingestion approaches handle both batch and streaming data from diverse sources.
- Specialized analytical stores optimize for different data types and query patterns.
- Azure's analytics services provide a comprehensive ecosystem for end-to-end analytics.

Beyond the Exam

While studying for the DP-900 exam provides an excellent foundation in Azure's large-scale analytics concepts and services, real-world implementations often involve additional considerations beyond exam coverage. Having implemented analytics solutions across industries, I've observed several factors that significantly influence success but might not appear directly in certification exams.

The Organizational Factor

While the technical aspects of large-scale analytics receive most of the attention in educational materials, the organizational dimensions often determine success or failure in practice. Technology represents only part of the analytics equation; organizational readiness plays an equally important role in achieving meaningful outcomes.

Perhaps the most critical organizational factor is analytics culture—the extent to which data-driven decision making is valued and practiced across the organization. Technical solutions can provide access to insights, but they can't force people to use those insights when making decisions. Organizations achieving the greatest analytics success foster cultures where leaders consistently ask for data to support proposals, teams habitually test hypotheses rather than relying solely on experience, and insights trump intuition when the two conflict. This cultural transformation often proves more challenging than implementing technical platforms, requiring sustained leadership commitment and demonstrated value to overcome entrenched habits.

Skills development represents another critical organizational dimension. The transition to large-scale analytics requires new capabilities across the organization—not just for technical teams but also for business users who must learn to leverage analytical insights effectively. Technical roles need skills in cloud platforms, distributed processing, and modern languages like Python and Scala. Business users need data literacy to interpret results correctly and analytical thinking to ask effective questions. Organizations that invest in comprehensive skills development across both technical and business teams achieve faster adoption and greater value from their analytics investments.

Cross-functional collaboration provides the foundation for effective analytics implementations. Traditional organizational boundaries between IT, business units, and analytical teams often impede the integrated approach that analytics requires. The most successful implementations establish collaborative structures that bring together domain expertise, technical capabilities, and analytical skills. These might take the form of dedicated analytics centers of excellence, cross-functional teams aligned to specific business domains, or matrix structures that maintain specialized expertise while enabling flexible teaming for specific initiatives.

I once worked with a government agency whose analytics initiative stalled despite substantial technology investments. The turning point came when the agency established cross-functional "insight teams" combining domain experts, analysts, and data engineers. These teams rapidly delivered targeted solutions to specific business problems, building momentum and demonstrating value that helped change the organizational culture. This structural change proved more important than any technical optimization in unlocking analytics value.

Implementation Realities

Real-world analytics implementations rarely follow the neat linear progression suggested in textbooks or certification materials. Several practical realities shape how organizations actually implement large-scale analytics in Azure.

Most organizations maintain hybrid environments that combine cloud and on-premises components, requiring careful integration and data movement strategies. The "all-cloud" architectures depicted in documentation rarely reflect reality, especially for established enterprises with significant existing investments. Successful implementations must address the complexity of connecting cloud analytics platforms with on-premises operational systems, often through carefully designed hybrid architectures that balance modernization with pragmatic reality.

The integration of modern analytics platforms with legacy systems creates significant complexity, particularly around data quality and synchronization. Many operational systems were designed decades before current analytics approaches emerged, with data models optimized for transactional efficiency rather than analytical utility. Creating coherent analytical views across these disparate systems requires sophisticated integration strategies that address differences in data formats, update frequencies, and semantic definitions. These integration challenges often consume more implementation effort than the analytics platforms themselves.

Rather than wholesale replacement, organizations typically migrate analytics workloads incrementally, maintaining parallel systems during transition periods. This evolutionary approach minimizes disruption but creates significant complexity as data flows between old and new environments. Practical implementations must manage this hybrid state through careful orchestration, ensuring consistency while gradually shifting workloads to modern platforms. This transitional complexity rarely appears in certification materials but represents a major focus for real-world implementations.

In one healthcare organization, we implemented a "sidecar" approach where Azure analytics services ran alongside existing on-premises systems. Each quarter, we migrated additional workloads to the cloud while maintaining business continuity. This gradual approach minimized risk while demonstrating incremental value. The architecture included robust synchronization mechanisms to ensure consistency between systems, with an eventual goal of complete migration. This pragmatic approach delivered more value than attempting a single "big bang" transition that would have created unacceptable business disruption.

The Scale Challenge

Storage patterns that work well in development can face challenges at production scale. In one project, we built a storage system for user-generated content with Hot tier storage (frequently accessed data) and Cool tier storage (infrequently accessed data) that performed perfectly in our test environment. However, when our Hot tier storage grew significantly in production, we needed to adjust our approach.

Our initial design followed standard best practices, but we hadn't fully accounted for our actual scale requirements. Operations that were fast in testing began to slow down as our data volume grew. We worked with experienced architects to implement proper partitioning and lifecycle management strategies, finding a balance between theoretical best practices and practical performance needs.

Real-World Insight

Testing with production-scale data volumes early in development helps identify potential performance issues before they impact users.

Emerging Directions

The analytics landscape continues to evolve rapidly, with several trends extending beyond current exam coverage

The boundary between analytics and AI continues to blur, with organizations increasingly embedding AI capabilities directly into analytical workflows. This integration moves beyond traditional predictive analytics to incorporate natural language understanding, computer vision, and automated decision making. Future analytics architectures will likely incorporate these capabilities as standard components rather than specialized extensions.

The concept of a semantic layer—which translates raw data into business-meaningful terms—has evolved beyond traditional approaches, now spanning both structured and unstructured information. Modern implementations use knowledge graphs, ontologies, and AI-assisted mapping to create unified business representations across diverse data types. This evolution addresses one of the most persistent challenges in analytics: ensuring consistent interpretation of information across different uses and tools.

Organizations increasingly use AI to generate synthetic datasets for analytics testing, training, and scenario planning, particularly in highly regulated industries. These approaches provide realistic data for development and testing without exposing sensitive information. They also enable exploration of hypothetical scenarios that haven't occurred in historical data, expanding analytical capabilities beyond historical analysis to sophisticated simulation and planning.

Advanced organizations are moving beyond descriptive and predictive analytics to decision intelligence frameworks that combine analytics with behavioral science and decision theory. These approaches recognize that deriving insights from data represents only part of the value chain—those insights must influence decisions and ultimately actions to deliver tangible business impact. Decision intelligence explicitly models this complete path from data to action, incorporating human factors alongside analytical capabilities.

These emerging approaches hint at where large-scale analytics is headed, though they may not yet appear in certification exams.

Real-World Insight

The most successful analytics implementations maintain flexibility to incorporate new approaches as they emerge, rather than locking into a static architecture.

As you move beyond certification to real-world implementation, remember that large-scale analytics represents a journey rather than a destination. Technologies will continue to evolve, but the fundamental principles of connecting diverse data sources, processing information at scale, and deriving valuable insights remain constant. The solid foundation provided by understanding Azure's analytics services will serve you well as you navigate this evolving landscape.

CHAPTER 10

Real-Time Analytics

The world today is hyperconnected, and analyzing data as it's created represents a transformative capability for organizations across industries. Whether monitoring financial transactions for fraud, optimizing traffic flow in smart cities, or personalizing customer experiences on ecommerce platforms, real-time analytics enables immediate insight and action that were impossible with traditional approaches. This shift from retrospective analysis to instantaneous understanding fundamentally changes how organizations operate and compete.

Think of real-time analytics as the difference between watching historical footage versus observing events as they unfold. Traditional batch analytics resembles reviewing security camera footage the next day—valuable for understanding what happened but too late for immediate intervention. Real-time analytics is like having security personnel monitor live camera feeds, enabling them to respond immediately to emerging situations. This fundamental shift from reactive to proactive analytics transforms both technological approaches and business capabilities.

Figure 10-1 illustrates how data flows from diverse sources through ingestion and processing to deliver immediate insights. The diagram shows streaming data entering the system on the top, passing through ingestion services and processing engines, and finally serving immediate insights through dashboards, alerts, and operational systems on the bottom.

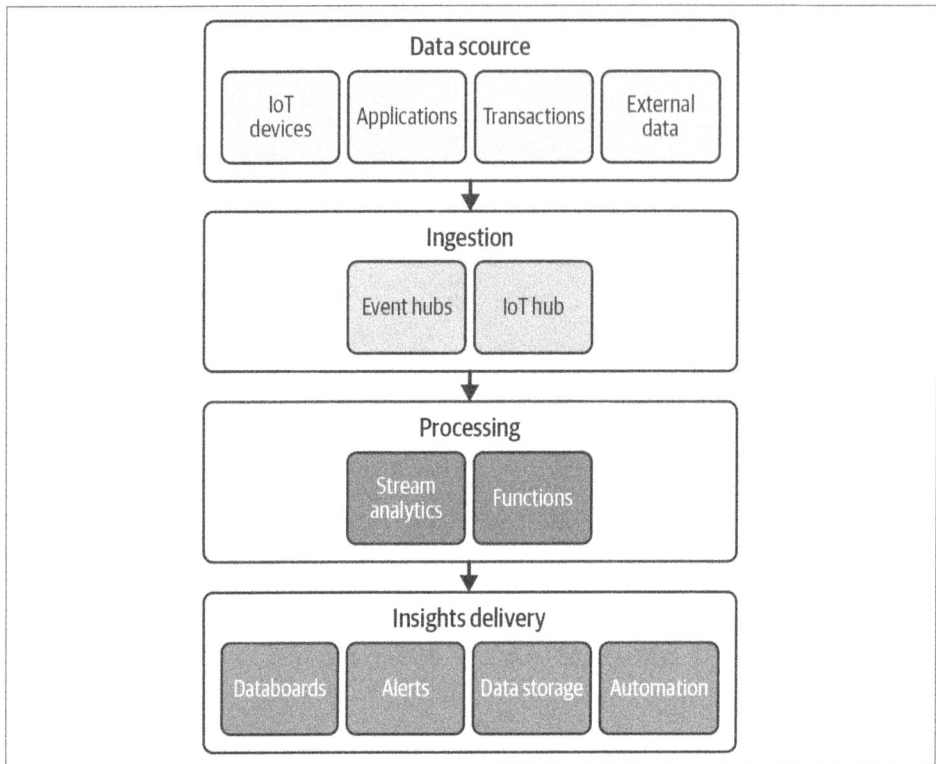

Figure 10-1. Real-time analytics pattern

For the DP-900 exam and anyone working with Azure, understanding real-time analytics is essential. Azure provides a comprehensive ecosystem of services designed specifically for ingesting, processing, analyzing, and acting on data in real time. These capabilities enable organizations to create systems that continuously monitor data streams and respond intelligently to changing conditions without human intervention.

Coverage of Curriculum Objectives

This chapter addresses the following DP-900 exam objectives:

- Describe considerations for real-time data analytics.
- Describe the difference between batch and streaming data.
- Identify Microsoft cloud services for real-time analytics.

Understanding Real-Time Analytics

Real-time analytics fundamentally changes the relationship between data and decision making. Traditional analytics often involves collecting data over time, storing it in databases or data warehouses, and then periodically analyzing it to identify patterns and insights. This approach, while valuable for historical analysis and long-term planning, introduces significant delays between when events occur and when organizations can react to them. Real-time analytics eliminates this delay, enabling immediate awareness and response to events as they happen.

Exam Tip

The DP-900 exam frequently tests your ability to differentiate scenarios where real-time analytics provides significant advantages over traditional batch processing. Look for clues in questions about time sensitivity, immediate response requirements, or continuous monitoring needs that indicate real-time approaches would be most appropriate.

The Time-Value Relationship of Data

The value of data often correlates directly with its freshness. Like many perishable goods, data can lose significant value as time passes from its creation to its analysis and application. This time-value relationship varies dramatically across different scenarios, creating a spectrum of analytical needs from truly real-time to near-real-time to periodic batch analysis.

Consider fraud detection in credit card transactions. When a fraudulent purchase occurs, the value of detecting it diminishes rapidly with time. Identifying fraud within milliseconds can block the transaction before it completes. Detection within seconds might prevent subsequent fraudulent purchases. Discovery within minutes could still limit financial damage. But finding the fraud during overnight batch processing likely means substantial losses have already occurred. In this scenario, the time-value curve drops precipitously, making real-time analysis essential.

Contrast this with inventory planning for a retail store. While recent sales data provides valuable input, the difference between analyzing sales patterns within seconds versus hours generally doesn't dramatically impact restocking decisions. The time-value curve declines much more gradually, making near-real-time or even batch processing potentially sufficient.

Understanding this time-value relationship helps organizations determine where real-time analytics delivers substantial business value versus where traditional approaches remain adequate. The most sophisticated organizations develop a nuanced view that applies different analytical approaches based on the specific time sensitivity of each use case.

When the time-value curve drops sharply—when immediate awareness and response significantly outperform delayed analysis—real-time analytics becomes essential. Following are some common scenarios where this occurs:

- Operational monitoring systems that detect equipment failures, network intrusions, or service disruptions require immediate awareness to minimize damage. Every second of delay in identifying issues can translate to significant financial or reputational costs.

- Customer experience optimization relies increasingly on real-time personalization based on current behaviors. Showing relevant recommendations while a customer browses an ecommerce site provides dramatically better results than sending suggestions the next day based on yesterday's behavior.

- Safety and security applications, from traffic management systems to industrial safety monitoring, depend on instantaneous detection of dangerous conditions. These scenarios have near-vertical time-value curves, where even seconds of delay can have severe consequences.

- Dynamic pricing systems in industries like transportation, hospitality, and energy adjust rates based on current supply and demand conditions. These mechanisms deliver optimal results when they incorporate the very latest market information in their calculations.

Exam Tip

The DP-900 exam emphasizes understanding when real-time analytics delivers substantial business value. Focus on recognizing scenarios where immediate insight and action provide significant advantages over delayed analysis.

The Evolution from Batch to Real-Time Analytics

To appreciate the transformative nature of real-time analytics, you need to understand how analytical approaches have evolved over time. This journey from periodic batch processing to continuous real-time analysis reflects both technological advances and changing business requirements.

Traditional batch analytics emerged in an era of more limited computational resources and simpler data environments. Organizations would collect data throughout the day, then process it during overnight windows when systems had spare capacity. This approach worked well when business processes operated on daily cycles and when competitive advantage didn't depend on immediate responsiveness. Reports generated each morning would inform the day's activities, creating a predictable rhythm of data collection, processing, and application.

As competitive pressures increased and digital transformation accelerated, organizations began to seek faster analytical cycles. This led to the development of microbatch processing, which reduced analytical windows from days to hours or even minutes. Instead of running major analysis jobs once daily, systems would process smaller batches of data more frequently. This approach maintained the fundamental batch paradigm but shortened the delay between data creation and analysis.

The true revolution came with stream processing, which fundamentally changed the analytical paradigm. Rather than collecting data and periodically processing it, stream analytics continuously processes each piece of information as it arrives. This eliminates the artificial boundaries between data collection and analysis, creating a continuous flow from event occurrence to insight generation and action. The result is analytical systems that can detect patterns, identify anomalies, and trigger responses within milliseconds of events occurring.

Exam Tip

While the DP-900 exam covers fundamental real-time analytics concepts, advanced patterns like Lambda and Kappa architectures that combine batch and streaming approaches are beyond the exam scope but worth noting for real-world implementations.

This evolution continues today with the development of complex event processing systems that can correlate multiple events across different streams to identify sophisticated patterns in real time. These advanced capabilities enable organizations to detect nuanced situations that would be invisible when looking at individual events or single data streams in isolation.

The technological progression from batch to stream processing parallels a business evolution from reactive to proactive to predictive operations. Real-time analytics enables organizations not just to respond quickly to events that have already occurred but increasingly to anticipate and prevent issues before they fully develop. This predictive capability represents the frontier of real-time analytics, where immediate analysis of current conditions informs predictions about future states, enabling truly proactive management.

The Architecture of Real-Time Analytics

Real-time analytics requires a fundamentally different architectural approach than traditional batch processing. While batch systems typically follow an ETL paradigm with clear separation between stages, real-time systems must continuously ingest, process, and deliver insights without these distinct boundaries. This architectural shift affects every component of the analytics pipeline.

A well-designed real-time analytics architecture generally includes several key components working together to convert continuous data streams into actionable insights.

The data source layer encompasses the diverse origins of streaming data—IoT devices sending telemetry, mobile applications reporting user activities, financial systems recording transactions, websites tracking visitor behaviors, and industrial equipment reporting operational metrics. Unlike batch systems that might connect to sources periodically, real-time architectures maintain continuous connections to these sources, often through publish-subscribe messaging patterns.

The ingestion layer receives and buffers incoming data streams, handling the potentially massive volume and velocity of real-time information. This critical component must scale dynamically to accommodate variable input rates while preventing data loss during volume spikes. Modern ingestion systems provide durability guarantees even under extreme load conditions, ensuring complete data capture regardless of downstream processing capacity.

The processing layer represents the analytical heart of the system, continuously analyzing incoming data to detect patterns, calculate metrics, identify anomalies, or recognize complex events. This component employs techniques like windowing (analyzing data within time-based or count-based boundaries), stateful processing (maintaining context across events), and pattern detection. The processing occurs continuously as data arrives, rather than waiting for batch boundaries.

The storage layer captures both raw streaming data and processed results, but with significant differences from batch storage. While batch systems might optimize primarily for analytical query performance, real-time storage must balance multiple requirements: low-latency access for immediate analysis, high-throughput ingestion for continuous data capture, and efficient long-term retention for historical analysis and compliance. This often leads to multitiered storage approaches where recent data resides in high-performance stores while older information moves to more cost-effective solutions.

The serving layer delivers insights to consumers through dashboards, alerts, APIs, or direct integration with operational systems. Unlike batch systems that might update reports daily, this layer continuously refreshes visualizations, triggers notifications, or invokes automated responses as new insights emerge. The focus shifts from comprehensive reports to targeted, actionable information delivered at the moment of maximum relevance.

Throughout these components, a monitoring and management layer provides observability into the health and performance of the real-time pipeline. This cross-cutting concern becomes especially critical in streaming systems, where issues can affect the accuracy and timeliness of ongoing analysis rather than simply delaying periodic batch jobs.

This architectural approach enables organizations to process data constantly rather than periodically, eliminating the inherent delays associated with batch processing. However, it also introduces new challenges around handling out-of-order data, managing system state, ensuring exactly-once processing semantics, and maintaining system performance under variable loads. Addressing these challenges requires specialized technologies and design patterns that differ significantly from traditional batch analytics.

Batch Versus Streaming Data

While we've touched on some differences between batch and streaming approaches, let's examine this distinction more thoroughly. Understanding the characteristics, advantages, and appropriate use cases for each paradigm helps organizations select the right approach for different analytical needs.

Figure 10-2 highlights the fundamental differences between batch and stream processing approaches. The batch model (top) shows data accumulating before periodic processing, while the streaming model (bottom) demonstrates continuous processing as each data point arrives. The diagram emphasizes how batch processing introduces inherent delays between data creation and insight generation, while streaming enables immediate analysis.

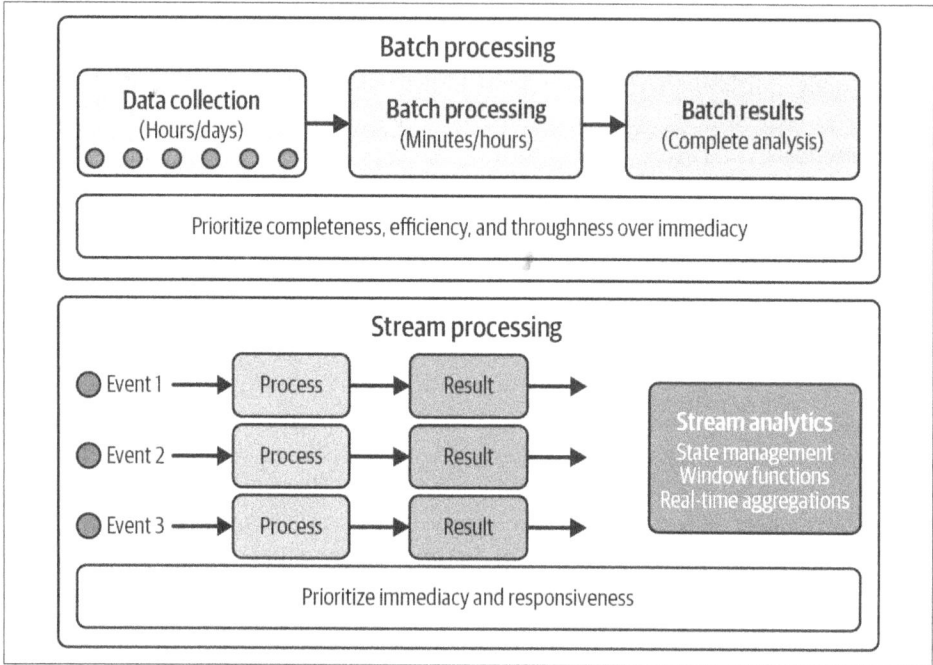

Figure 10-2. Comparing batch and stream processing

Characteristics of Batch Processing

Batch processing represents the traditional approach to data analytics, with a history stretching back to the earliest days of computing. Despite technological advances and the rise of streaming alternatives, batch processing remains appropriate and efficient for many scenarios. To understand when to use this approach, we need to recognize its fundamental characteristics.

At its core, batch processing operates on bounded datasets—collections of data that have definite beginning and ending points. These might be daily transaction records, monthly customer activity logs, or quarterly financial results. The bounded nature of these datasets enables several key characteristics of batch processing.

First, batch processes typically have complete visibility into the entire dataset before producing results. This completeness enables sophisticated analytical techniques that require multiple passes through the data or that analyze relationships across the entire dataset. Complex aggregations, joins between different data sources, and global optimizations become possible when the full dataset is available for processing.

Second, batch processes generally prioritize throughput over latency. Since they operate on data that's already been collected rather than requiring immediate processing of new events, they can optimize for efficient resource utilization and maximum data processing rates. This often leads to higher overall throughput at the cost of increased end-to-end processing time.

Third, batch processes tend to follow predictable, scheduled execution patterns. Organizations typically run batch jobs at regular intervals—nightly, weekly, or monthly—creating a rhythmic cycle of data collection, processing, and analysis. This predictability simplifies resource planning, as systems can allocate computing capacity according to known processing windows.

Finally, batch processing typically employs sophisticated fault tolerance mechanisms that prioritize data completeness and accuracy over processing speed. If errors occur during processing, batch systems can retry operations, restore from checkpoints, or even restart entire jobs to ensure accurate results. This approach acknowledges that getting the right answer eventually is more important than getting an approximate answer immediately.

These characteristics make batch processing well suited for several scenarios.

For example, historical analysis and reporting thrive under batch processing, where completeness and accuracy outweigh immediacy. Financial reporting, compliance documentation, and business intelligence dashboards comparing performance across extended periods benefit from the thoroughness of batch approaches.

Complex analytical workloads that require multiple processing stages or that integrate diverse datasets often work best as batch processes. Data science workflows, machine learning model training, and complex pattern detection across historical data leverage the computational efficiency of batch processing.

Resource-intensive processing that would strain systems if attempted in real time can operate efficiently through scheduled batch windows. Tasks like rebuilding recommendation models, recalculating complex network relationships, or processing high-resolution images benefit from the controlled resource allocation of batch approaches.

Real-World Scenario

A financial institution processes loan applications through a nightly batch system that incorporates credit history, income verification, property appraisals, and risk assessments. This approach allows comprehensive analysis of all factors before making lending decisions, prioritizing accuracy and completeness over immediate approvals. While not providing instant decisions, this overnight batch process still meets customer expectations for mortgage applications while ensuring thorough risk evaluation.

Characteristics of Streaming Data

In contrast to the bounded, periodic nature of batch processing, streaming data represents a continuous, never-ending flow of information. This fundamental difference in data characteristics necessitates entirely different processing approaches. Understanding these characteristics helps clarify when streaming analytics delivers substantial advantages.

Streaming data is inherently unbounded—it has no defined beginning or end but continues flowing indefinitely. This continuous nature reflects many real-world processes: customer interactions with websites, sensor readings from IoT devices, financial market transactions, and social media activity. These information sources don't produce cleanly packaged datasets with clear boundaries but generate endless sequences of events.

The unbounded nature of streaming data leads to several important characteristics. First, streaming data typically arrives with time sensitivity, where the value of each data point diminishes rapidly after creation. While batch data might retain consistent value whether processed immediately or hours later, streaming data often contains signals requiring prompt detection and response. This time sensitivity drives the need for immediate processing rather than periodic analysis.

Second, streaming data generally arrives at variable rates rather than in predictable volumes. A social media monitoring system might see dramatic spikes during major events, while an IoT platform might experience daily patterns reflecting human activity cycles. This variability challenges processing systems to scale dynamically rather than allocating fixed resources as many batch systems do.

Third, streaming data often requires stateful processing that maintains context across events. While batch processes can analyze complete datasets to identify patterns, streaming systems must detect meaningful signals incrementally as data arrives. This requires maintaining state information—tracking cumulative metrics, remembering recent events, or building evolving profiles—to provide the context needed for analysis.

Finally, streaming data frequently contains time-based relationships that affect its processing. Events might arrive out of chronological order due to network delays or device characteristics. Analytical windows might need to span time periods to identify patterns. Common windowing approaches include tumbling windows (fixed, nonoverlapping time periods), sliding windows (overlapping time periods), and session windows (variable periods based on activity). These temporal aspects introduce complexities that don't exist in batch processing, where the entire dataset is available for analysis regardless of creation time.

These characteristics make streaming analytics essential for several key scenarios.

Monitoring and alerting applications depend on continuous data analysis to detect anomalies, threshold violations, or emerging patterns that require attention. Whether monitoring network security, industrial equipment performance, or patient vital signs, these applications need immediate awareness of changing conditions.

Real-time decision systems leverage streaming analytics to make automated choices based on current conditions. Dynamic pricing engines, fraud detection systems, and automated trading platforms all require instantaneous analysis to function effectively.

Customer experience optimization increasingly depends on understanding and responding to user behavior as it happens. Personalization engines, recommendation systems, and contextual assistance features deliver maximum value when they incorporate the most recent user actions.

Operational intelligence across transportation networks, utility grids, telecommunications systems, and supply chains relies on continuous awareness of current conditions. These complex systems benefit from real-time dashboards and control systems that reflect actual conditions rather than historical states.

Exam Tip

The DP-900 exam tests your understanding of when streaming analytics provides essential capabilities versus where batch processing remains appropriate. Focus on recognizing time sensitivity, continuous data characteristics, and immediate response requirements that indicate streaming approaches are needed.

When to Use Each Approach

Given their fundamental differences, how should organizations determine which processing approach best fits their analytical needs? Several key considerations influence this decision, helping to match technical approaches with business requirements.

Time sensitivity represents perhaps the most crucial factor. When the value of insights diminishes rapidly after events occur—when minutes or seconds matter—streaming analytics becomes essential. Applications requiring immediate anomaly detection, real-time decision making, or instantaneous personalization benefit from the minimal latency of streaming approaches. Conversely, when analytical value remains relatively constant whether delivered immediately or hours later, batch processing may provide sufficient timeliness while offering advantages in efficiency and completeness.

Analytical complexity influences approach selection significantly. Batch processing excels at complex, multistage analytical workflows that require multiple passes through data or sophisticated joins across diverse datasets. The ability to see the entire dataset enables global optimizations and complex algorithms that may be difficult or impossible in streaming contexts. Streaming analytics, while increasingly sophisticated, still faces greater challenges with complex analytical requirements due to its incremental processing nature.

Data completeness requirements affect paradigm choice substantially. Some analytical scenarios demand exhaustive processing of every relevant data point to deliver valid results. Financial reconciliation, compliance reporting, and certain scientific analyses fall into this category, generally favoring batch approaches that can ensure comprehensive data inclusion. Other scenarios can deliver valuable insights from partial or sampled data, making them suitable for streaming approaches even with their inherent possibility of missing information during processing transitions or failures.

Technical infrastructure considerations often influence processing decisions. Organizations with substantial investments in batch processing systems may extend these platforms rather than adopting entirely new streaming architectures. Conversely, cloud native organizations building new analytical capabilities may embrace streaming-first approaches that leverage modern cloud services designed for real-time analytics.

The most sophisticated organizations recognize that batch and streaming aren't competing alternatives but complementary approaches addressing different analytical needs. These organizations develop nuanced strategies that apply each paradigm where it delivers maximum value, often implementing lambda architectures that combine both approaches within unified analytical frameworks. This pragmatic perspective focuses on matching processing characteristics to business requirements rather than advocating universally for either batch or streaming.

Exam Warning

The DP-900 exam often presents scenarios asking you to select the most appropriate processing approach. Be careful not to automatically choose streaming for every scenario. Instead, recognize when batch processing provides adequate timeliness while offering advantages in completeness, efficiency, or analytical complexity.

Microsoft Cloud Services for Real-Time Analytics

Having explored the concepts and characteristics of real-time analytics, let's examine how Microsoft implements these capabilities in Azure. The cloud has revolutionized real-time analytics by providing fully managed services that eliminate much of the infrastructure complexity traditionally associated with stream processing. Azure offers a comprehensive ecosystem of services designed specifically for ingesting, processing, analyzing, and visualizing streaming data.

Azure Event Hubs

At the foundation of many real-time analytics architectures lies Azure Event Hubs, a cloud native event ingestion service designed to capture and buffer massive volumes of streaming data. Think of Event Hubs as a specialized digital funnel—capable of receiving millions of events per second from distributed sources, preserving their order within partitions, and making them available for downstream processing.

Event Hubs serves as the entry point for streaming data from diverse sources: IoT devices sending telemetry, web applications tracking user activities, logging systems recording service operations, or custom applications producing event streams. Its primary responsibility involves efficiently capturing this continuous flow of information, providing temporary buffering, and enabling multiple downstream systems to process the same events independently.

Several key capabilities make Event Hubs particularly valuable for real-time analytics scenarios.

Massive scalability enables ingestion of millions of events per second with submillisecond latency. This performance capacity handles both consistent high-volume streams and unexpected traffic spikes that might overwhelm less robust ingestion systems. Organizations can start with minimal capacity and scale dynamically as streaming volumes grow.

Partitioning provides the fundamental organizing principle for streaming data within Event Hubs. The service distributes incoming events across partitions based on partition keys, maintaining strict ordering of events within each partition. This structure enables parallel processing while preserving sequence relationships for events sharing the same key—a critical capability for analyzing related events in the correct order.

The publisher-subscriber model allows multiple independent consumers to process the same event streams without interfering with each other. Each consumer tracks its own position within the stream, enabling diverse applications to analyze the same events at different rates or using different processing approaches. This capability supports sophisticated architectures where multiple analytical systems operate concurrently on the same data streams.

Time retention features maintain events for configurable periods, typically between one and seven days. This temporary persistence enables replay of recent events for analytical purposes or recovery after downstream processing failures. The retention provides a buffer that decouples event producers from consumers, allowing each component to operate at its own pace within reasonable time frames.

Event Hubs particularly excels in high-volume ingestion scenarios that benefit from its partitioning approach and temporary retention capabilities.

IoT telemetry collection represents a perfect fit for Event Hubs, with its ability to handle millions of device messages while preserving their sequence within device-specific partitions. The service's support for AMQP (Advanced Message Queuing Protocol, an enterprise messaging standard) and MQTT (Message Queuing Telemetry Transport, a lightweight protocol designed for IoT devices) enables direct integration with many IoT devices and gateways.

Application monitoring systems increasingly adopt event-driven architectures (systems that respond to events as they occur rather than operating on fixed schedules) that feed operational metrics, logs, and trace information into analytics pipelines. Event Hubs serves as an ideal ingestion point for these monitoring events, enabling real-time operational awareness across distributed applications.

Activity tracking for websites, mobile applications, and digital services generates valuable behavioral data for analysis. Event Hubs efficiently captures these user interaction events, making them available for immediate processing to power personalization, anomaly detection, or experience optimization.

Exam Tip

For the DP-900 exam, understand that Azure Event Hubs specializes in high-volume event ingestion and temporary buffering for streaming data. Its particular strengths include massive scalability, partitioned event organization, and support for multiple concurrent consumers of the same event streams.

Azure Stream Analytics

While Event Hubs excels at capturing streaming data, Azure Stream Analytics provides the analytical engine needed to derive meaning from these continuous information flows. Stream Analytics enables real-time querying of data streams using a SQL-like language, making sophisticated streaming analysis accessible to the many data professionals already familiar with SQL.

Stream Analytics processes continuous streams of data through persistent queries that analyze events as they arrive rather than waiting for batch boundaries. These queries apply filtering, aggregation, pattern detection, and joining operations to incoming events, producing analytical results with minimal latency. The service handles the complexity of distributed processing, state management, and fault tolerance, allowing developers to focus on analytical logic rather than infrastructure concerns.

Several distinctive capabilities make Stream Analytics particularly valuable for real-time analytical scenarios.

Temporal processing represents a core strength, with built-in support for time-based operations like windowing, filtering by time properties, or handling late-arriving data. The service intelligently manages event timestamps, enabling analysis based on when events occurred rather than when they arrived for processing. This temporal awareness is crucial for analyzing real-world event sequences where network delays or device limitations might affect transmission timing.

Its SQL-based query language dramatically simplifies streaming analytics development. Rather than requiring specialized programming skills, Stream Analytics enables analysts with SQL experience to create powerful streaming queries using familiar syntax. The language extends standard SQL with streaming-specific features like windowing functions, geospatial operations, and pattern matching, creating an accessible yet powerful analytical environment.

Reference data joins combine streaming events with static datasets to provide essential context. For example, a stream of IoT sensor readings might join with a device metadata table to incorporate location, type, and configuration information. This capability connects real-time events with the organizational context needed for meaningful analysis, bridging between streaming and batch data worlds.

Integration with the broader Azure ecosystem enables end-to-end streaming pipelines. Stream Analytics connects natively with Event Hubs and IoT Hub for input, while supporting diverse output destinations including databases, storage services, analytical systems, and visualization tools. This connectivity simplifies the construction of complete streaming solutions that transform raw events into actionable insights.

Figure 10-3 illustrates how Azure Stream Analytics processes data streams through persistent queries. Input adapters connect to event sources like Event Hubs or IoT Hub; event data flows through SQL-like analytical queries that filter, aggregate, and transform the information; and output adapters deliver results to destinations ranging from databases to visualization tools. The architecture emphasizes how Stream Analytics maintains continuous processing of incoming events, delivering analytical results with minimal latency.

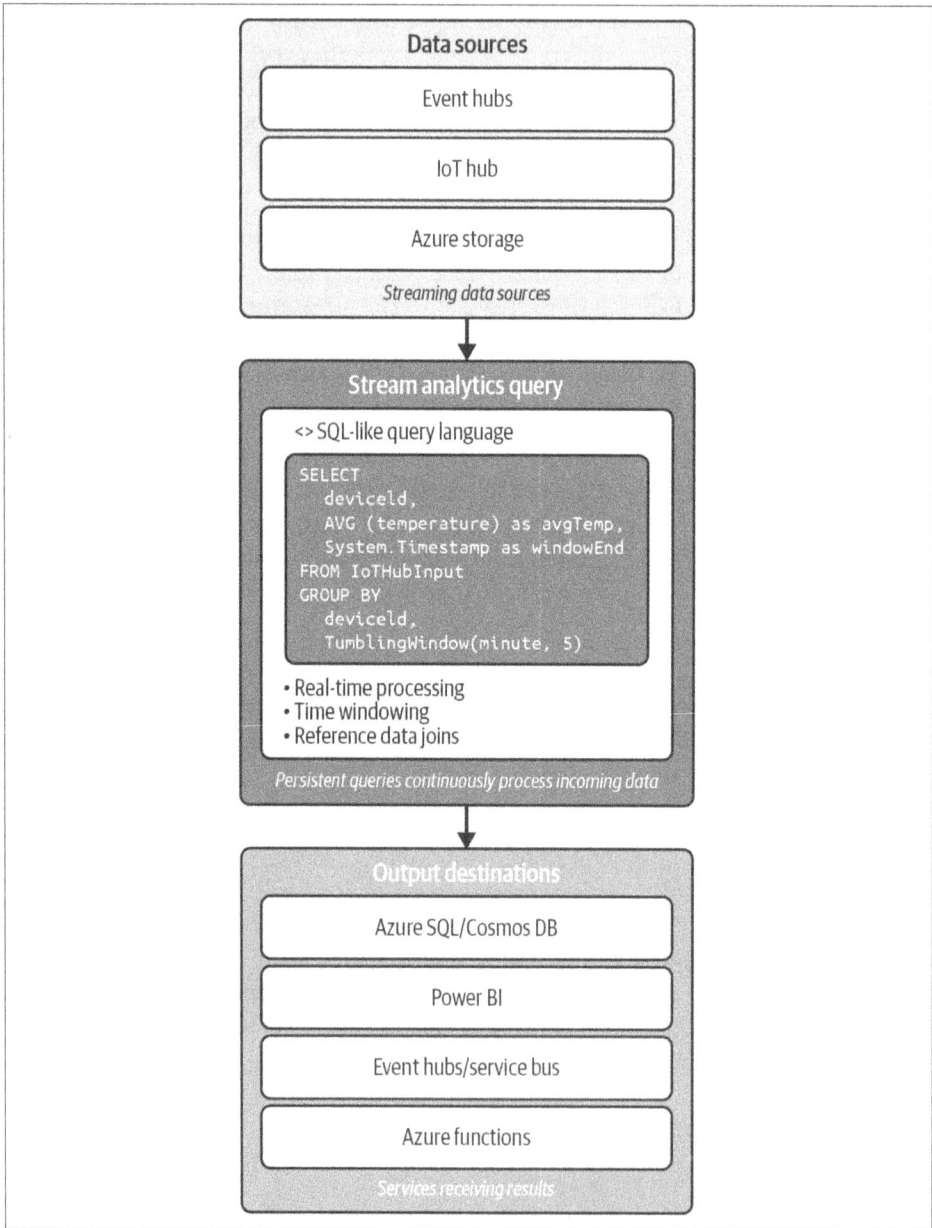

Figure 10-3. Persistent queries with Azure Stream Analytics

Stream Analytics particularly excels in analytical scenarios requiring continuous query processing with SQL-like semantics.

IoT analytics leverages Stream Analytics to monitor and analyze telemetry from connected devices. The service can detect threshold violations, calculate moving averages across measurement windows, identify anomalous patterns, or trigger alerts based on complex event combinations. These capabilities enable scenarios from industrial monitoring to smart building management.

Note that Stream Analytics has limitations with complex multiway joins and built-in machine learning support. For these advanced scenarios, consider Azure Databricks with Spark Structured Streaming.

Business activity monitoring applies Stream Analytics to operational event streams, providing real-time visibility into organizational processes. The service can track key performance indicators, detect process bottlenecks, or identify exceptional conditions requiring intervention. This continuous monitoring transforms traditional business processes into adaptively managed operations responding to actual conditions.

Media stream analysis employs Stream Analytics for processing metadata from media streams, social platforms, or content delivery networks. While not processing the media content itself, the service analyzes viewer behaviors, quality metrics, or consumption patterns, enabling adaptive content delivery and personalized experiences.

Real-World Scenario

A utility company uses Stream Analytics to process millions of smart meter readings hourly, detecting anomalous consumption patterns that might indicate meter tampering, infrastructure leaks, or billing issues. The streaming queries compare current usage against historical patterns, time-of-day expectations, and neighborhood averages to identify outliers requiring investigation. This real-time awareness enables proactive service management that would be impossible with traditional batch processing of meter data.

Azure Synapse Analytics

While we explored Azure Synapse Analytics in detail in the previous chapter focusing on large-scale analytics, it deserves mention here for its significant real-time analytics capabilities. Synapse Analytics provides integrated streaming support within its comprehensive analytics platform, enabling organizations to incorporate real-time data processing alongside batch analytics, data warehousing, and machine learning.

Synapse Analytics integrates streaming analytics through several key capabilities.

Synapse Link creates change data capture connections to operational databases like Cosmos DB, automatically streaming changes into analytical storage for immediate analysis. This capability eliminates traditional ETL delays between operational systems and analytical environments, enabling near-real-time analytics on operational data without impacting transaction processing.

Synapse Pipelines supports streaming data ingestion through integration with Event Hubs, IoT Hub, and other real-time sources. These pipelines can continuously move streaming data into Synapse analytical environments, making it available for immediate processing without manual intervention.

Spark Structured Streaming leverages Apache Spark within Synapse to provide code-based stream processing using Python, Scala, or .NET. This capability enables sophisticated streaming analytics that might require complex algorithms, machine learning models, or custom processing logic beyond what's possible with SQL-based approaches.

Integration with Stream Analytics allows organizations to incorporate Stream Analytics queries within larger Synapse analytical workflows. This integration enables scenarios that combine the SQL-based simplicity of Stream Analytics with the comprehensive analytical capabilities of the broader Synapse platform.

Synapse Analytics particularly excels at scenarios requiring integration between streaming and batch analytics.

Operational analytics benefits from Synapse's ability to combine real-time operational data with historical context. Organizations can monitor current business metrics while simultaneously analyzing longer-term trends and patterns, providing both immediate awareness and deeper understanding of performance drivers.

Combined streaming and batch pipelines enable sophisticated lambda architectures where systems process data through both real-time and batch paths. Synapse supports these hybrid approaches within a unified platform, simplifying the implementation of architectures that deliver both immediate insights and comprehensive analytical results.

Near-real-time data warehousing leverages Synapse's streaming capabilities to continuously update dedicated SQL pools with fresh information. This approach reduces the latency between operational events and their availability for analytical querying, supporting business intelligence scenarios that benefit from current rather than day-old information.

Azure Data Explorer

For organizations dealing with particularly high-volume telemetry data or requiring specialized time-series analysis, Azure Data Explorer (ADX) provides unique capabilities optimized for these scenarios. ADX offers a fully managed analytics service designed specifically for high-volume log and telemetry data analysis, with exceptional performance for interactive querying of massive datasets.

While not exclusively focused on real-time processing, ADX includes significant streaming capabilities that make it valuable for near-real-time analytics on continuous data streams. The service can ingest millions of events per second directly from Event Hubs or IoT Hub, making them available for querying within seconds of creation. This combination of massive ingestion capacity and immediate query availability supports scenarios requiring interactive analysis of high-volume telemetry.

Several distinctive capabilities make ADX particularly valuable for certain streaming analytics scenarios:

Kusto Query Language (KQL)
This expressive language provides a powerful purpose-built language for analyzing log and telemetry data. It combines elements of SQL with unique operators designed specifically for time-series data, pattern matching, and telemetry analysis. While requiring some learning investment, KQL enables remarkably concise and powerful analytical queries against streaming and historical data.

Time-series optimizations
Having these throughout the system delivers exceptional performance for time-based queries. The service employs specialized indexing, storage formats, and query processing techniques designed specifically for the patterns common in log and telemetry data. These optimizations enable fast performance even when querying billions of events across extended time periods.

Multitier storage architecture
This automatically manages data across performance tiers based on age. Recent data remains in memory and SSD storage for fast interactive querying, while older information transitions to cooler storage tiers for cost-effective retention. This automated tiering ensures optimal performance for recent data while maintaining access to historical information for long-term analysis.

Interactive querying at scale
This sets ADX apart from many streaming technologies. Rather than focusing exclusively on continuous processing of new events, ADX enables analysts to interactively explore massive telemetry datasets, iteratively refining queries to investigate patterns or anomalies. This interactive capability bridges between streaming and exploratory analytics paradigms.

These capabilities combine to create a uniquely powerful platform for organizations dealing with massive volumes of time-series data. The seamless integration of streaming and historical analysis enables use cases that would otherwise require multiple specialized systems.

Azure Data Explorer particularly excels in scenarios involving high-volume telemetry and log analytics:

Application performance monitoring
This leverages ADX to collect and analyze telemetry from thousands of application instances, enabling detection of performance issues, usage patterns, or error conditions. The service's ability to handle billions of daily events while providing interactive query performance enables effective monitoring of large-scale application deployments.

IoT platform analytics systems
These systems employ ADX to analyze telemetry from massive device fleets, identifying patterns, anomalies, or maintenance requirements. The service's time-series optimizations and scalable architecture make it ideal for scenarios involving millions of connected devices generating continuous data streams.

Security monitoring systems
These increasingly use ADX to analyze authentication events, network traffic logs, and security signals at scale. The service's pattern matching capabilities and performance with high-cardinality datasets enable sophisticated threat hunting and anomaly detection across enterprise security telemetry.

For organizations with demanding telemetry analysis requirements, Azure Data Explorer offers a compelling combination of scalability, performance, and specialized capabilities. As data volumes continue to grow exponentially, particularly in IoT and application monitoring domains, ADX provides a future-proof foundation for extracting actionable insights from massive telemetry streams.

Azure Event Grid

While not a processing engine itself, Azure Event Grid deserves mention for its central role in reactive real-time architectures. Event Grid provides a fully managed event routing service that enables event-driven architectures and real-time integration between systems. This service handles the complexity of event distribution, connecting event producers with interested consumers without requiring direct integration between components.

Event Grid serves as the nervous system for many real-time applications, propagating events through the architecture to trigger analytical and operational responses. It follows a publish-subscribe model where sources publish events to topics, and subscribers receive those events through filtered subscriptions. This decoupled approach enables flexible, extensible architectures where new event handlers can be added without modifying existing components.

Several key capabilities make Event Grid valuable for real-time analytical architectures:

Event-driven triggering

This enables analytical processes to execute in response to specific events rather than running on fixed schedules. This reactive approach ensures that analytical resources activate only when relevant events occur, improving efficiency while maintaining responsiveness to important signals.

Filtering mechanisms

These allow subscribers to only receive events matching specific patterns. This targeted delivery ensures that analytical components process only relevant events, reducing unnecessary computation and focusing resources on valuable analyses. Filters can select events based on event types, subject patterns, or data attributes.

Reliable delivery with retry logic

This ensures that critical events reach their destinations despite temporary network or system issues. Event Grid automatically retries delivery when subscribers are unavailable, maintaining persistence until successful delivery or expiration. This reliability proves crucial for analytical systems that must process every relevant event without gaps.

Serverless integration

This enables event-driven analytical architectures without managing messaging infrastructure. Event Grid connects natively with Azure Functions, Logic Apps, and other serverless components, enabling sophisticated event processing without dedicated infrastructure. This approach simplifies implementation of real-time analytical workflows triggered by specific events.

These capabilities combine to make Event Grid a foundational service for modern event-driven architectures. By separating event producers from consumers and providing reliable, scalable event routing, Event Grid enables more modular, maintainable, and responsive real-time analytical systems.

Event Grid particularly excels at scenarios requiring event-driven analytics and integration:

Analytical workflow orchestration

This uses Event Grid to coordinate processing across distributed analytical components. When one processing stage completes, it publishes events that trigger subsequent stages, creating dynamic analytical pipelines that respond to actual data flows rather than operating on fixed schedules.

Cross-service integration

This leverages Event Grid to connect operational systems with analytical environments. When important business events occur in operational applications, Event Grid routes notifications to analytical systems for immediate processing, maintaining tight coupling between business operations and analytical insights.

Reactive analytics

This employs Event Grid to activate specialized analytical processes in response to specific conditions. Rather than continuously analyzing all data, these systems conserve resources by performing detailed analysis only when trigger events indicate potentially interesting situations requiring investigation.

As organizations increasingly adopt event-driven architectures, Event Grid's role as a central nervous system for real-time applications becomes even more vital. Its combination of reliability, flexibility, and native integration with both operational and analytical services makes it an essential component in modern cloud native analytical platforms.

> **Exam Tip**
>
> For the DP-900 exam, understand that Azure Event Grid specializes in event routing and reactive architecture patterns rather than stream processing. Its value in real-time analytics comes from orchestrating event-driven workflows and connecting event sources with analytical systems.

Azure Functions

When real-time analytics requires custom processing logic, Azure Functions provides the ideal serverless compute environment for implementing specialized analytical components. Functions enables event-driven code execution without managing infrastructure, allowing developers to focus on analytical logic rather than computing platforms. This serverless approach perfectly complements streaming analytics by providing flexible, scalable processing for events flowing through real-time architectures.

Azure Functions integrates directly with many event sources, including Event Hubs, Event Grid, Cosmos DB change feed, and IoT Hub. These native bindings enable Functions to trigger automatically when new data arrives, process the information using custom code, and output results to downstream systems. The result is responsive event-driven analytics that scales automatically with incoming data volume.

Azure Functions excels at implementing custom processing logic beyond what SQL-based approaches can express, with support for multiple programming languages and automatic scaling based on event volume.

These capabilities make Azure Functions a versatile and powerful component in real-time analytical architectures. The combination of event-driven execution, language flexibility, and seamless integration provides a foundation for implementing custom analytical logic that responds immediately to incoming data.

Figure 10-4 illustrates how Azure Functions enables event-driven analytics within a real-time architecture. Event sources on the left generate data that flows through Azure Service Bus, triggering functions that execute custom analytical logic. These functions process the events and produce outputs that flow to downstream systems on the right for storage, visualization, or operational action. The architecture demonstrates how Azure Functions provides responsive, customizable analytical capabilities that scale automatically with event volume.

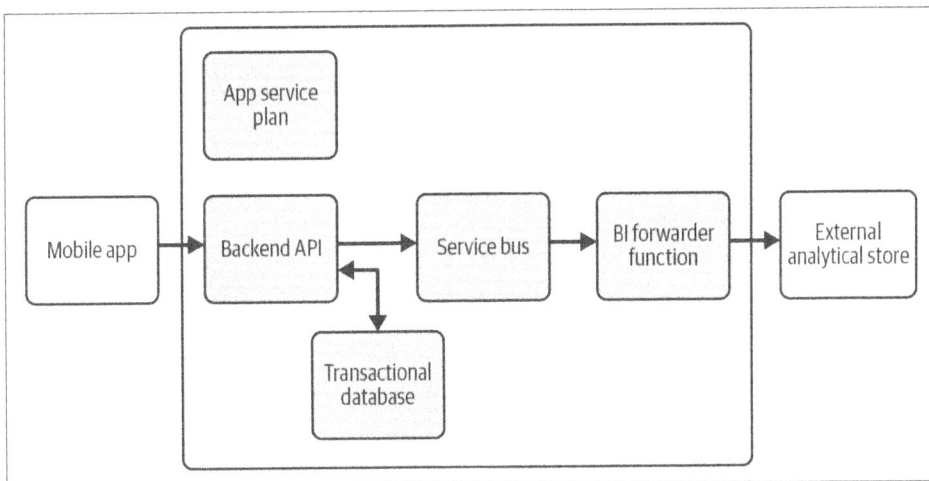

Figure 10-4. Azure Functions as BI forwarder

Azure Functions particularly excels at scenarios requiring custom analytical processing:

- Custom analytics beyond standard query capabilities leverage Functions to implement specialized algorithms not easily expressed in SQL-like languages. Whether applying domain-specific business rules, complex statistical techniques, or proprietary analytical methods, Functions provides the flexibility to execute custom code against streaming data.

- Machine learning inferencing in real time applies trained models to streaming events through Functions. While model training typically occurs in batch environments, Functions can apply these trained models to incoming events, enabling immediate scoring and classification within streaming pipelines. This approach combines the thoroughness of batch training with the responsiveness of real-time application.

- Multistep analytical pipelines employ Functions to orchestrate complex processing across multiple stages. Using Durable Functions, organizations can implement sophisticated workflows that maintain state across event boundaries, aggregate information over time windows, or coordinate parallel processing paths within analytical architectures.

As organizations increasingly adopt event-driven architectures for real-time analytics, Azure Functions provides the essential capabilities for implementing custom processing logic without infrastructure management overhead. Its combination of scalability, language flexibility, and integration capabilities makes it an ideal platform for extending streaming analytics beyond standard query capabilities.

Real-World Scenario

An energy trading company uses Azure Functions to apply proprietary pricing models to streaming market data. When new pricing information arrives from exchanges, Functions triggers immediately to recalculate optimal trading positions using algorithms embodying the company's unique market insights. These calculations incorporate both the latest prices and contextual information about market conditions, energy demand forecasts, and current portfolio positions. The results flow to trading dashboards and automated trading systems, enabling rapid response to market opportunities that might exist for only seconds before others identify them.

Azure IoT Hub

For real-time analytics specifically focused on Internet of Things scenarios, Azure IoT Hub provides specialized capabilities beyond general-purpose event ingestion. While Event Hubs excels at generic event streams, IoT Hub adds device-centric features essential for IoT scenarios: bidirectional communication, device management, per-device authentication, and protocol support specifically designed for connected devices.

From an analytics perspective, IoT Hub serves as both a data source feeding telemetry into streaming analytics pipelines and an action channel for returning analytical results to devices. This bidirectional capability enables closed-loop systems where analytics drives immediate device behavior rather than simply recording information for later analysis. The result is responsive IoT systems that adapt to changing conditions based on real-time analytical insights.

Several key capabilities make IoT Hub valuable for real-time IoT analytics.

For example, device telemetry ingestion provides the foundation for IoT analytics, capturing measurements, status information, and event data from connected devices. IoT Hub scales to millions of simultaneously connected devices, each sending continuous telemetry streams for analysis. This ingestion includes built-in support for protocols common in IoT scenarios, including MQTT, AMQP, and HTTPS.

Built-in routes direct device data to different analytical systems based on message properties or content. This message routing enables sophisticated architectures where critical telemetry flows to real-time processing while routine information takes different paths. The routing occurs without device awareness, allowing analytical architectures to evolve independently from device firmware.

Device-to-cloud and cloud-to-device messaging enables bidirectional communication essential for analytical feedback loops. After processing device telemetry through analytical pipelines, systems can send commands back to specific devices through IoT Hub's reliable messaging infrastructure. This bidirectional capability enables architectures where analytics directly influence device behavior in near-real time.

Integration with the broader Azure analytics ecosystem connects IoT Hub with Stream Analytics, Functions, Event Grid, and other analytical services. This native integration simplifies construction of end-to-end IoT analytics pipelines from device telemetry acquisition through processing to insight delivery and action.

IoT Hub particularly excels at scenarios requiring device-aware analytics with feedback loops.

For example, predictive maintenance analytics leverages IoT Hub to collect equipment telemetry, process it through analytical pipelines to detect potential failures, and deliver maintenance commands back to devices or field service systems. The bidirectional communication enables both monitoring and intervention within a single architecture.

Smart environment management employs IoT Hub to connect building systems, environmental sensors, and control devices into analytical feedback loops. Telemetry from throughout the environment feeds real-time analytics that optimize comfort, energy efficiency, and space utilization, with results driving immediate adjustments to building systems.

Connected vehicle platforms use IoT Hub to manage bidirectional communication with vehicle fleets, enabling real-time analytics for route optimization, predictive maintenance, and operational monitoring. The device management capabilities provide secure, reliable connectivity even in challenging network environments with intermittent connectivity.

How to Choose the Right Real-Time Analytics Services

With multiple Azure services supporting real-time analytics, how should organizations select the appropriate components for their specific scenarios? Rather than viewing these services as competing alternatives, it's more helpful to recognize how they complement each other within end-to-end analytical pipelines. Most real-time analytics solutions combine multiple services, each addressing specific requirements within the overall architecture.

Several key considerations guide service selection for different architectural components.

Data ingestion requirements significantly influence the choice between Event Hubs and IoT Hub for the initial capture of streaming data. When scenarios focus specifically on IoT, with requirements for device management, bidirectional communication, and IoT-specific protocol support, IoT Hub provides the ideal foundation. For more general event streaming scenarios without these device-specific needs, Event Hubs offers a more streamlined approach focused purely on high-volume event ingestion.

Processing requirements guide the selection of analytical engines for real-time data. Stream Analytics provides the simplest approach for scenarios where SQL-like queries can express the required analytical logic. Functions becomes essential when scenarios require custom processing beyond what query languages can express. For high-volume telemetry analysis with interactive exploration needs, Data Explorer offers unique capabilities optimized specifically for these workloads.

Integration patterns influence architectural choices substantially. Event Grid becomes particularly valuable when architectures require event-driven coordination across multiple components, decoupling producers from consumers while ensuring reliable event delivery. Synapse Analytics deserves consideration when real-time analytics needs to integrate with broader data warehousing and big data processing within unified analytical environments.

Skill sets and organizational capabilities often guide practical service choices. Teams with strong SQL skills might leverage Stream Analytics as their primary processing engine, while those with data science backgrounds might prefer code-based approaches using Functions or Spark Structured Streaming. The most successful implementations align technology choices with existing team capabilities while strategically building new skills where they deliver significant value.

Most sophisticated real-time analytics solutions in Azure combine multiple services into integrated pipelines addressing end-to-end scenarios. These architectures typically include specialized components for ingestion, processing, storage, and visualization, all working together to transform raw data streams into actionable insights.

Bringing It All Together: Real-Time Analytics in Practice

Now that you've explored the concepts, components, and architectures of real-time analytics, let's examine how these elements come together in a real-world scenario. This practical perspective helps illustrate how organizations translate technical capabilities into business value.

Consider TransGlobal Logistics, a fictional international transportation and logistics organization managing complex supply chains across multiple transportation modes, warehouses, and distribution centers. The organization is implementing real-time analytics in Azure to gain comprehensive visibility into its operations, detect potential disruptions, and respond proactively to changing conditions. Its journey illustrates the practical application of the concepts we've discussed throughout this chapter.

The Data Landscape

TransGlobal Logistics faces classic real-time analytics challenges that exemplify why traditional batch approaches no longer suffice. Its global operations generate continuous streams of time-sensitive information that requires immediate analysis for maximum value.

Vehicle telemetry flows continuously from thousands of trucks, ships, and aircraft, reporting location, speed, fuel levels, engine performance, cargo conditions, and environmental factors. This telemetry arrives from diverse device types using multiple communication protocols, with update frequencies varying based on criticality and connectivity.

Logistics systems track every step in complex supply chains, from initial order placement through warehouse operations to final delivery. These systems generate transactional events for shipment status changes, inventory movements, documentation processing, and customer interactions, creating a detailed digital record of physical operations.

IoT sensors throughout warehouses and distribution centers monitor temperature, humidity, motion, access control, and equipment status. These sensors detect environmental conditions affecting cargo, security events requiring immediate response, and operational metrics revealing process efficiency.

External data streams provide essential context for logistics operations, including weather conditions affecting transportation routes, traffic congestion impacting delivery times, port congestion affecting maritime operations, and customs delays influencing international shipments. These external factors often determine whether shipments arrive as scheduled or face disruptions.

The combined data landscape presents classic volume, velocity, and variety challenges, with thousands of data sources generating millions of events hourly in diverse formats. More importantly, the time-value relationship for this information drops precipitously—insights that might prevent delivery delays provide enormous value when available immediately but offer little benefit when discovered after shipments are already late.

The Analytics Architecture

To address these challenges, TransGlobal Logistics implemented a comprehensive real-time analytics architecture in Azure, leveraging multiple services in an integrated ecosystem. Its solution transforms continuous data streams into actionable insights that improve operational efficiency, customer satisfaction, and financial performance.

For data ingestion, TransGlobal Logistics deployed a hybrid approach addressing both IoT and business event streams. Azure IoT Hub manages connectivity with its transportation fleet and warehouse sensors, providing device authentication, bidirectional communication, and protocol support for diverse device types. Event Hubs captures business events from logistics applications, external data feeds, and partner systems, providing high-throughput ingestion for these nondevice sources. Both services feed their real-time analytical pipeline while maintaining event copies in Azure Data Lake Storage Gen2 for later batch analysis.

The processing layer employs multiple technologies addressing different analytical needs. Azure Stream Analytics provides the primary analytical engine, continuously analyzing telemetry and events using SQL-like queries that identify important patterns, calculate real-time metrics, and detect anomalous conditions. Azure Functions handles specialized processing requirements beyond Stream Analytics capabilities, implementing proprietary algorithms for route optimization, delivery time prediction, and risk assessment. Azure Data Explorer stores and analyzes historical telemetry alongside real-time data, enabling interactive investigation of patterns and anomalies across both current and historical information.

For insight delivery, the organization created a multifaceted approach addressing different consumer needs. Power BI real-time dashboards provide operational visibility for logistics managers, displaying current fleet status, shipment progress, warehouse conditions, and potential disruptions with automatic updates as conditions change. An alerting system leverages Event Grid to deliver targeted notifications for specific conditions requiring human intervention, routing these alerts to appropriate personnel based on event characteristics. A Cosmos DB operational data store maintains current state information for all active shipments, providing a continuously updated view accessible through custom applications.

Throughout this architecture, Event Grid provides the integration fabric connecting components into a cohesive system. When Stream Analytics detects anomalies, Event Grid routes these events to appropriate notification systems, operational dashboards, and response workflows. When Functions completes route optimizations, Event Grid delivers the results to fleet management systems and driver applications. This event-driven approach maintains loose coupling between components while ensuring reliable event delivery throughout the architecture.

Implementation Approach

Rather than attempting to build this entire architecture at once, TransGlobal Logistics took an incremental approach that delivered value at each stage while building toward its comprehensive vision.

The organization began with a focused implementation addressing high-value transportation visibility. This initial phase connected the TransGlobal Logistics vehicle fleet through IoT Hub and implemented Stream Analytics processing to track shipment progress, detect potential delays, and calculate real-time fleet metrics. Power BI dashboards provided dispatchers with current fleet visibility, while an alerting system notified relevant personnel about potential delivery issues. This targeted implementation delivered immediate operational improvements while establishing the foundation for broader capabilities.

Building on this foundation, the organization next incorporated warehouse and distribution center monitoring. This phase expanded its IoT footprint to include environmental and operational sensors throughout physical facilities, with Stream Analytics processing to detect inventory conditions, security events, and process inefficiencies. The resulting insights enabled improved inventory management, reduced product damage from environmental factors, and enhanced warehouse productivity.

With both transportation and warehouse visibility established, the organization implemented predictive disruption detection leveraging Azure Functions and machine learning models. In this phase, sophisticated algorithms were developed to predict potential supply chain disruptions before they affected customer deliveries, analyzing patterns across transportation telemetry, warehouse operations, and external factors. The resulting predictive capabilities enabled proactive rerouting, resource reallocation, and customer communication that transformed potential disruptions into managed situations.

The most recent phase implemented closed-loop optimization that continuously refines operations based on real-time conditions. This capability analyzes current fleet positions, delivery commitments, traffic conditions, and warehouse status to dynamically optimize routing, loading, and scheduling decisions. The system continuously adapts to changing conditions throughout the day rather than following static plans, resulting in improved asset utilization and delivery performance.

This phased approach delivered value at each stage while building toward a comprehensive real-time analytics ecosystem. It allowed the organization to learn from each phase before proceeding to the next, adjusting its implementation based on real-world experience rather than theoretical planning. It also enabled the organization to demonstrate tangible business impact early in the process, building organizational momentum and support for continued investment.

Summary

The shift to real-time analytics represents a fundamental transformation in how organizations derive value from their data. Azure provides a comprehensive ecosystem of services designed to address the unique challenges of ingesting, processing, analyzing, and acting on data in real time.

Throughout this chapter, you explored how:

- Real-time analytics fundamentally changes the relationship between data and decision making by eliminating delays between event occurrence and insight generation.
- The distinction between batch and streaming approaches involves fundamental differences in data characteristics, processing paradigms, and architectural patterns.
- Azure offers specialized services for real-time analytics, including Event Hubs, Stream Analytics, IoT Hub, Functions, and Data Explorer.

Exam Tip

The DP-900 exam frequently presents scenarios asking you to select the most appropriate real-time analytics services for specific requirements. Focus on understanding the primary purpose and strengths of each service rather than memorizing detailed features or configuration options.

Exam Essentials

For success on the DP-900 exam, focus on these key areas:

- Understanding real-time analytics fundamentals:
  - Know the characteristics that distinguish real-time from traditional batch analytics.
  - Understand the time-value relationship for data and how it influences analytical approaches.
  - Recognize scenarios where real-time analytics provides essential capabilities.
  - Identify the key components of real-time analytical architectures.
- Grasping batch versus streaming differences:
  - Understand the fundamental differences between batch and streaming data characteristics.
  - Know the contrasting processing paradigms for batch and streaming analytics.
  - Recognize when each approach provides appropriate capabilities for specific scenarios.
  - Understand how organizations combine batch and streaming approaches in comprehensive architectures.
- Identifying Azure real-time analytics services:
  - Know the primary purpose of each Azure service supporting real-time analytics.
  - Understand which service is most appropriate for different streaming scenarios.
  - Recognize how these services integrate into end-to-end analytical architectures.

Beyond the Exam

While studying for the DP-900 exam provides an excellent foundation in understanding Azure's real-time analytics concepts and services, real-world implementations often involve additional considerations beyond exam coverage. Having implemented real-time analytics solutions across industries, I've observed several factors that significantly influence success but might not appear directly on certification exams.

Organizational Readiness

Despite its technical nature, successful real-time analytics depends as much on organizational factors as on technological capabilities. Several key organizational elements significantly influence implementation outcomes.

Operational culture represents perhaps the most critical success factor for real-time analytics initiatives. Organizations accustomed to daily or weekly decision cycles often struggle initially with the immediacy that real-time analytics enables. Successful implementations include change management efforts that help operational teams adapt to continuous awareness and more frequent decision making. This cultural evolution often proves more challenging than the technical implementation itself.

Process integration determines whether real-time insights actually drive operational improvements. Analytics that doesn't connect to decision processes creates "interesting but not actionable" information that rarely justifies its implementation cost. The most successful organizations explicitly redesign operational processes to incorporate real-time insights, creating clear pathways from analytical detection to operational response. These pathways might involve human decision makers for complex situations or automated responses for well-understood scenarios.

Skills development across both technical and business teams significantly influences adoption success. Technical teams need skills in streaming technologies, event-driven architectures, and real-time visualization approaches that differ from traditional batch analytics. Business teams need familiarization with real-time capabilities, understanding of detection limitations, and training in effective response to the immediate insights these systems provide.

I worked recently with a transportation company whose real-time analytics implementation initially struggled despite solid technical architecture. The turning point came when the company established a cross-functional "control tower" team combining technical and operational expertise with explicit authority to respond to emerging situations. This organizational innovation, combined with process redesign and targeted training, transformed analytical capabilities into operational improvements that delivered substantial business value.

Implementation Realities

Beyond the conceptual understanding that certification exams assess, real-world implementations face practical challenges that require pragmatic approaches.

Legacy integration presents significant challenges when implementing real-time analytics alongside existing systems. Many operational applications weren't designed for event-driven integration or real-time data exposure, requiring creative approaches to extract actionable information without disrupting critical business systems. Successful implementations often employ change data capture (CDC), log parsing, API polling, or agent-based approaches to derive real-time events from systems designed for batch interaction.

Edge-cloud architecture decisions significantly impact real-time analytics implementations, particularly for IoT scenarios with remote or bandwidth-constrained devices. Rather than sending all raw telemetry to cloud analytics, sophisticated implementations employ edge processing to filter, aggregate, or analyze data locally before transmission. This approach reduces bandwidth requirements, limits cloud processing costs, and enables faster response to critical conditions through local detection and action.

Hybrid deployment models predominate in real-world implementations, combining cloud analytics with on-premises operational systems. While certifications often focus on cloud native architectures, practical implementations must bridge between cloud analytics and existing infrastructure. Successful designs include gateway components, hybrid networking, and secure integration patterns that connect cloud analytics with on-premises operational technology.

A manufacturing client recently implemented real-time quality monitoring using a pragmatic hybrid approach. Edge devices performed initial analysis of production line sensor data, detecting potential quality issues locally for immediate intervention. These devices also sent filtered telemetry to Azure for fleet-wide pattern analysis, model training, and cross-facility optimization. This hybrid architecture balanced immediate response needs against comprehensive analytics, delivering value without requiring complete infrastructure replacement.

Emerging Directions

The real-time analytics landscape continues to evolve rapidly, with several emerging directions extending beyond current certification coverage:

Digital twin approaches increasingly complement traditional telemetry analytics, providing contextual models that enhance real-time understanding. Rather than analyzing raw sensor data in isolation, digital twin architectures maintain virtual representations of physical assets that incorporate design specifications, maintenance history, and relationship models. This contextual foundation enables more sophisticated real-time analytics that understands not just what's happening but also what it means within the broader operational context.

Converged OLTP-OLAP architectures blur traditional boundaries between operational and analytical systems. Technologies like Cosmos DB Analytical Store, SQL Hyperscale with read replicas, and Synapse Link enable near-real-time analytics directly against operational data without traditional ETL delays. This convergence enables analytical insight within the operational decision window, transforming analytics from a separate activity into an integrated aspect of operational systems.

Edge-to-cloud intelligence distribution creates sophisticated analytical pipelines spanning from device endpoints through edge computing to cloud platforms. These architectures distribute analytical workloads based on latency requirements, bandwidth constraints, and centralization benefits. Time-critical detection occurs at the edge for immediate response, while pattern recognition across devices leverages cloud analytics for comprehensive understanding. This distributed approach optimizes both responsiveness and analytical depth.

As you move beyond certification to real-world implementation, remember that real-time analytics represents a journey rather than a destination. Technologies will continue to evolve, but the fundamental principles of capturing time-sensitive data, processing it immediately, and delivering actionable insights remain constant. The solid foundation provided by understanding Azure's real-time analytics services will serve you well as you navigate this evolving landscape.

CHAPTER 11

Data Visualization with Power BI

In a world awash with data, the ability to transform raw numbers into meaningful insights represents one of the most valuable skills in modern business. Data visualization stands at the intersection of analytical thinking and visual communication, enabling us to discover patterns, identify trends, and communicate findings in ways that drive understanding and action. Microsoft Power BI has emerged as a transformative tool in this space, democratizing access to sophisticated data visualization and analysis capabilities that were once available only to specialized analysts.

Think of Power BI as the bridge between your organization's data and the decisions it informs. Traditional approaches to business intelligence often created bottlenecks where technical experts had to mediate between data and business users. Power BI fundamentally changes this dynamic by providing intuitive tools that enable business professionals to directly explore data, create visualizations, and share insights without requiring deep technical expertise. This democratization accelerates the journey from data to insight to action, enabling organizations to become truly data driven in their decision making.

The Power BI visualization framework shown in Figure 11-1 shows how data flows from diverse sources through transformation and modeling to create interactive visualizations and dashboards. The diagram illustrates the progression from data connection on the left through preparation, modeling, visualization, and sharing on the right, highlighting how Power BI unifies these previously separate processes into a cohesive analytical experience.

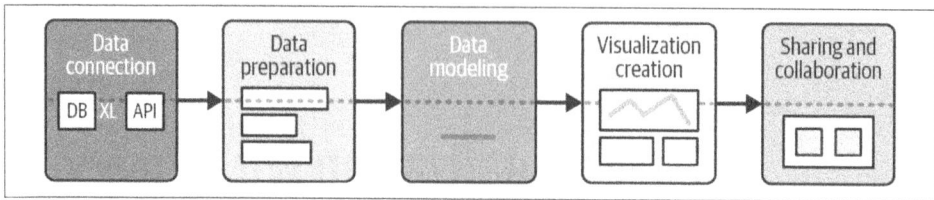

Figure 11-1. Power BI overall framework

For the DP-900 exam and anyone working with Azure's data ecosystem, understanding Power BI is essential. As Microsoft's flagship business intelligence platform, Power BI integrates seamlessly with Azure data services, forming a crucial component in the modern data toolkit. Whether you're visualizing results from Azure Synapse Analytics, creating dashboards from Azure Data Explorer queries, or building reports from Azure SQL Database, Power BI provides the visualization layer that translates sophisticated data processing into accessible business insights.

Coverage of Curriculum Objectives

This chapter addresses the following DP-900 exam objectives:

- Describe data visualization in Microsoft Power BI.
- Identify capabilities of Power BI.
- Describe features of data models in Power BI.
- Identify appropriate visualizations for data.

Understanding Data Visualization

Before diving into the specifics of Power BI, it's important to understand the foundational principles of data visualization and why it has become such a critical component of modern data strategies. At its core, data visualization leverages the human brain's remarkable capacity for visual processing to make complex information more accessible, patterns more obvious, and insights more compelling.

Exam Tip

The DP-900 exam often presents scenarios asking you to identify appropriate visualization approaches for specific business requirements. Focus on understanding the connection between business questions and data types, and the visualizations that effectively answer those questions.

The Power of Visual Communication

The human brain processes visual information extraordinarily efficiently—neuroscience research indicates that most of the brain is devoted to visual processing when compared to touch and hearing.[1] This biological advantage gives visual communication tremendous power to convey complex information quickly and memorably. Effective data visualizations leverage this neural capacity to translate abstract numbers into visual patterns that we can intuitively grasp, often revealing insights that might remain hidden in rows and columns of numbers.

This visual advantage becomes increasingly important as organizations contend with the growing volume and complexity of data. When an analyst reviews a spreadsheet with dozens of columns and thousands of rows, identifying patterns requires substantial mental effort and time. The same data presented through thoughtful visualization can reveal patterns, outliers, and trends almost immediately. This efficiency doesn't just save time. It fundamentally changes how we interact with information, enabling more exploratory approaches and rapid iteration through analytical questions.

Beyond mere efficiency, visualization often reveals insights that might never emerge from examining raw data. Our visual system excels at pattern recognition in ways that complement statistical analysis. A skilled analyst might identify a correlation coefficient between variables, but visualization can reveal whether that correlation is consistent across the data range, is influenced by outliers, or contains interesting subpatterns that warrant further investigation. This complementary relationship between quantitative analysis and visual exploration forms the foundation of modern business intelligence.

Visualization also transforms how we communicate findings to others. While technical specialists might comfortably interpret complex tables or statistical outputs, most business decision makers absorb information more effectively through visual formats. A well-designed dashboard or report doesn't merely present data. It tells a story, highlights key insights, and guides viewers toward informed decisions. This narrative quality makes visualization particularly valuable for driving organizational alignment around data-informed strategies.

The Evolution of Business Intelligence

To appreciate Power BI's significance, it helps to understand the evolution of business intelligence and the challenges that traditional approaches face. Early business intelligence followed a highly centralized model where IT departments controlled data

---

1 David C. Van Essen, "Organization of Visual Areas in Macaque and Human Cerebral Cortex," in *Visual Neurosciences*, ed. L. Chalupa and J. Werner, March 2, 2020, *https://www.cns.nyu.edu/csh/csh04/Articles/Vanessen-03.pdf*.

access and specialized analysts created reports. While this model ensured data quality and governance, it created significant bottlenecks: business users often waited weeks or months for new reports, limiting the organization's ability to respond quickly to new questions or changing conditions.

The first wave of democratization came through self-service reporting tools that gave business users more direct access to data and reporting capabilities. However, these tools often separated different aspects of the analytical workflow across multiple systems: data preparation might occur in one tool, modeling in another, visualization in a third, and sharing through yet another platform. This fragmentation created friction in the analytical process and required users to develop expertise across multiple systems.

Power BI represents the next evolution—a unified platform that integrates the complete analytical workflow from data connection through preparation, modeling, visualization, and sharing. This integrated approach dramatically reduces the technical barriers to sophisticated analysis, enabling business users to answer their own questions without waiting for specialized support. The result is more agile, responsive decision making that leverages data assets more effectively across the organization.

This democratization doesn't eliminate the need for data professionals. Rather, it transforms their role from report creators to platform enablers who establish data models, governance frameworks, and analytical patterns that business users can leverage. The result is a collaborative ecosystem where technical specialists and business experts work together more effectively, with each contributing their unique expertise to the analytical process.

Exam Tip

For the DP-900 exam, understand that Power BI represents a unified approach to business intelligence that integrates previously separate processes (data connection, preparation, modeling, visualization, and sharing) into a cohesive platform accessible to both business users and data professionals.

The Analytical Workflow

Understanding how Power BI supports the complete analytical workflow helps contextualize its various components and capabilities. This workflow represents the journey from raw data to actionable insights, incorporating several key stages that work together to transform information into understanding.

The analytical journey typically begins with data connection—accessing the diverse sources where relevant information resides. Modern organizations rarely store all their valuable data in a single location; instead, it's distributed across operational systems, data warehouses, cloud platforms, SaaS applications, and local files. Power BI provides hundreds of built-in connectors that simplify access to this distributed landscape, enabling analysts to bring together information regardless of where it physically resides.

Once connected, data often requires transformation before it's suitable for analysis. Raw operational data typically contains inconsistencies, missing values, or structural issues that must be addressed to enable reliable analysis. Sometimes the required information exists but needs restructuring to answer specific analytical questions. The data preparation stage addresses these challenges, cleaning and shaping information into a form that supports the intended analysis.

With clean, properly structured data available, the modeling stage establishes relationships between different data elements and defines the analytical foundation. This stage creates a semantic layer that translates raw data into business concepts, establishing metrics, hierarchies, and relationships that align with how the organization understands its operations. Effective modeling makes complex data accessible to business users by expressing it in familiar terms rather than technical structures.

The visualization stage transforms modeled data into charts, graphs, maps, and other visual formats that reveal patterns and communicate findings. This stage leverages visual design principles to highlight important insights, provide context for interpretation, and enable interactive exploration. Effective visualization doesn't merely present data attractively. It thoughtfully selects visual formats that highlight the most important aspects of the information for the specific questions being addressed.

Finally, the sharing stage delivers insights to stakeholders who can take action based on the analysis. This might involve publishing interactive dashboards, distributing static reports, embedding visualizations in operational applications, or collaborating on analytical findings. The sharing stage closes the loop from data to decision, ensuring that analytical work drives real business impact rather than remaining isolated in analytical tools.

Throughout this workflow, Power BI provides integrated capabilities that enable smooth progression from one stage to the next without switching between disparate tools. This integration significantly reduces the technical barriers to sophisticated analysis, enabling business users to complete the entire journey from question to insight within a unified environment.

Figure 11-2 shows the analytical workflow as implemented in Power BI, highlighting how different Power BI tools support each stage of the journey from data to insight. The diagram shows Power BI Desktop spanning the connection, preparation, modeling, and visualization stages, while Power BI Service extends across visualization and sharing. Power BI Dataflows support the preparation stage, and Power BI Report

Builder provides additional visualization capabilities. The workflow emphasizes how Power BI provides integrated capabilities across the entire analytical process.

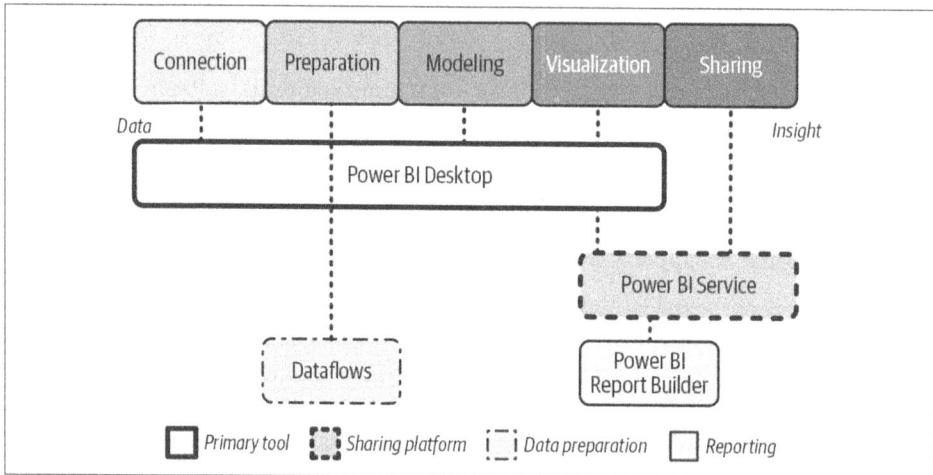

Figure 11-2. Power BI suite of capabilities

Power BI Capabilities

With this foundational understanding of data visualization and the analytical workflow, let's explore the specific capabilities that Power BI provides to support data-driven decision making. Power BI isn't a single application but rather a family of connected tools and services that work together to deliver a comprehensive business intelligence platform.

Power BI Components

The Power BI ecosystem includes several core components that serve different parts of the analytical workflow and different user needs. Understanding these components and how they interrelate helps organizations implement effective Power BI strategies that balance self-service flexibility with appropriate governance and control.

Power BI Desktop represents the primary authoring environment for creating reports and data models. This free Windows application provides comprehensive capabilities for connecting to data, transforming it into suitable analytical structures, establishing data models, and creating interactive visualizations. Desktop serves as the development environment where most complex analytical work occurs before publishing to the Power BI Service for broader consumption.

Power BI Service provides the cloud-based platform for sharing, collaborating on, and consuming Power BI content. After developing reports in Desktop, analysts publish them to Power BI Service, where they can be organized into workspaces, assembled into dashboards, scheduled for automatic refresh, and shared with appropriate audiences. Service also provides web-based editing capabilities for creating and modifying reports directly in the browser, though with somewhat fewer capabilities than the full Desktop application.

Power BI Mobile offers tailored applications for iOS, Android, and Windows devices that enable consumption of Power BI content while on the go. These applications provide secure access to reports and dashboards optimized for touch interfaces and smaller screens, ensuring that decision makers can access critical insights regardless of their location. Mobile apps support both online access to the latest data and offline viewing of previously accessed reports when connectivity isn't available.

Power BI Report Builder supports paginated reports—precisely formatted, pixel-perfect documents optimized for printing or PDF generation. While standard Power BI reports excel at interactive analysis, paginated reports address scenarios requiring exact layout control, such as invoices, statements, or regulatory documents. Report Builder complements the core Power BI tools by addressing these specialized formatting requirements that interactive reports aren't designed to handle.

Power BI Dataflows enable centralized data preparation that multiple reports can leverage. Rather than having each report implement its own data transformation logic, dataflows establish reusable preparation pipelines that promote consistency and efficiency. These dataflows can be created through the same visual interface available in Power BI Desktop or through more advanced options for data engineers, providing appropriate tools for different user expertise levels.

Real-World Scenario

A healthcare provider uses different Power BI components for different audiences and needs. Clinical analysts use Power BI Desktop to develop sophisticated reports analyzing patient outcomes and treatment effectiveness. They publish these reports to Power BI Service where department heads access interactive dashboards showing key performance indicators. Doctors and nurses use the Power BI Mobile app to check patient metrics while making rounds. The finance department uses Report Builder to create precisely formatted cost reports for regulatory submission. Throughout the organization, dataflows ensure that patient, treatment, and financial data is consistently prepared for analysis regardless of which team is using it.

These components work together to form a comprehensive ecosystem that supports different aspects of the analytical workflow and different organizational roles. Power BI Desktop provides the robust development environment needed by analysts creating sophisticated reports. Power BI Service delivers the sharing and collaboration platform that connects creators with consumers. Mobile apps ensure access regardless of location. Report Builder addresses specialized formatting needs. Dataflows promote reusability and consistency in data preparation. By providing integrated components tailored to different needs, Power BI enables effective collaboration between technical and business users throughout the analytical process.

Connectivity and Data Access

The journey from data to insight necessarily begins with accessing relevant information. Power BI excels at connecting to the remarkably diverse data landscape that modern organizations maintain, providing hundreds of built-in connectors that simplify integration across data sources. This connectivity capability transforms how organizations leverage their distributed data assets, enabling comprehensive analysis across previously siloed information.

Power BI's database connectivity spans the spectrum from traditional on-premises databases to modern cloud platforms. Built-in connectors support Microsoft SQL Server, Oracle, MySQL, PostgreSQL, and other common database systems regardless of whether they're hosted on premises or in cloud environments. These connectors handle the technical complexities of database connectivity while providing options for importing data into the Power BI model or querying it directly through Direct-Query mode.

Cloud platform integration provides seamless connectivity with Azure data services and other cloud platforms. Power BI connects natively to Azure SQL Database, Azure Synapse Analytics, Azure Data Explorer, Cosmos DB, and other Azure data services. This integration extends beyond Microsoft's ecosystem to include AWS services like Redshift and S3, Google's BigQuery, and other cloud platforms, enabling comprehensive analysis regardless of where data resides.

Application connectivity enables analysis of data from hundreds of business applications and services. Built-in connectors for Salesforce, Dynamics 365, SAP, Service-Now, Google Analytics, and many other applications provide access to valuable operational data without requiring technical extraction processes. These application connectors particularly benefit business analysts who need to analyze data from the systems they use daily but lack the technical expertise to extract it through custom integration methods.

File and content system support ensures access to information stored in less structured formats across organizational repositories. Power BI easily connects to data in Excel files, CSV documents, XML files, JSON data, and other common formats. This connectivity extends to content systems like SharePoint, OneDrive, Google Drive, Dropbox, and other platforms where organizations store document-based information, enabling analysis of data regardless of its storage format.

Internet and service connectivity provides access to online data sources ranging from web services and REST APIs to public datasets. Power BI can connect to OData feeds, web APIs, Azure DevOps, GitHub, and many other service-based data sources. The platform also provides access to curated public datasets through the Power BI Datamarket, enabling enrichment of internal data with external information for more comprehensive analysis.

This exceptional connectivity transforms how organizations approach analysis by dramatically reducing the technical barriers to comprehensive data integration. Rather than requiring specialized ETL processes or developer resources to access distributed information, business analysts can directly connect to relevant sources through intuitive interfaces. The result is more agile, responsive analysis that leverages more of the organization's data assets to drive better decision making.

Data Transformation and Preparation

Raw data rarely arrives in the perfect form for analysis. Power BI provides robust capabilities for transforming and preparing data, enabling analysts to clean, reshape, and enhance information before visualization. These capabilities bridge the gap between how data is stored for operational purposes and how it needs to be structured for effective analysis.

Power Query serves as the primary data preparation engine within Power BI, providing a visual interface for defining transformation steps without requiring programming expertise. Through this interface, analysts can filter rows, remove or rename columns, change data types, split or merge columns, unpivot data for better analysis, and perform hundreds of other transformations through intuitive dialogues. Behind the scenes, Power Query generates M code (Power Query Formula Language) that defines these transformations as a reproducible sequence that applies automatically when data refreshes.

For advanced users, Power Query supports direct editing of the underlying M code, enabling more sophisticated transformations beyond what the visual interface provides. This multilayered approach makes data preparation accessible to business analysts while providing the depth needed by data professionals, accommodating different skill levels within the same platform.

Data cleansing capabilities address the quality issues commonly found in raw operational data. Power BI can automatically detect and fix inconsistent values, handle missing data through removal or replacement, and standardize formatting for dates, numbers, and text. These cleansing capabilities ensure that analysis builds on reliable information rather than being undermined by data quality issues.

Structural transformations reshape data to better support analytical needs. Power BI can pivot or unpivot data to convert between wide and tall formats, split hierarchical fields into separate columns, generate date tables that enable time intelligence, and implement other structural changes that align data with analytical requirements. These transformations bridge between how systems naturally store data and how it needs to be structured for effective visualization and analysis.

Data enrichment features enhance source information with additional context that improves analytical value. Power BI can merge multiple tables to combine related information, append similar tables to consolidate data from different periods or systems, add custom columns calculated from existing fields, and implement sophisticated grouping operations. These enrichment capabilities enable more nuanced analysis by connecting and extending data beyond what individual source systems provide.

Query folding optimization automatically pushes appropriate transformations back to source database systems rather than processing them within Power BI. When connecting to databases like SQL Server or Azure Synapse Analytics, Power BI intelligently translates transformation steps into native SQL queries that execute on the source system. This optimization leverages the processing power of database platforms while minimizing data transfer, significantly improving performance for large datasets.

Data Modeling

At the heart of effective business intelligence lies the data model—the semantic layer that transforms raw data into business-meaningful concepts, relationships, and calculations. Power BI provides sophisticated modeling capabilities that establish the analytical foundation upon which visualizations build, enabling business users to interact with data in familiar terms rather than technical structures.

Relationship management establishes connections between different tables in the model, enabling integrated analysis across related information. Power BI automatically detects potential relationships based on column names and values, while also providing manual controls for defining more complex connections. These relationships enable natural navigation across business dimensions—such as analyzing sales by customer, product, and time period—without requiring users to understand the technical joins that connect underlying tables.

The relationships in Power BI support various cardinality types (one-to-many, many-to-one, many-to-many) and filtering behaviors (single direction, bidirectional), accommodating complex business models while maintaining performance. This flexibility enables representation of sophisticated business relationships while providing appropriate control over how filters propagate through the model during analysis.

Power BI's tabular modeling approach, based on the Microsoft Analysis Services engine, organizes data into tables and columns that users can understand without database expertise. Rather than exposing technical structures like database schemas, the model presents information in business terms—sales amount rather than `transac tion.amount_decimal` and customer name rather than `cust_lname_tx`. This business-oriented representation makes data more accessible to nontechnical users while maintaining the necessary analytical rigor.

The Data Analysis Expressions (DAX) language provides a formula language specifically designed for analytical calculations within tabular models. DAX enables the definition of calculated columns that derive new values within tables, measures that calculate aggregations based on user selections, and calculated tables that generate new structures based on existing data. Through these calculation capabilities, Power BI transforms basic data into rich analytical metrics that directly answer business questions.

DAX particularly excels at time intelligence calculations that analyze performance over time periods, comparisons between different periods, and cumulative values across time. Functions like `SAMEPERIODLASTYEAR`, `TOTALYTD`, and `DATEADD` simplify otherwise complex time-based analysis, enabling business users to track performance trends without implementing sophisticated date handling logic. These time intelligence capabilities prove especially valuable for monitoring business performance against historical benchmarks and targets.

Advanced modeling features address more complex analytical requirements through sophisticated capabilities. Row-level security restricts data access based on user identity, ensuring that individuals see only information appropriate for their role. Perspectives create focused views of the model for different business purposes. Model calculation groups establish reusable calculation patterns. Composite models combine imported data with DirectQuery connections to balance performance with freshness. These advanced features enable Power BI to support enterprise-scale analytical needs while maintaining appropriate governance.

Exam Tip

For the DP-900 exam, understand that Power BI's modeling capabilities create a semantic layer that translates technical data structures into business-meaningful concepts and calculations, enabling business users to analyze information in familiar terms rather than technical structures.

Visualization and Analysis

With data connected, prepared, and modeled, Power BI's visualization capabilities transform information into interactive insights that reveal patterns and drive decisions. Rather than providing just a fixed library of charts, Power BI delivers a comprehensive visualization platform that combines a rich selection of built-in visuals with extensive customization options and an expandable framework for specialized needs.

The built-in visualization library includes dozens of standard charts and graphs covering the core analytical requirements that most business scenarios demand. Bar and column charts for comparing values across categories, line and area charts for analyzing trends over time, scatter and bubble charts for examining relationships between variables, pie and donut charts for showing composition, tables and matrices for presenting detailed information—these fundamental visuals address the most common analytical needs directly out of the box.

Beyond these standard options, Power BI includes specialized visualizations for particular analytical purposes: maps for geographic analysis, treemaps and sunbursts for hierarchical data, waterfalls for cumulative impact, funnels for sequential processes, gauges and cards for key metrics, decomposition trees for multilevel analysis, and many others. This specialized library ensures appropriate visualization options for diverse analytical requirements without requiring custom development.

Figure 11-3 showcases the diverse visualization options available in Power BI, arranged by analytical purpose. The top section displays comparison visuals like bar charts, column charts, and radar charts. The middle section shows trend visualizations including line charts, area charts, and waterfalls. The bottom section illustrates relationship visualizations such as scatterplots, treemaps, and network diagrams. Each visual type is shown with a small example illustration in the right pane, demonstrating the range of visualization approaches available for different analytical purposes.

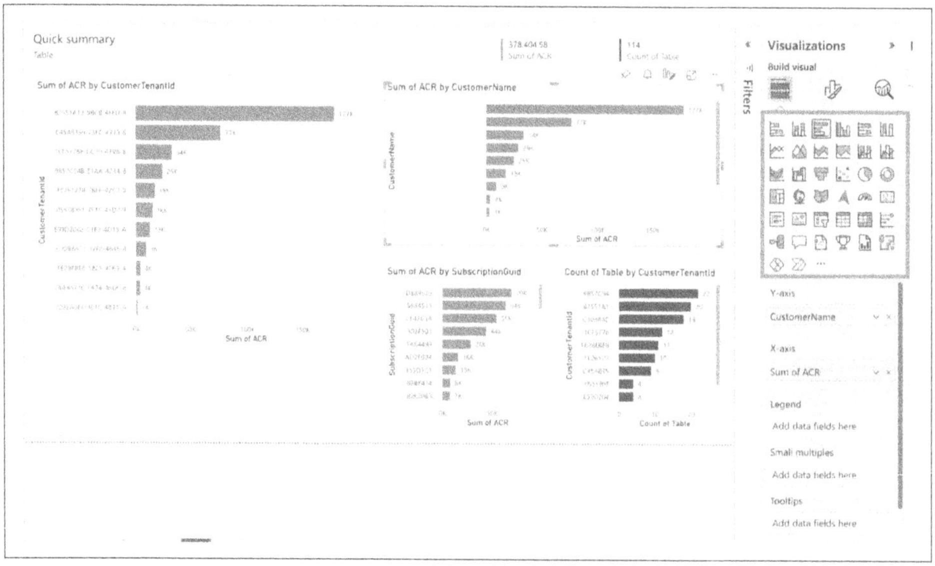

Figure 11-3. Power BI visualizations

Interactive features transform static visualizations into dynamic analytical tools that users can manipulate to explore data from different perspectives. Cross-filtering enables selection in one visual to automatically highlight related information in other visuals, revealing relationships across different aspects of the data. Slicers and filters provide intuitive controls for focusing analysis on specific dimensions or values. Drill-down capabilities enable navigation from summary information to increasing levels of detail. These interactive elements transform the analytical experience from passive consumption to active exploration.

The custom visualization framework extends Power BI's capabilities through an open platform for specialized visuals. The marketplace includes hundreds of custom visuals created by Microsoft and third-party developers, addressing specialized needs from advanced statistical analysis to industry-specific visualizations. Organizations can also develop proprietary visuals using the open source Power BI Custom Visuals SDK, enabling visualization approaches tailored to specific business requirements or corporate design standards.

Visual formatting options provide extensive control over the appearance and behavior of visualizations, enabling reports that align with organizational branding while maximizing analytical clarity. Power BI includes comprehensive settings for colors, fonts, labels, backgrounds, borders, and other visual elements, along with responsive layout capabilities that adapt to different screen sizes and form factors. These formatting options balance aesthetic quality with analytical functionality, ensuring that reports are both visually appealing and informative.

AI-assisted analysis enhances traditional visualization with AI capabilities that automatically discover patterns and explain trends. Power BI can automatically identify key influencers driving a metric, detect anomalies in time-series data, perform decomposition analysis to explain changes over time, and generate natural language summaries of key findings. These AI features help users discover insights they might otherwise miss, accelerating the analysis process while revealing deeper patterns within the data.

Sharing and Collaboration

The value of analytical insights emerges when they reach the people who can take action based on the information. Power BI provides comprehensive capabilities for sharing and collaborating on analyses, ensuring that insights flow effectively throughout the organization to drive better decisions.

Power BI workspaces serve as collaborative containers for organizing and managing related content. These workspaces function as shared environments where teams can collectively develop, publish, and maintain reports, dashboards, and datasets. Access controls determine who can contribute to the workspace versus who can simply view its contents, enabling appropriate governance while promoting collaboration among analytical teams. Workspaces typically align with organizational structures like departments or project teams, creating natural boundaries for content organization and security.

Dashboards provide curated views that combine visualizations from multiple reports into unified analytical surfaces. Unlike reports, which typically organize multiple visualizations about a single business area, dashboards integrate the most important visuals from different reports to provide comprehensive overviews. These dashboards enable executives and managers to monitor key metrics across business functions without navigating multiple reports, simplifying high-level performance monitoring while providing paths to detailed analysis when needed.

Apps package related content for distribution to broader audiences throughout the organization. A Power BI app might include multiple reports and dashboards organized into a coherent experience for a particular user group or analytical purpose. Apps support phased release management where content developers can stage and test changes before updating the production version, ensuring quality while enabling continuous improvement. For consumers, apps provide a curated entry point to related content without requiring navigation through the broader workspace structure.

Mobile experiences ensure that insights remain accessible regardless of user location. Power BI's mobile applications provide optimized interfaces for phones and tablets, with responsive layouts that adapt visualizations to smaller screens and touch-based interaction. Mobile annotations allow on-the-go collaboration, enabling field personnel to highlight findings or raise questions directly within the mobile experience. Location-based filtering can automatically focus reports on the user's current geography, a capability that is particularly valuable for regional sales or service teams.

Exam Warning

The DP-900 exam may ask about data refresh and access limitations in different Power BI licensing levels. Remember that free Power BI accounts cannot access refresh capabilities in Power BI Service, while Pro and Premium licenses provide different refresh frequencies and sharing options. Know the basic differences between these licensing tiers from a technical capability perspective.

Embedding capabilities integrate Power BI analytics directly into operational applications, portals, and websites. Rather than requiring users to switch contexts between their operational systems and analytical tools, embedding delivers insights within the applications people already use daily. This integration ranges from simple iframe embedding in internal portals to sophisticated integration in customer-facing applications using the Power BI API. The embedded approach particularly benefits operational users who need analytical context for transactional decisions without switching to separate analytical tools.

Export and integration options connect Power BI with other productivity and collaboration tools. Users can export visualizations and data to Excel for additional analysis, PowerPoint for presentations, or PDF for distribution. Integration with Microsoft Teams embeds reports directly in collaborative workspaces, enabling data-driven discussions without leaving the team environment. These integration capabilities ensure that insights flow freely between analytical and productivity contexts, enhancing collaboration around data-driven decisions.

Data Models in Power BI

While visualizations provide the visible interface that users interact with, the underlying data model determines what questions they can effectively answer and how intuitively they can navigate between different analytical perspectives. Understanding how Power BI implements data modeling helps explain why some reports provide fluid, responsive analytical experiences while others feel limited or fragmented.

Model Structures and Relationships

The foundation of effective Power BI modeling lies in properly structured tables connected through well-defined relationships. These structures determine how data elements relate to each other and how users can navigate between different analytical dimensions during exploration.

The star schema design represents the most common and effective approach for analytical models in Power BI. This design organizes data into fact tables containing quantitative measurements (like sales amounts or production quantities) and dimension tables containing the contextual attributes for analyzing those measurements (like products, customers, or time periods). The fact tables connect to dimension tables through relationships, creating a starlike structure with the fact table at the center connected to surrounding dimension tables.

This star schema approach aligns perfectly with how users naturally think about analysis—examining measurements (facts) across different business dimensions. It enables intuitive exploration where users can seamlessly analyze sales by product category, then by customer segment, and then by time period, without having to understand the technical relationships connecting these tables. The star schema also optimizes performance by clearly separating the typically large fact tables from the smaller dimension tables that provide analytical context.

For more complex business scenarios, snowflake schemas extend the star approach by normalizing dimension tables into multiple related tables. For example, rather than having a single product dimension with all product-related attributes, a snowflake might separate products, categories, and manufacturers into distinct tables. This normalization can improve data management for rapidly changing dimensions but introduces additional relationship complexity that may impact both performance and user comprehension. Power BI supports these more complex structures when necessary while generally recommending star schemas for their analytical clarity and performance characteristics.

Relationship types in Power BI determine how filters propagate between tables during analysis. Most relationships follow a one-to-many cardinality where each row in the "one" table can relate to multiple rows in the "many" table, but each row in the "many" table relates to exactly one row in the "one" table. For example, each product category contains many products, but each product belongs to exactly one category. These one-to-many relationships reflect natural business hierarchies and enable intuitive filtering from the "one" side to the "many" side.

In more complex scenarios, Power BI supports many-to-many relationships where rows in each table can relate to multiple rows in the other table. For example, each customer might purchase many products, and each product might be purchased by many customers. These many-to-many relationships often require bridge tables containing the associations between entities, adding complexity to the model structure. While Power BI handles these relationships, they require careful design to maintain performance and analytical clarity.

Filter direction controls how selections in one table affect related tables during analysis. By default, filters flow from the "one" side of relationships to the "many" side but not in the reverse direction. This single-direction filtering prevents unexpected query results where selections in fact tables might inadvertently filter dimension tables, causing confusion for users. In specific scenarios where bidirectional filtering benefits the analytical experience, Power BI allows explicit configuration of bidirectional relationships, though these require careful consideration due to their performance implications and potential for creating ambiguous filter contexts.

Exam Tip

For the DP-900 exam, understand that effective Power BI data models typically follow star schema designs with dimension tables connected to fact tables through one-to-many relationships. This structure optimizes both analytical clarity and query performance while enabling intuitive navigation across business dimensions.

Calculated Columns and Measures

Beyond the base tables and relationships, Power BI's calculation capabilities extend the data model with derived values that directly answer business questions. These calculations transform raw data into meaningful business metrics, enabling analysis in terms that directly align with how organizations measure performance.

Calculated columns derive new values within tables based on other columns, creating permanently stored results that appear like any other column. These calculations might standardize formatting (converting names to proper case), create flags based on conditions (marking high-value customers), or derive new attributes from existing ones (extracting year from date). Calculated columns are computed when data refreshes and consume storage within the model, making them appropriate for values that many visualizations will reference or that support row-level filtering.

Measures, by contrast, define aggregations that calculate dynamically based on the current filter context rather than storing predetermined results. A measure for "Total Sales" dynamically calculates the appropriate sum based on whatever filters the user has applied—whether viewing all sales, sales for a specific region, or sales for a particular product category in a specific time period. This dynamic calculation enables consistent metric definitions that automatically adapt to the user's analytical focus, providing reliable results regardless of visualization context.

The distinction between calculated columns and measures significantly impacts both model performance and analytical flexibility. Calculated columns consume storage but offer faster retrieval for frequently used values. Measures require computation during analysis but provide more dynamic results that adapt to filtering context. Understanding when to use each approach represents a key modeling skill that experienced Power BI developers cultivate through practice and performance testing.

DAX provides the formula language for defining these calculations, offering specific functions for common analytical needs:

Time intelligence functions
> These simplify analysis across time periods, enabling comparisons like year-over-year growth, rolling averages, or year-to-date accumulations. Functions like `SAME PERIODLASTYEAR`, `DATEADD`, and `TOTALYTD` handle the complexity of calendar logic, enabling business users to track performance trends without implementing sophisticated date manipulation.

Filter context functions
> These control how calculations respond to the current selection state, enabling conditional logic based on user interactions. `CALCULATE` allows explicit modification of context, `ALL` removes filters to provide baseline comparisons, and `FILTER`

applies additional conditions within measures. These context functions enable sophisticated analytical patterns that adapt to user exploration paths.

Iterator functions

THese perform row-by-row operations and aggregations beyond simple summation. SUMX, AVERAGEX, and related functions calculate expressions for each row before aggregating the results, enabling weighted averages, conditional aggregations, and other complex calculations that basic aggregates cannot express. These iterators prove particularly valuable for financial and statistical analysis requiring nuanced computation logic.

The combination of these calculation capabilities transforms raw data into a rich analytical model that directly answers business questions in familiar terminology. Rather than requiring users to mentally calculate key metrics from base fields, a well-designed model provides these metrics as predefined measures that ensure consistent definition and interpretation throughout the organization.

Row-Level Security

As organizations share data more broadly through Power BI, controlling who can access specific information becomes increasingly important. Row-level security (RLS) provides a sophisticated approach to data access control, enabling a single report to automatically show different data to different users based on their identity or role.

Unlike traditional security models that control access at the report or dashboard level, RLS operates at the data row level within the model. This granular approach enables scenarios where regional managers see only data for their own regions, sales representatives access only their own customer information, or department heads view only their own departmental financials—all from the same report and without creating separate versions for each audience.

The implementation of RLS centers on roles and rules defined within the data model. Security roles define groups of users with similar access requirements, such as "West Region Managers" or "Finance Department Analysts." Within each role, DAX filter expressions establish rules that determine which data rows members of that role can access. For example, a region-based rule might specify [Region] = "West" or [Region] = USERPRINCIPAL("Region"), dynamically filtering based on attributes in the user's organizational profile.

This role-based approach simplifies security management by enabling permission assignment at the role level rather than requiring individual user configuration. When organizational changes occur, administrators simply update role membership rather than reconfiguring data access rules. For users with multiple access profiles—such as a regional manager who also has global reporting responsibilities—Power BI supports membership in multiple roles, showing all data accessible through any assigned role.

The dynamic filtering provided by RLS operates automatically and transparently during report interaction. Users see only the data they have permission to access, with all visualizations, filters, and calculations respecting these security boundaries. The security remains enforced regardless of how users interact with reports—whether through the Power BI Service, mobile applications, embedded reports, or exported data—ensuring consistent protection across access methods.

Real-World Scenario

A global retail organization implements row-level security in its store performance dashboard based on the organizational hierarchy. Store managers see data only for their individual locations, district managers view information for all stores in their districts, regional directors access data across their regions, and corporate executives see the complete global dataset. This approach delivers personalized analytics to each management level from a single report definition, ensuring consistent metrics and visualization while respecting organizational data access boundaries.

For the DP-900 exam, understanding the basic concept of row-level security matters more than implementation details. Remember that RLS enables a single report to show different data to different users based on their identity, with security enforced at the data row level rather than through separate reports for different audiences.

DirectQuery and Import Modes

Power BI offers different storage modes that determine how data is accessed and processed during analysis. These modes present important trade-offs between data freshness, query performance, and model size limitations that influence architectural decisions for Power BI implementations.

Import mode represents the default and most common approach, where Power BI imports a copy of the source data into its highly compressed, in-memory storage engine. This imported data powers all visualizations and calculations within the report, enabling extremely fast query performance as all data resides in memory in an optimized format. The import approach particularly benefits scenarios with moderate data volumes where analytical responsiveness outweighs real-time data requirements.

Several key advantages make import mode the preferred choice for many scenarios. Query performance remains consistently excellent regardless of source system capabilities, as all queries run against the optimized in-memory copy. The full Power BI calculation engine supports sophisticated DAX expressions and relationships that might not translate to source system queries. Users can continue analyzing imported data even when disconnected from source systems, enabling offline scenarios through Power BI Desktop or mobile applications.

However, import mode also presents limitations. Imported data represents a snapshot from the time of refresh rather than live information, creating potential delays between operational changes and their analytical visibility. The entire dataset must fit within Power BI's memory limitations (generally 10 GB for Power BI Premium and 1 GB for shared capacity). Complex models with numerous tables and relationships may approach these limits, requiring careful optimization. Frequent refresh requirements can place substantial load on source systems and consume significant Power BI resource capacity.

DirectQuery mode takes a fundamentally different approach by leaving data in the source system and translating Power BI interactions into native queries against that source. When users interact with visualizations, Power BI dynamically generates queries (typically SQL) that execute directly against the source database rather than against imported data. This approach ensures that visualizations always reflect the latest source data while avoiding the need to import potentially massive datasets into Power BI's memory.

This direct approach particularly benefits several scenarios. For datasets too large to practically import into Power BI's memory, DirectQuery provides analytical access without size limitations beyond what the source system can handle. When data changes frequently and analysis requires the very latest information, DirectQuery ensures that visualizations always reflect current values without waiting for scheduled refreshes. For organizations with substantial investments in source system optimization, DirectQuery leverages these capabilities rather than duplicating data processing within Power BI.

Like import mode, DirectQuery presents its own trade-offs. Query performance depends heavily on source system capabilities, with slow source databases creating potentially frustrating analytical experiences. Not all DAX functions and modeling capabilities are available in DirectQuery mode, as calculations must translate into operations the source system can execute. Filter operations affect query scope and complexity, sometimes creating performance challenges for highly interactive reports with numerous slicers and filters.

Composite models provide a hybrid approach that combines import and DirectQuery tables within a single model. Some tables import their data for optimal performance, while others remain in DirectQuery mode for real-time access or to avoid importing excessively large dimensions. This flexible approach enables architects to make appropriate mode decisions for each table rather than applying a single approach to the entire model. Dual storage mode takes this flexibility further by allowing individual tables to operate in both modes simultaneously, dynamically choosing the appropriate mode based on the specific query context.

Exam Tip

For the DP-900 exam, understand the fundamental trade-off between import mode (which offers superior performance but with point-in-time data) and DirectQuery mode (which provides real-time data access but depends on source system performance). Remember that composite models can combine both approaches within a single analytical solution.

Visualizations in Power BI

With a comprehensive data model established, visualization represents the final step in transforming raw information into accessible insights. Power BI offers a rich library of visualization types, each designed to communicate specific aspects of data effectively. Understanding which visualization types best suit different analytical purposes helps create reports that reveal patterns clearly rather than obscuring them behind inappropriate visual choices.

Choosing the Right Visualization

The selection of appropriate visualizations directly impacts how effectively users understand the underlying data. Rather than simply choosing visualizations based on aesthetic preferences or variety, effective Power BI development matches visualization types to the specific analytical questions they best address.

Comparison visualizations help users understand differences between values across categories or groups. Bar and column charts excel at this purpose, leveraging the human brain's ability to compare the lengths of bars accurately. These charts work particularly well for comparing discrete categories like products, regions, or departments. For comparisons involving multiple measures across categories, clustered column charts or small multiples might reveal patterns more clearly. When comparing current values against targets, bullet charts provide specialized designs that show progress toward goals within the context of performance ranges.

When visualization needs extend beyond simple comparisons to understanding part-to-whole relationships, different approaches become appropriate. Pie and donut charts show the composition of a whole divided into categories, though they become difficult to interpret accurately with more than five to seven slices. Treemaps provide an alternative that uses nested rectangles sized according to value, enabling visualization of hierarchical categories while still showing relative proportions. Stacked bar charts combine comparison and composition by showing both total values and their constituent parts, though at the cost of making comparisons between components more difficult.

Trend analysis over time requires visualizations designed specifically for temporal patterns. Line charts excel at showing continuous trends, making them ideal for metrics tracked over time periods. Area charts extend this capability by filling the area below the line, emphasizing cumulative impact or showing stacked components over time. When analysis needs to focus on changes between specific time points rather than continuous trends, column charts might prove more effective despite their discrete nature. For complex time-based analysis showing both seasonality and long-term trends, small multiples of line charts organized by time period can reveal patterns that single charts might obscure.

Relationship analysis between variables requires specialized visualizations that reveal connections, correlations, and distributions. Scatter charts plot individual data points along two axes to reveal correlations between variables, optionally using point size and color to incorporate additional dimensions. For network relationships between entities, network diagrams show connection patterns that might remain hidden in traditional charts. When analyzing how values distribute across ranges, histograms group data into bins to show frequency distributions that reveal central tendencies and outliers.

Geographic analysis presents unique visualization requirements addressed through specialized map visuals. Filled maps (choropleth) shade geographic regions based on associated values, effectively showing regional patterns across countries, states, or custom territories. Point maps display individual locations as dots or bubbles, optionally sized by associated measures to show both position and magnitude. For scenarios involving movement between locations, flow maps connect origins and destinations with lines weighted by volume, revealing transportation patterns or migration flows.

These various visualization types each excel at specific analytical purposes while potentially creating confusion when misapplied. An effective Power BI developer matches visualization types to analytical requirements, considering both the question being answered and the characteristics of the underlying data. This thoughtful matching transforms visualization from mere decoration into a powerful analytical tool that reveals patterns effectively and accurately.

The DP-900 exam often presents scenarios asking you to identify the most appropriate visualization type for specific analytical questions. Focus on understanding which visualizations best serve different purposes: bar/column charts for comparisons, line charts for trends, scatterplots for relationships, and maps for geographic data. Remember that the best visualization depends on the specific question being answered rather than visual appeal alone.

Understanding Dashboard and Report Design

Beyond individual visualizations, effective Power BI implementation requires thoughtful organization of visuals into cohesive reports and dashboards. This design process transforms collections of individual charts into integrated analytical experiences that guide users through data exploration and understanding.

Visual hierarchy establishes the relative importance of information through size, position, and emphasis. Major metrics and key insights typically appear prominently in larger visuals at the top or left of reports (following natural reading patterns), with supporting details in smaller visuals in less prominent positions. This hierarchy guides users through the analytical narrative from high-level findings to supporting details, helping them absorb information in a logical progression rather than becoming overwhelmed by undifferentiated data.

Layout and grouping organizes related visualizations into logical sections that reinforce relationships between metrics and dimensions. Effective reports group visuals addressing the same business questions or processes, using consistent section layouts across pages to create predictable patterns that users can navigate intuitively. This thoughtful organization reduces cognitive load by establishing clear information architecture rather than presenting disconnected collections of visualizations.

Interactivity design determines how visualizations respond to user interactions and work together to enable exploration. Cross-filtering connections allow selection in one visual to highlight related information in others, revealing relationships that might otherwise remain hidden. Drill-through actions enable users to navigate from summary visuals to detailed reports that provide deeper context. Bookmarks save specific report states that capture important analytical views for future reference. These interactive elements transform static reports into dynamic exploration tools that adapt to user inquiry paths.

Information density balances comprehensiveness against clarity based on user needs and usage context. Executive dashboards typically emphasize clarity through focused metrics with minimal detail, enabling quick understanding of organizational performance. Analytical reports for business analysts might incorporate higher information density with multiple detailed visualizations, supporting deeper exploration and investigation. Mobile experiences require careful density management for smaller screens, often focusing on fewer metrics with progressive disclosure of details through interaction. This density calibration should align with both user expertise and consumption context to avoid overwhelming inexperienced users while still providing sufficient detail for sophisticated analysis.

Accessibility and inclusivity ensure that reports remain effective for all users regardless of abilities or circumstances. Color choices should maintain sufficient contrast and include redundant encodings beyond color alone to support users with color vision deficiencies. Text sizes need to accommodate different visual acuities, with important information conveyed through more than just small text. Alt text descriptions for visualizations enable screen reader interpretation for users with visual impairment. These accessibility considerations extend the reach of analytical content to diverse audiences while often improving usability for all users regardless of ability.

Performance optimization ensures that reports respond quickly to user interactions, maintaining the flow of analytical exploration without frustrating delays. Effective optimization strategies include limiting visuals per page to essential elements, using appropriate aggregations instead of row-level details, implementing efficient filter relationships, and leveraging incremental refresh for large datasets. These optimizations become particularly important for DirectQuery reports where each interaction potentially generates queries against source systems, making thoughtful performance management essential for satisfactory user experiences.

Implementing Advanced Visualization Techniques

Beyond basic charts and design principles, Power BI offers advanced visualization capabilities that address sophisticated analytical needs and enhance communication effectiveness. These techniques extend the platform's capabilities for both analytical depth and presentation impact.

Custom visualizations from the AppSource marketplace extend Power BI's built-in library with specialized visuals for particular analytical purposes. These range from advanced statistical visuals like box plots and violin plots to specialized business visuals like Gantt charts and waterfall charts. The marketplace includes both free visuals from Microsoft and the community alongside premium offerings from third-party vendors. For organizations with unique visualization requirements, the custom visual SDK enables development of proprietary visuals tailored to specific business needs or corporate standards.

Conditional formatting dynamically changes visual appearance based on data values or analytical context. Simple implementations might change color based on value ranges—showing metrics in green, yellow, or red based on performance thresholds. More sophisticated approaches might adjust multiple visual properties simultaneously, such as combining color, icon, and font weight changes to highlight important values. This dynamic formatting draws attention to significant information without requiring separate visuals for different conditions, enabling more compact and intuitive presentations.

Small multiples (also called *trellis charts*) repeat the same visualization for different category values, enabling comparison across categories while maintaining consistent visual structure. Rather than combining multiple categories into a single complex visual, this approach creates separate instances of the same visual type for each category—showing the same metrics for different regions, products, or time periods in identical mini-charts arranged in a grid. This technique particularly helps when comparing patterns or trends across categories rather than just individual values, revealing similarities and differences that might be obscured in consolidated visuals.

Narrative text and annotations complement quantitative visualizations with explanatory context that helps users interpret the significance of what they're seeing. Text boxes provide narrative overviews that explain key findings or methodological context. Text annotations within charts highlight specific data points or patterns deserving attention. Together, these textual elements transform collections of charts into analytical stories that guide users through key insights rather than leaving interpretation entirely to the viewer.

Advanced interactivity extends beyond basic filtering to create guided analytical experiences that adapt to user exploration. Tooltip pages replace simple data tooltips with rich mini-reports that appear when hovering the cursor over data points, providing multidimensional context without cluttering the main report. Drill-through filters enable navigation from summary views to detailed analysis pre-filtered to the selected context. Bookmarks linked to buttons allow users to switch between different analytical perspectives with a single click. These advanced interactions transform reports from static presentations into dynamic exploration tools that respond intelligently to user interests.

AI-powered visualizations leverage AI to automatically discover and explain patterns within data. Key influencer analysis identifies factors most strongly associated with particular outcomes, helping to explain what drives specific results. Decomposition trees enable multidimensional exploration guided by AI that highlights the most significant paths. Smart narrative automatically generates textual summaries of key findings within visualizations. Q&A visuals interpret natural language questions to create appropriate visualizations on demand. These AI capabilities accelerate insight discovery while making sophisticated analytical techniques accessible to users without specialized expertise.

Bringing It All Together: Power BI in Practice

Now that you've explored the concepts, components, and capabilities of Power BI, let's examine how these elements come together in a real-world scenario. This practical perspective helps illustrate how organizations leverage Power BI to transform raw data into actionable insights that drive better business decisions.

Consider Northern Distributors, a fictional regional distribution company managing a complex supply chain across multiple product categories, warehouses, and retail partners. The company is implementing Power BI to gain comprehensive visibility into its operations, identify optimization opportunities, and deliver targeted insights to different roles throughout the organization. Its journey illustrates the practical application of the concepts we've discussed throughout this chapter.

The Data Landscape

Northern Distributors faces classic business intelligence challenges that require a unified analytical approach spanning multiple systems and data sources.

Its operational environment includes an ERP system tracking inventory, orders, and financials; a warehouse management system monitoring product movement and storage; a transportation management system tracking shipments and fleet performance; and a CRM platform managing customer relationships and sales activities. Each system contains valuable information, but the fragmentation makes comprehensive analysis challenging without a unified analytical layer.

Product and partner data spans thousands of SKUs across dozens of categories, with different profit margins, storage requirements, and inventory turnover rates. The company works with hundreds of retail partners ranging from major chains to independent stores, each with unique ordering patterns, delivery requirements, and payment terms. Understanding performance requires analyzing these complex relationships across multiple dimensions simultaneously.

Financial data includes revenue, costs, and profitability metrics tracked at different levels of granularity. The finance team needs to analyze profitability by product, customer, region, and time period to identify both opportunities and concerns. Historical trends help forecast future performance, while variance analysis identifies areas requiring attention or intervention.

Operational metrics track inventory levels, order fulfillment rates, delivery times, return rates, and other KPIs that indicate distribution efficiency and service quality. These metrics require both high-level monitoring for executives and detailed analysis for operational managers responsible for specific areas or processes.

This diverse data landscape creates significant analytical challenges without a unified business intelligence approach. Individual systems provide limited reporting focused on their specific domains, but understanding cross-functional relationships requires integrated analysis that connects information across organizational boundaries. Power BI provides the platform to create this integrated view while delivering appropriate insights to different roles throughout the company.

The Power BI Implementation

To address these challenges, Northern Distributors implemented a comprehensive Power BI solution that integrates data across systems and delivers targeted analytics to different user groups.

For data integration, the company established a multilayered approach addressing both immediate reporting needs and long-term analytical governance. Power BI Dataflows handle initial data extraction and standardization, creating reusable transformation logic that multiple reports leverage. These dataflows connect to source systems through a combination of direct database connections and API integrations, extracting relevant data while applying consistent business rules and transformations.

For the core analytical foundation, it created a comprehensive data model following star schema principles. Fact tables contain quantitative measurements like sales, shipments, inventory transactions, and financial entries. Dimension tables provide analytical context through product hierarchies, customer classifications, geographic regions, and detailed date dimensions with fiscal periods and seasonality flags. Relationships connect these tables, enabling intuitive navigation across business dimensions without requiring users to understand the underlying data structure.

Its calculation layer transforms raw data into meaningful business metrics through DAX measures and calculated columns. Standard financial measures ensure consistent definitions for revenue, costs, margin, and profitability across all reports. Inventory measures track stock levels, turnover rates, and days-of-supply with appropriate business logic. Service measures calculate order fulfillment rates, on-time delivery percentages, and other KPIs that indicate operational performance. These calculations provide consistent metric definitions that everyone in the organization uses, eliminating debates about how numbers are derived.

For insight delivery, the company created role-focused reports and dashboards targeting specific user needs. Executive dashboards provide high-level metrics with drill-down capabilities for exploring concerning areas. Sales reports analyze customer and product performance with detailed filtering and comparative analysis. Operations dashboards monitor warehouse and transportation metrics with alerts for exceptions requiring attention. These targeted experiences deliver relevant insights to each role while maintaining consistent definitions and visualizations across reports.

Throughout the implementation, security ensures appropriate data access based on organizational roles. Row-level security restricts sales representatives to their assigned accounts and regions, while allowing managers to see broader performance within their areas. The security model balances appropriate access restrictions with sufficient visibility for effective decision making, ensuring that users can see what they need without exposing sensitive information inappropriately.

The Implementation Approach

Rather than attempting to build this entire solution at once, Northern Distributors took an incremental approach that delivered value at each stage while building toward its comprehensive vision.

The company began with a focused sales analysis implementation addressing the most pressing business questions. This initial phase connected core sales and customer data, built fundamental measures for revenue and profitability, and created reports analyzing performance by product, customer, and region. The resulting insights enabled the sales team to identify both growth opportunities and concerning trends, delivering immediate value while establishing the foundation for broader capabilities.

Building on this foundation, the company next incorporated operational analytics across warehousing and transportation. This phase expanded the data model to include inventory movements, shipment details, and service metrics. Power BI reports provided visibility into operational efficiency, highlighting bottlenecks and optimization opportunities. The integration between sales and operations data revealed valuable connections between customer ordering patterns and fulfillment challenges, enabling process improvements that enhanced service levels.

With both sales and operations visibility established, Northern Distributors implemented financial analytics that connected performance metrics to profitability outcomes. This phase incorporated cost allocations, budget comparisons, and trend analysis that helped explain financial results through operational and sales activities. The resulting insights enabled more sophisticated profitability analysis that identified the true drivers of financial performance beyond simple revenue metrics.

The company's most recent phase focused on predictive analytics and proactive alerting. This capability analyzes historical patterns to forecast future outcomes, identifying potential inventory shortages, delivery delays, or customer churn risks before they materialize. Automated alerts notify appropriate personnel when metrics trend toward concerning thresholds, enabling proactive intervention rather than reactive response.

This phased approach delivered value at each stage while building toward a comprehensive analytics ecosystem. It allowed the organization to learn from each phase before proceeding to the next, adjusting its implementation based on user feedback and emerging requirements. It also enabled the organization to demonstrate tangible business impact early in the process, building organizational momentum and support for continued investment.

The Business Outcomes

The Power BI implementation delivered significant business impact for Northern Distributors, transforming how the company operated across multiple dimensions.

Inventory optimization improved dramatically, with reductions in excess stock while maintaining service levels. By analyzing historical sales patterns, seasonal trends, and lead times within a unified view, company personnel were able to identify opportunities to reduce safety stock for stable products while ensuring adequate inventory for volatile items. The resulting working capital improvements enhanced financial performance while maintaining the service levels customers expected.

Customer profitability analysis revealed surprising insights about the company's account portfolio. The integrated view of sales, operations, and finance data demonstrated that some high-revenue customers generated minimal profits due to challenging delivery requirements, frequent returns, or substantial service demands. Conversely, some smaller accounts delivered exceptional profitability through efficient ordering patterns and low service costs. This analysis enabled targeted strategy adjustments that improved overall profitability without sacrificing key customer relationships.

Operational efficiency increased through data-driven process improvements identified through Power BI analysis. Cross-functional metrics revealed how decisions in one area affected performance in others—how purchasing patterns influenced warehouse efficiency, how delivery scheduling affected transportation utilization, and how product packaging choices impacted handling costs. By understanding these relationships, the company implemented process changes that improved overall efficiency rather than simply optimizing individual functions in isolation.

Decision agility improved substantially as Power BI replaced monthly static reports with near-real-time analytics available on demand. When market conditions or operational challenges emerged, managers could immediately analyze relevant data rather than waiting for scheduled reporting cycles. This timely insight enabled faster, more confident decisions that addressed issues before they escalated into significant problems. The self-service capabilities empowered business users to answer their own analytical questions without requiring IT assistance for each new inquiry.

These outcomes demonstrate how Power BI transforms technical capabilities into business value. By focusing implementations on specific business challenges and measuring outcomes in business terms, Northern Distributors ensured that its analytics investment delivered tangible returns beyond creating attractive dashboards. The unified analytical view across previously siloed systems revealed insights that would have remained hidden in fragmented reporting, enabling more effective strategy and operations throughout the organization.

Summary

The evolution of Power BI represents a fundamental transformation in how organizations approach business intelligence, democratizing access to sophisticated analytical capabilities while integrating previously separate processes into a cohesive experience. Power BI enables the complete analytical journey from data connection through preparation, modeling, visualization, and sharing within a unified platform accessible to both business users and data professionals.

Throughout this chapter, we explored how:

- Power BI integrates the complete analytical workflow from data connection through preparation, modeling, visualization, and sharing.

- The platform includes connected components (Desktop, Service, Mobile, Report Builder, Dataflows) that address different aspects of this workflow.

- Data models establish the semantic foundation that transforms raw data into business-meaningful structures and calculations.

- Visualization selection should align with analytical purpose rather than aesthetic preference alone.

Exam Tip

The DP-900 exam frequently presents scenarios asking you to identify appropriate Power BI capabilities for specific requirements. Focus on understanding which components and features address different analytical needs, from data preparation to modeling to visualization to sharing.

Exam Essentials

For success on the DP-900 exam, focus on these key areas:

- Understanding Power BI components:
  - Know the primary purpose of each Power BI component (Desktop, Service, Mobile, Report Builder, Dataflows).
  - Understand how these components work together to support the analytical workflow.
  - Recognize which component best addresses specific requirements in different scenarios.
  - Understand the basic differences between licensing tiers from a technical capability perspective.

- Grasping data modeling concepts:
  - Understand star schema design principles and their application in Power BI models.
  - Know the differences between calculated columns and measures and when to use each.
  - Recognize how relationships establish connections between tables and how they affect filtering.
  - Understand the basic concept of row-level security for data access control.

- Identifying appropriate visualizations:
  - Know which visualization types best serve different analytical purposes.
  - Understand the relationship between data characteristics and suitable visualization choices.
  - Recognize basic design principles for effective dashboards and reports.
  - Identify appropriate visualization techniques for comparison, relationship, trend, and compositional analysis.

- Comprehending Power BI's connectivity and deployment:
  - Understand the different ways Power BI can connect to data sources.
  - Know the differences between Import and DirectQuery modes and their appropriate use cases.
  - Recognize how Power BI integrates with other Microsoft services and platforms.
  - Understand basic sharing and collaboration capabilities within the Power BI ecosystem.

Beyond the Exam

While DP-900 certification provides an excellent foundation in Power BI's concepts and capabilities, real-world implementations often involve additional considerations beyond exam coverage. Having implemented Power BI solutions across industries, I've observed several factors that significantly influence success but might not appear directly in certification exams.

Organizational Factors

Despite its technical nature, successful Power BI implementation depends as much on organizational factors as on technical capabilities. Several key organizational elements significantly influence implementation outcomes.

Analytics culture represents perhaps the most critical success factor for Power BI initiatives. Organizations where decisions historically rely on intuition rather than data analysis often struggle to adopt even well-designed Power BI solutions. Successful implementations include change management efforts that demonstrate analytical value through specific business examples, train leaders in data-driven approaches, and recognize teams that effectively leverage insights. This cultural foundation determines whether beautiful reports actually influence decisions or simply become ignored artifacts.

Governance structures balance self-service flexibility with appropriate controls that ensure quality and consistency. Effective governance establishes clear roles and responsibilities, defining who can create official reports versus personal analysis, who publishes to specific workspaces, and who maintains shared datasets. Naming conventions, visual standards, and metadata management ensure that users can find and understand relevant content. These governance frameworks enable organizational scale without creating either excessive restrictions or unmanaged analytical chaos.

Skills development across different roles significantly influences adoption success. While Power BI offers intuitive interfaces, effective use still requires understanding analytical concepts, data modeling principles, and visualization best practices. The most successful organizations implement role-appropriate training paths—fundamentals for casual consumers, report creation for business analysts, data modeling for power users, and administration for IT teams. This tiered approach ensures that everyone develops capabilities appropriate to their analytical responsibilities.

I recently worked with a manufacturing company whose initial Power BI rollout struggled despite solid technical implementation. The turning point came when the company established a "Center of Excellence" combining business and technical experts who provided training, consultation, and report certification. This organizational innovation, combined with executive sponsorship that publicly used Power BI in leadership meetings, transformed adoption rates and analytical impact throughout the company.

Implementation Realities

Beyond the conceptual understanding that certification exams assess, real-world implementations face practical challenges that require pragmatic approaches.

Data quality issues invariably emerge when implementing Power BI against real business data. Missing values, inconsistent formats, duplicate records, and conflicting information across systems challenge the creation of reliable analytics. Effective implementations incorporate data cleaning strategies, quality monitoring, and appropriate handling of exceptions within the Power BI model. Rather than waiting for perfect source data (which rarely exists), successful approaches implement progressive improvement while ensuring that users understand data limitations.

Performance optimization becomes increasingly important as reports grow more complex and user bases expand. Real-world implementations require careful attention to model design (minimizing calculated columns, leveraging appropriate storage modes), query optimization (restricting unnecessary data retrieval, implementing efficient relationships), and report design (limiting visuals per page, using appropriate aggregations). These technical optimizations ensure responsive analytical experiences that maintain user engagement rather than creating frustration through excessive wait times.

Integration with Microsoft 365 significantly influences deployment approaches for many organizations. Power BI's connections with Teams, SharePoint, Excel, and other Microsoft tools enable integrated experiences that embed analytics within collaboration and productivity environments. Successful implementations leverage these integrations to deliver insights within tools users already use daily, reducing context switching while increasing analytical adoption. The most effective approaches align Power BI deployment with broader Microsoft 365 governance strategies rather than treating it as an isolated platform.

I once worked with a healthcare organization that implemented a particularly effective approach by embedding Power BI reports directly within Microsoft Teams channels organized around specific improvement initiatives. This integration placed analytics directly within the collaborative environment where teams discussed issues and planned interventions, making data a natural part of these conversations rather than a separate tool to access. This contextual delivery dramatically increased analytical engagement compared to their previous portal-based approach requiring separate navigation.

Emerging Directions

The Power BI platform continues to evolve rapidly, with several emerging directions extending beyond current certification coverage.

AI-powered capabilities increasingly complement traditional visualization with automated insight discovery and natural language interfaces. Power BI's AI features can automatically identify key influencers driving metrics, detect anomalies in data series, decompose complex changes into contributing factors, and generate narrative summaries explaining key findings. These capabilities make sophisticated analytical techniques accessible to business users without requiring specialized expertise, accelerating insight discovery while expanding analytical reach throughout organizations.

Fabric integration represents Microsoft's evolution toward an integrated analytics platform spanning business intelligence, data science, data engineering, and real-time analytics. Power BI now forms one component within this broader Microsoft Fabric ecosystem, sharing a common foundation with other analytical capabilities. This integration enables smoother transitions between different analytical approaches—from standard reporting to advanced analytics to machine learning—without requiring data movement or platform switching. Organizations increasingly view Power BI within this broader Fabric context rather than as an isolated visualization tool.

Composite models and hybrid tables extend Power BI's architectural flexibility by enabling mixed storage modes within individual tables and models. These capabilities enable sophisticated approaches that optimize for both performance and freshness, importing aggregated historical data while directly querying real-time detail. The resulting architectures provide responsive analytical experiences even against massive datasets that would exceed import capacity, while still leveraging the performance benefits of imported data where appropriate.

As you move beyond certification to real-world implementation, remember that effective Power BI deployment represents a journey rather than a destination. Technologies will continue to evolve, but the fundamental principles of connecting diverse data, creating appropriate models, and designing effective visualizations remain constant. The solid foundation provided by understanding Power BI's core capabilities will serve you well as you navigate this evolving landscape.

PART V

Beyond DP-900

This part looks beyond the scope of the foundational exam to the strategic enablers of sustainable, scalable data value: governance, lineage, cataloging, responsible AI integration, and performance + cost stewardship. It frames how disciplined data practice becomes the multiplier for AI acceleration rather than a bottleneck.

- Chapter 12, "Advanced Azure Data Concepts", synthesizes governance frameworks, the role of Microsoft Purview in catalog + classification + lineage, emergent AI-assisted data interaction (LLMs and intelligent agent patterns), and forward-looking architectural considerations.

By completing this part, you'll be able to articulate why governance maturity precedes trustworthy AI, explain how lineage underpins auditability and metric confidence, and identify where AI augmentation speeds up—and doesn't replace—data professional workflows.

Common failure patterns include applying governance post implementation, launching AI pilots against uncurated datasets, conflating prototype model capability with production readiness, and underestimating compliance obligations as data exposure grows.

Exam Alignment: Conceptual awareness here prepares you for advanced certifications (DP-300, DP-420, DP-500) and architectural specializations.

Advanced Azure Data Concepts

The data landscape has evolved dramatically since the early days of isolated databases and simple reporting. Today's organizations face unprecedented challenges: data scattered across cloud and on-premises systems, regulatory requirements that change more quickly than technology can adapt, and the explosive rise of AI that demands both governed data and responsible implementation. This final chapter explores two critical domains that extend beyond the DP-900 exam but represent the future of data work: comprehensive data governance and the integration of AI technologies, particularly large language models (LLMs) and intelligent agents.

Beyond the Exam Scope

This chapter explores advanced Azure data concepts that extend beyond the DP-900 exam scope:

- Microsoft Purview for comprehensive data governance
- LLMs and AI agents in Azure
- The convergence of governed data and AI

Think of your DP-900 knowledge as mastering the fundamentals of navigation—understanding maps, compasses, and basic wayfinding. This chapter equips you with advanced instruments: satellite GPS for data governance that provides real-time visibility across your entire data estate, and AI technologies that act like intelligent copilots, helping you discover insights and automate decisions you never thought possible.

Whether you're preparing for advanced certifications, solving complex business challenges, or simply curious about where data technology is headed, this chapter provides essential context for your continued journey. You'll explore how Microsoft Purview brings order to data chaos, how LLMs are transforming how we interact with information, and how these capabilities combine to create the next generation of intelligent data systems.

The Modern Data Governance Imperative

As organizations accumulate vast amounts of data across multiple systems, clouds, and formats, the challenge isn't just storing and processing this information. It's understanding what you have, where it lives, who can access it, and how it flows through your organization. Data governance has evolved from a compliance check-box to a strategic capability that enables everything from regulatory compliance to AI innovation.

Consider a global retail organization with POS systems in thousands of stores, ecommerce platforms spanning multiple countries, customer service systems, supply chain databases, and marketing analytics platforms. Each system contains valuable data, but without governance, this becomes a liability rather than an asset. Customer information might be duplicated across systems with different quality standards. Sensitive data could be accessible to unauthorized users. Critical business data might be stored in formats that prevent effective analysis.

Modern data governance addresses these challenges through comprehensive discovery, classification, lineage tracking, and access management. But unlike traditional approaches that required manual cataloging and extensive IT involvement, cloud native governance solutions provide automated discovery and intelligent classification that scales with your data estate.

Understanding Microsoft Purview

Microsoft Purview represents a fundamental shift in how organizations approach data governance, providing unified visibility and control across their entire data landscape. Rather than treating governance as an afterthought or compliance requirement, Purview positions data governance as an enabling capability that makes data more valuable and accessible while maintaining appropriate controls.

Figure 12-1 illustrates how Microsoft Purview operates as an intermediary hub between diverse data sources and end users. On the left, various data sources, including Azure services, on-premises systems, third-party platforms, cloud environments, and APIs, feed into Purview through automated scanning and cataloging processes. The central Purview platform performs core functions of data discovery, classification, governance, and compliance management. On the right, different user groups including data analysts, data scientists, data stewards, business users, and compliance teams access the governed data through Purview's unified interface. This architecture enables organizations to maintain centralized control and visibility over their entire data estate while providing users with streamlined access to trusted, well-governed data assets.

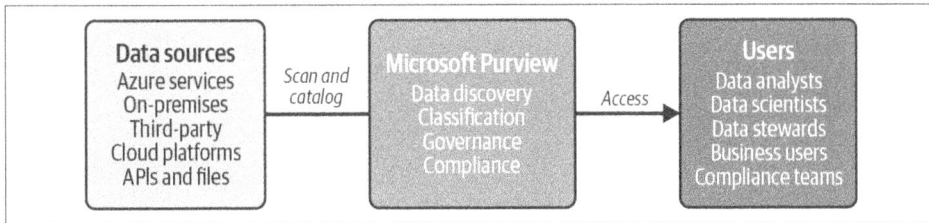

Figure 12-1. Microsoft Purview serves as a centralized governance layer connecting data sources to users

At its core, Purview creates a comprehensive map of your data estate, automatically discovering and cataloging information across cloud and on-premises systems. But this isn't just about creating an inventory. Purview understands the content, context, and connections within your data, providing insights that transform how organizations work with information.

The platform combines several critical capabilities into a unified experience:

- *Automated discovery and cataloging* eliminates the manual effort traditionally required to maintain data inventories. Purview continuously scans your data sources, automatically identifying new datasets and changes to existing information. This automated approach ensures that your governance layer stays current with your evolving data landscape.

- *Intelligent classification* goes beyond simple data types to understand the business meaning and sensitivity of your information. Using built-in classifiers and machine learning, Purview can identify personally identifiable information (PII), financial data, health records, and other sensitive content across diverse file formats and database structures.

  While Purview includes pre-built classifiers for common data types, organizations can also create custom classifiers tailored to industry-specific or company-specific requirements, such as proprietary product codes or internal document classifications.

- *Data lineage visualization* traces how information flows through your systems, from original sources through various transformations to final consumption. This capability is crucial for understanding data dependencies, impact analysis, and compliance requirements.

  Purview integrates seamlessly with Azure Data Factory and other Azure resources to automatically capture lineage information as data flows through pipelines, providing real-time visibility into data transformations and dependencies.

- A *collaborative data catalog* enables business users to discover and understand available data through search, browsing, and business glossaries. Rather than relying on IT teams to locate relevant data, users can self-serve while maintaining appropriate governance controls.

Real-World Scenario

A healthcare organization implemented Purview to prepare for a major analytics initiative. Within the first month, Purview automatically discovered over 2,000 datasets across the organization's environment and identified 847 tables containing patient information that weren't previously cataloged. This discovery enabled the organization to implement proper access controls and compliance measures before beginning its analytics project, avoiding potential regulatory violations.

Implementing Data Governance at Scale

Traditional ad hoc data management often results in siloed information, inconsistent naming conventions, duplicate datasets, and unknown data quality issues. Teams struggle to find relevant data, leading to redundant work and missed insights.

The transition from ad hoc data management to comprehensive governance requires careful planning and phased implementation. Organizations that attempt to implement governance across their entire data estate simultaneously often become overwhelmed by the scope and complexity. Successful implementations start with high-value, high-risk data and gradually expand coverage while delivering incremental value.

Microsoft Purview supports this incremental approach through its flexible deployment model. Organizations typically begin by connecting their most critical data sources—perhaps their customer database and financial systems—to establish foundational governance capabilities. This initial phase focuses on discovery, classification, and basic access management for the most sensitive or valuable data.

Consider how a financial services organization might approach Purview implementation:

Phase 1: Critical Data Discovery

The organization begins by connecting its core banking systems, CRM platform, and regulatory reporting databases to Purview. The automated scanning immediately provides visibility into data it never had before, including discovery of shadow IT databases and forgotten data stores.

Here's an example of how Purview automatically classifies sensitive data elements in a typical customer database:

```
-- Example of sensitive data automatically classified by Purview
SELECT
    customer_id,
    full_name,          -- Classified as "Person Name"
    ssn,                -- Classified as "U.S. Social Security Number"
    account_balance,    -- Classified as "Financial Information"
    credit_score        -- Classified as "Credit Information"
FROM customer_accounts
```

Phase 2: Access Management and Lineage

With critical data cataloged and classified, the organization implements RBACs and begins mapping data lineage across its most important business processes. This phase reveals how customer data flows from origination through various systems to regulatory reports, enabling better impact analysis and change management. Access controls integrate with Microsoft Entra ID (formerly Azure Active Directory), enabling organizations to leverage existing identity management infrastructure and security policies.

Phase 3: Business Enablement

The final phase focuses on making governed data accessible to business users through self-service discovery and business glossaries. Data analysts can now find and understand available data without requiring IT assistance, while maintaining compliance with established governance policies.

This phased approach delivers value at each stage while building organizational confidence and expertise with governance processes.

The Rise of AI and Large Language Models

While data governance provides the foundation for responsible data management, AI—particularly LLMs—represents a revolutionary shift in how we interact with and derive value from data. The emergence of technologies like ChatGPT, Claude, and Azure OpenAI has fundamentally changed what's possible when humans and machines collaborate on data analysis, content generation, and decision support.

LLMs represent a breakthrough in AI that enables machines to understand and generate humanlike text at unprecedented scale and quality. Unlike traditional analytics that require precise queries and specific data structures, LLMs can understand natural language questions and provide contextual responses that feel conversational and intuitive.

Understanding Large Language Models in Azure

Azure OpenAI Service brings the power of advanced language models to enterprise environments with the security, compliance, and integration capabilities that organizations require. Rather than accessing these capabilities through consumer interfaces, Azure OpenAI provides enterprise-grade access to models like GPT-4o, o1-preview, and o1-mini, enabling organizations to build sophisticated AI applications while maintaining control over their data and ensuring compliance with regulatory requirements.

Figure 12-2 demonstrates how Azure OpenAI Service acts as the central intelligence hub that transforms raw data into intelligent applications. On the left, diverse data sources including governed data, business documents, knowledge bases, and real-time data streams feed into the Azure OpenAI platform through retrieval-augmented generation (RAG) patterns and grounding techniques. The central Azure OpenAI Service provides advanced language models like GPT-4o and o1-preview, along with multimodal capabilities through DALL-E and Whisper, all backed by enterprise-grade security and responsible AI frameworks. On the right, these capabilities power various AI applications including autonomous agents, copilot interfaces, and custom business applications that can process natural language and automate complex tasks. Supporting services at the bottom—Azure AI Search for data retrieval, Azure ML for model customization, and Prompt Flow for orchestration—enhance the platform's capabilities and enable sophisticated AI workflows that blend enterprise data with LLM intelligence.

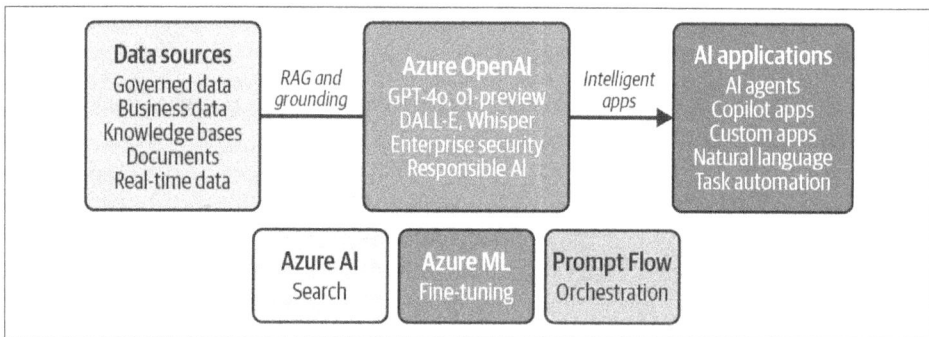

Figure 12-2. Azure AI ecosystem combining governed data with enterprise-grade language models

Technology Spotlight: Azure OpenAI Service 2025 Updates

Azure OpenAI Service has seen significant enhancements in 2025, including:

Latest models
> Access to GPT-4o, o1-preview, and o1-mini for advanced reasoning and problem-solving tasks

Computer use preview
> An experimental model that can control mouse and keyboard input while getting context from screenshots

Global batch processing
> Generally available for large-scale, high-volume processing tasks

Enhanced fine-tuning
> Vision fine-tuning with GPT-4o now generally available, allowing images in training data

AutoGen integration
> Multiagent conversation framework enabling multiple specialized AI assistants to collaborate

Data zone deployments
> Dynamic traffic routing to optimal data centers for improved availability

Note that some advanced models may have limited availability and require special access approval from Microsoft.

The service includes enterprise features like virtual network support, private endpoints, and customer-managed encryption keys, ensuring that AI capabilities can be deployed securely within enterprise environments.

Consider how an LLM might transform data analysis for a business user. Instead of learning SQL syntax or navigating complex business intelligence tools, they could ask natural language questions. Here's how the two approaches compare:

Traditional Approach

```
SELECT
    product_category,
    SUM(revenue) as total_revenue,
    AVG(customer_satisfaction) as avg_satisfaction
FROM sales_data s
JOIN customer_feedback c ON s.order_id = c.order_id
WHERE s.sale_date >= '2024-01-01'
GROUP BY product_category
ORDER BY total_revenue DESC
```

LLM-Enabled Approach

> Query: "Show me which product categories generated the most revenue this year, along with average customer satisfaction scores for each category."

> The LLM understands the intent, generates the appropriate query, executes it against the data, and presents results in a conversational format with insights and recommendations.

While LLMs simplify data access, organizations should maintain technical oversight to verify that generated queries are appropriate/optimized for the specific context.

Building AI Agents with Azure

Beyond simple question-and-answer interactions, Azure enables the creation of sophisticated AI agents—autonomous systems that can perform complex tasks, make decisions, and take actions based on data and business rules. These agents represent the next evolution of AI, moving from passive response systems to proactive assistants that can manage workflows, analyze trends, and even execute business processes. An AI agent differs from a simple chatbot in its ability to:

- *Maintain context* across long conversations and complex tasks.
- *Access multiple data sources* to gather comprehensive information.
- *Execute actions* beyond just providing information.
- *Learn and adapt* based on feedback and results.
- *Collaborate* with other systems and agents.

Consider how an AI agent might support a supply chain manager. Here's an example of how an AI agent might handle a complex supply chain scenario.

User: "We're seeing delivery delays from our Southeast Asia suppliers. Can you analyze the situation and recommend adjustments?"

The AI agent:

1. Accesses real-time shipping data from logistics systems
2. Analyzes weather patterns affecting transportation routes
3. Reviews supplier performance metrics and alternative vendors
4. Calculates cost implications of route changes
5. Generates recommendations with risk assessments
6. Automatically creates purchase orders for alternative suppliers
7. Schedules follow-up analysis to monitor improvements

This agent doesn't just answer questions. It performs comprehensive analysis, takes action, and continues monitoring the situation autonomously. While agents can automate many tasks, human oversight remains essential for critical business decisions, ensuring accountability and intervention when needed.

> **Exam Tip**
>
> While AI agents extend beyond the scope of the DP-900 exam, understanding the foundational data concepts they require is crucial for success in advanced certifications and real-world implementations. Agents need access to well-governed, high-quality data to function effectively, demonstrating why data fundamentals remain essential even as AI capabilities advance.

Practicing Responsible AI and Data Ethics

The power of LLMs and AI agents brings significant responsibilities. Organizations must ensure that these technologies are used ethically, fairly, and transparently while protecting individual privacy and maintaining human oversight of critical decisions.

Microsoft's Responsible AI framework provides guidelines for developing and deploying AI systems that are:

Fair and inclusive
AI systems should treat all people equitably and avoid discriminatory outcomes based on protected characteristics.

Reliable and safe
AI systems should perform consistently and safely, with appropriate safeguards against harmful or unintended behaviors.

Transparent and explainable
Users should understand how AI systems make decisions, particularly for high-stakes scenarios.

Private and secure
AI systems should protect individual privacy and maintain security throughout the data lifecycle.

Accountable
Organizations should maintain human oversight and responsibility for AI system outcomes.

These principles become particularly important when AI systems work with sensitive data or make decisions that affect people's lives, livelihoods, or well-being.

The Convergence: Governed AI

The most exciting developments occur at the intersection of comprehensive data governance and advanced AI capabilities. When organizations combine Microsoft Purview's governance foundation with Azure OpenAI's intelligent capabilities, they create systems that are both powerful and responsible—AI that understands not just what data exists but also what data should be used for specific purposes and who should have access to different insights.

Governance-Aware AI Systems

Traditional AI implementations often struggle with data quality, bias, and compliance issues because they lack comprehensive understanding of their underlying data. By integrating governance capabilities with AI systems, organizations can build "governance-aware" AI that makes better decisions about data usage and provides more trustworthy results.

Consider how a governance-aware AI agent might handle a business intelligence request.

User request: "Analyze customer churn patterns and identify the top factors driving customer departures."

Governance-aware AI process:

1. *Access validation:* Confirms user has permissions for customer data analysis
2. *Data quality assessment:* Identifies high-quality customer datasets through Purview metadata
3. *Compliance check:* Ensures that analysis complies with data retention and privacy policies
4. *Bias detection:* Reviews data for potential biases that might skew analysis
5. *Lineage awareness:* Understands data sources and transformations affecting accuracy
6. *Result contextualization:* Provides insights with appropriate caveats about data limitations

This governance-aware approach produces more reliable insights while maintaining compliance with organizational policies and regulatory requirements.

Building the Future of Data Work

The combination of comprehensive governance and advanced AI capabilities enables entirely new approaches to data work. Instead of requiring specialized technical skills to extract value from data, organizations can democratize data access while maintaining appropriate controls and safeguards:

Self-service analytics with governance
Business users can ask natural language questions and receive accurate, compliant answers without requiring IT intervention or risking data misuse.

Automated compliance monitoring
AI agents continuously monitor data usage patterns, identifying potential compliance issues before they become violations.

Intelligent data discovery
AI-powered search helps users find relevant data across the organization while respecting access controls and data sensitivity classifications.

Proactive quality management
AI systems automatically monitor data quality, identifying and flagging potential issues before they impact business decisions.

This future isn't hypothetical. Organizations are implementing these capabilities today, combining Microsoft Purview's governance foundation with Azure OpenAI's intelligent capabilities to create data platforms that are both powerful and responsible.

Your Journey Beyond DP-900

As you conclude your exploration of Azure's data fundamentals, it's important to recognize that DP-900 certification represents not an endpoint but a beginning. The concepts, services, and approaches you've learned provide a solid foundation for an exciting journey into the future of data and AI.

The Skills That Matter

The data landscape continues to evolve rapidly, but several foundational skills remain consistently valuable:

Data thinking
The ability to understand how data flows through organizations, how it creates value, and how it should be governed and protected. This conceptual understanding transcends specific technologies and remains valuable as tools evolve.

Business alignment
The capability to connect technical possibilities with business needs, translating between data capabilities and organizational objectives. This skill becomes more important as data systems become more sophisticated and AI capabilities expand.

Ethical reasoning
> The judgment to evaluate the responsible use of data and AI technologies, considering privacy, fairness, and societal impact alongside technical and business requirements.

Continuous learning
> The mindset and methods for staying current with rapidly evolving technologies while maintaining focus on enduring principles and practices.

These skills, combined with the technical foundation provided by DP-900 certification, position you to succeed regardless of how specific technologies evolve.

Pathways Forward

Your DP-900 certification opens doors to numerous specialization paths, each building on the fundamentals you've mastered:

Data engineering
> This focuses on building and managing the infrastructure that moves, transforms, and stores data at scale. This path emphasizes Azure Data Factory, Synapse Analytics, and Databricks, with advanced certifications like DP-203.

Data analysis
> This concentrates on extracting insights and creating visualizations that drive business decisions. This path emphasizes Power BI, Azure Synapse Analytics, and statistical analysis techniques, with certifications like PL-300.

Data science
> This develops predictive models and advanced analytics that enable organizations to anticipate trends and optimize decisions. This path emphasizes Azure Machine Learning, Python/R programming, and statistical modeling, with certifications like DP-100.

AI engineering
> This builds intelligent applications that incorporate language models, computer vision, and other AI capabilities into business solutions. This path emphasizes Azure OpenAI, Cognitive Services, and responsible AI practices, with emerging certifications in AI development.

Data architecture
> designs comprehensive data strategies that align technical capabilities with business requirements while ensuring governance, security, and scalability. This path combines elements from all other specializations with enterprise architecture principles.

These paths aren't mutually exclusive. Many successful data professionals develop expertise across multiple areas while maintaining primary focus on their core specialty.

The Azure Advantage

Azure's comprehensive ecosystem provides unique advantages for your continued data journey:

Integrated services
> Work together seamlessly, reducing the complexity typically associated with multivendor environments—the foundation you've built with DP-900 certification will apply across Azure's entire data platform.

Enterprise-grade capabilities
> Ensure that solutions you build can scale from prototype to global production while maintaining security, compliance, and reliability requirements

An innovation platform
> Provides early access to emerging technologies like advanced AI models, ensuring that you can stay current with the latest developments in data and AI

Global reach
> Enables solutions that serve users worldwide, with data residency and compliance capabilities that support international operations

Hybrid flexibility
> Accommodates existing investments while enabling cloud modernization, supporting organizations regardless of their current technology landscape

These advantages compound over time, making Azure expertise increasingly valuable as organizations expand their data and AI capabilities.

Summary

This chapter explored advanced Azure capabilities that extend beyond DP-900 fundamentals, focusing on three critical areas that represent the future of data work.

Microsoft Purview for data governance provides comprehensive visibility and control across entire data estates, enabling organizations to understand what data they have, where it lives, and how it flows through their systems. Through automated discovery, intelligent classification, and collaborative cataloging, Purview transforms data governance from a compliance burden into an enabling capability.

AI and LLMs revolutionize how we interact with data, enabling natural language queries, intelligent automation, and sophisticated analysis that was previously impossible. Azure OpenAI Service brings enterprise-grade AI capabilities to data platforms, while AI agents enable autonomous task execution and decision support.

The convergence of governance and AI creates the most exciting possibilities, where governance-aware AI systems make better decisions about data usage while maintaining compliance and ethical standards. This convergence enables new forms of self-service analytics, automated compliance monitoring, and intelligent data discovery.

These advanced capabilities build directly on the DP-900 fundamentals you've mastered, demonstrating how foundational knowledge in data storage, processing, and security enables participation in the next generation of data and AI systems.

Beyond the Exam

While these topics extend beyond the scope of the DP-900 exam, understanding their relationship to foundational concepts is valuable:

- Data governance evolution:
  - Manual processes becoming automated AI augmenting human decision making
  - Governance enabling rather than restricting innovation
  - Security and compliance remaining paramount
- AI integration:
  - Natural language interfaces transforming data access
  - Agents enabling autonomous task execution
  - Foundation knowledge remaining crucial
  - Ethical considerations gaining importance
- Future readiness:
  - Technical skills providing the foundation
  - Business alignment determining value
  - Continuous learning ensuring relevance
  - Responsible practices building trust

Conclusion: Your Data Future Starts Now

As we reach the end of our DP-900 journey together, take a moment to appreciate how much ground we've covered. We began with fundamental concepts of data storage and processing, explored the rich ecosystem of Azure data services, and concluded with a glimpse into the future of governed AI. You've built a comprehensive understanding of how modern organizations create value from data while managing complexity, ensuring security, and enabling innovation.

But this conclusion is really a commencement. The data revolution is accelerating, not slowing down. Every day brings new possibilities for how data and AI can solve problems, create opportunities, and improve lives. The foundation you've built through DP-900 certification will position you to be part of this exciting future.

The world needs skilled data professionals who understand not just how to work with data but also how to do so responsibly, effectively, and ethically. You now possess the foundational knowledge to be one of those professionals. Whether you specialize in engineering the infrastructure that powers analytics, creating the visualizations that illuminate insights, building the models that predict the future, or architecting the strategies that align technology with business goals, you're equipped to make a meaningful contribution.

The future of data work is bright, and with your DP-900 foundation, you're well positioned to help shape that future. The next chapter of your journey begins now. Where will you take your data skills next?

Remember, you're not just learning about data systems; you're preparing to be part of the generation that transforms how humanity understands and acts on information. That's an exciting opportunity and a significant responsibility. Embrace both with confidence, knowing that your solid foundation in Azure data fundamentals will serve you well no matter where your journey leads you.

The future of data is yours to build. Go forth and build it well.

Beyond This Book

While this book provided comprehensive coverage of DP-900 concepts and glimpses into advanced capabilities, your learning journey is just beginning. The data and AI landscape evolves continuously, requiring ongoing education and hands-on experience to maintain expertise.

Practical Next Steps

Hands-on experience remains the most effective way to deepen your understanding. Create Azure free accounts, experiment with the services covered in this book, and build small projects that reinforce theoretical knowledge with practical application.

Community engagement accelerates learning through shared experiences and diverse perspectives. Join Azure user groups, participate in online forums, and attend conferences where you can learn from others' successes and challenges.

Continuous experimentation with new services and features keeps your skills current as Azure evolves. Microsoft regularly releases new capabilities that extend existing services in powerful ways.

Real-world application provides the context that transforms technical knowledge into business value. Look for opportunities to apply what you've learned in your current role or through volunteer projects.

How to Stay Current

The Microsoft Learn platform (*https://learn.microsoft.com*) provides free, continuously updated training on Azure services, including new capabilities and emerging best practices. This resource ensures that you can stay current with platform evolution.

Microsoft's official Azure blog (*https://azure.microsoft.com/blog*) and documentation provide authoritative information about service updates, best practices, and emerging capabilities. Following these sources helps you understand not just what's new but also why changes matter.

Industry publications and analyst reports provide broader context about trends affecting data and AI technologies, helping you understand how Azure capabilities fit within the broader technology ecosystem.

Final Thoughts

Your DP-900 certification represents the beginning of an exciting journey into the world of data and AI. The foundation you've built provides the knowledge and confidence needed to tackle complex challenges, contribute to innovative solutions, and help shape the future of how organizations work with data.

The skills you've developed—understanding data concepts, working with Azure services, thinking about governance and security—will serve you well regardless of how specific technologies evolve. But more importantly, you've developed the mindset needed to approach data challenges systematically and responsibly.

The future belongs to organizations and individuals who can harness the power of data and AI while maintaining human values and ethical practices. With your solid foundation in Azure data fundamentals, you're well equipped to be part of that future.

Index

JOIN operations, 111
language categories, 105
SELECT statement, 106-107
    filtering with WHERE, 106
    sorting with ORDER BY, 107
UPDATE statement, 108

T
Table API, 180-181
    (see also Azure Cosmos DB, APIs; Azure
    Table Storage)
table relationships, 102-105
    (see also foreign key)
    many-to-many, 103
        (see also junction table)
    one-to-many, 103
    one-to-one, 102
table scan, 114
    (see also database objects, indexes)
tables (database), 99-101
    (see also primary keys; foreign key; data
    types (database))
time-value relationship of data, 225-226
    (see also real-time analytics)
transactional versus analytical processing, 202
transactional workloads (OLTP), 59-64
    (see also high concurrency)
    characteristics of, 61-63

use cases, 63-64

U
unstructured data, 13-17
    (see also Binary Large Objects (BLOBs))
    Azure services, 16
    benefits and limitations of, 17
    characteristics of, 14

V
virtual machines (VMs), 129
Volume, Variety, and Velocity (the three Vs of
    big data), 197
    (see also large-scale analytics)

W
windowing (in stream processing), 232
    (see also streaming data)
workload spectrum, 57-58

X
XML (see eXtensible Markup Language (XML))

Y
YAML Ain't Markup Language (YAML), 10
    (see also semi-structured data)

About the Author

Michael John Peña is a principal data and application engineer who thrives on innovation, leadership, and learning. With 15+ years of experience in cloud, big data, IoT, and AI, he's recognized as a tech leader and community contributor. MJ also cofounded a crypto startup, has held the roles of CTO and solutions architect, and is a Microsoft Data Platform and AI Services MVP.

Colophon

The animal on the cover of *Azure Data Fundamentals* is a racket-tailed roller (*Coracias spatulatus*), a bird native to parts of sub-Saharan Africa, most notably Mozambique, Malawi, Zimbabwe, and parts of Tanzania and Zambia. It typically inhabits dry, open woodlands and mopane tree forests, where it can find suitable perches and open spaces for hunting predominantly grasshoppers, beetles, scorpions, and small lizards.

The racket-tailed roller gets its name from the distinctive extensions on its elongated tail feathers. The male variety displays vibrant plumage, with a mix of turquoise blue, purple, and brown tones. Its wings are especially striking in flight, revealing bright blue and black patterns that contrast vividly with its surroundings.

Racket-tailed rollers are highly territorial, especially during the breeding season. They defend their chosen territories by performing dramatic dives, rolls, and sharp calls aimed at potential rivals.

The racket-tailed roller is currently listed as Least Concern on the IUCN Red List. Many of the animals on O'Reilly covers are endangered; all of them are important to the world.

The color illustration by Karen Montgomery, based on an antique line engraving from Shaw's *Zoology*. The series design is by Edie Freedman, Ellie Volckhausen, and Karen Montgomery. The cover fonts are Gilroy Semibold and Guardian Sans. The text font is Adobe Minion Pro; the heading font is Adobe Myriad Condensed; and the code font is Dalton Maag's Ubuntu Mono.

O'REILLY®

Learn from experts.
Become one yourself.

60,000+ titles | Live events with experts | Role-based courses
Interactive learning | Certification preparation

**Try the O'Reilly learning platform
free for 10 days.**